NORMALIZING INEQUALITY

NORMALIZING INEQUALITY

HOW CALIFORNIANS MAKE SENSE OF THE GROWING DIVIDE

G. Cristina Mora and Tianna S. Paschel

Russell Sage Foundation NEW YORK

THE RUSSELL SAGE FOUNDATION
The Russell Sage Foundation, one of the oldest of America's general purpose foundations, was established in 1907 by Mrs. Margaret Olivia Sage for "the improvement of social and living conditions in the United States." The foundation seeks to fulfill this mandate by fostering the development and dissemination of knowledge about the country's political, social, and economic problems. While the foundation endeavors to assure the accuracy and objectivity of each book it publishes, the conclusions and interpretations in Russell Sage Foundation publications are those of the authors and not of the foundation, its trustees, or its staff. Publication by Russell Sage, therefore, does not imply foundation endorsement.

ROR: https://ror.org/02yh9se80
DOI: https://doi.org/10.7758/uybx4321

LIBRARY OF CONGRESS CATALOGING-IN-PUBLICATION DATA

Names: Mora, G. Cristina, 1980- author | Paschel, Tianna S. author
Title: Normalizing inequality : how Californians make sense of the growing divide / G. Cristina Mora and Tianna S. Paschel.
Description: New York : Russell Sage Foundation, [2026] | Includes bibliographical references and index. | Summary: "While we know a lot about class inequality, its patterns, how it has shifted over time, and how it is shaped by racial dynamics, we know much less about how ordinary people make sense of it all, and how they navigate it in their daily lives. In this book, G. Cristina Mora and Tianna S. Paschel set out to understand how a precarious middle class understands, lives with, and navigates these pervasive inequalities. The authors argue that while individuals are largely aware of the structural conditions that shape the inequalities they experience and see around them, they lean toward minimizing them in favor of more individualist understandings of these divisions. More specifically, the authors show how individuals do this by using three specific narrative strategies: exceptional framing, spatial comparison, and bounded blame. Mora and Paschel contend that while such strategies are helpful for allowing people to live with and navigate inequality, they also help to passively reproduce it. The authors examine these issues in the context of California, one of the most unequal regions in one of the most unequal countries in the world. Drawing on a trove of interview and survey data, they tell the story of how people make sense of the changes they see around them, and the meanings that they ascribe to the ever-changing nature of opportunity, racial inequality, and social mobility"— Provided by publisher.
Identifiers: LCCN 2025045926 (print) | LCCN 2025045927 (ebook) | ISBN 9780871545367 paperback | ISBN 9781610449465 ebook
Subjects: LCSH: Social classes—California | Social stratification—California | Equality—California | California—Social conditions—21st century | California—Economic conditions—21st century
Classification: LCC HN79.C23 S657 2026 (print) | LCC HN79.C23 (ebook)
LC record available at https://lccn.loc.gov/2025045926
LC ebook record available at https://lccn.loc.gov/2025045927

The paper used in this publication meets the minimum requirements of American National Standard for Information Sciences—Permanence of Paper for Printed Library Materials. ANSI Z39.48-1992.

Text design by Matthew T. Avery. Front matter DOI: https://doi.org/10.7758/uybx4321.1548

RUSSELL SAGE FOUNDATION
112 East 64th Street, New York, New York 10065
10 9 8 7 6 5 4 3 2 1

We dedicate this book to our children, Camilo, Marshawn, and Adela.
We dream of a better future for you and for all of those
that come after you.

CONTENTS

ILLUSTRATIONS

Figures

ABOUT THE AUTHORS

G. Cristina Mora is Chancellor's Professor of Sociology and co-director of the Institute of Governmental Studies at the University of California, Berkeley.

Tianna S. Paschel is associate professor of African American studies and sociology at the University of California, Berkeley.

PREFACE

We were both raised in California, albeit in different kinds of communities and in different parts of the state. We found each other in this profession where people with working class roots like us were few and far between. We became close when we both were starting on the tenure track, with one of us moving from California to Chicago, and one back to California from Chicago. That time away from California spurred many conversations with friends and colleagues from California but living elsewhere about whether this place was actually as unique as it seemed to be when it came to inequality and belonging. Some years later, and already sisters, we would become colleagues at the University of California, Berkeley, where we became serious about studying the contradictory discourses and realities around race, class, and immigration in California. We were incensed at so much going on here, and yet we also loved this place. In 2018, we embarked on this collaborative book project to tackle these very questions that had been swirling around in our heads. We also came to understand that our experiences—both the daughters of (im)migrants but growing up differently—uniquely positioned us to do this work. We offer this preface both as a way of situating ourselves in this story and also as a guide for how you might read the rest of this book.

G. Cristina Mora

I grew up in the northeastern edge of Los Angeles County, in and around Pacoima, a place synonymous with hypersegregation, hyperpolicing, and Latino working poverty—the kind that is hard to shake, no matter how many jobs you work. There, everyone seemed to be Latino—primarily Mexican. There were those from Durango, those from Jalisco, and those from Michoacán—like my parents. In some ways, the neighborhood often felt like a family, with all its beauty and struggles. It felt like someone was related to us on every block, a distant cousin from my parents' hometown.

Pacoima and its surroundings were far, so very far, from the LA paradise broadcast in the movies but, to my parents, it represented a new start and a new world of opportunities not afforded elsewhere. You see, my father never finished elementary school. The eldest son of a Mexican Bracero, he grew up sleeping on dirt floors and working in the fields. As a teen, he came to the United States to pick apples in California's Silicon Valley and Central Valley, following the harvest cycles alongside his farmworker father. While his stories about that time are sometimes infused with nostalgia—he tells me of "torteando" over campfires on Sundays so that he could have food for the week—they are also inflicted with pain, about missing his mother and siblings, about backbreaking labor in the heat, and about being robbed of an occasional weekly wage by dishonest employers. In California, farmworkers still have one of the lowest life expectancy rates in the state, sometimes dying decades before their working-class counterparts. I was lucky. My father made it out of the fields and eventually migrated to Los Angeles to find work in the factories.

It was in Los Angeles that my father would meet my mother. Daughter of an aspiring entrepreneur, she came to the United States by way of Tijuana with her seven siblings to go to school and work alongside her parents in a dry cleaning shop. Yet despite being one of the top students in her class and having a deep love of reading, she quit the ninth grade to work full-time when her mother suddenly found herself a single parent. As the oldest, my mother worked long hours to help keep her family out of poverty. But still, she read. Between full-time work shifts, she read history, science fiction, classical literature, and mystery novels, which would transport her out of her forty-plus-hour work weeks. My mother's love of reading would later also become the basis of our strong bond. When, at the age of fifteen, my mother met my father, both understood that they would need to continue to support their parents and extended families in this new country.

For my parents, Los Angeles was a world of new beginnings, different from the small agricultural towns where they were born, where rigid class hierarchies closed off opportunities for the poor. Young newlyweds in the late 1970s, they quickly grew a family. Comparatively lenient immigration policies and wide-scale reform at the time allowed them to adjust their immigration status and eventually afforded them labor market opportunities in the city's growing textile industry. They bought a modest home, opened their own business, and raised my brothers and me in a neighborhood close to the factories where they toiled, sometimes seven days a week. And in my family, nearly every adult worked in the garment factories—spending hours on end using loud machines to sew women's blouses, baby hats, and jackets for brand name companies. To this day, my father has hearing loss, likely related to his years spent operating those machines.

But what seemed better than Michoacán to my parents was more nuanced for my brothers and me. We knew, because we sometimes visited and because our parents told us, that social mobility was much harder in Mexico. Still, it was hard for us to see Los Angeles as a land of great promise. Regular helicopter patrols, gangs, and intense policing surrounded our neighborhood and schools back in the 1990s. "No cruising" signs lined the streets near my home; kids with baggy pants and crisp white shirts were regularly searched and questioned by authorities; and schools boasted tall, wraparound chain-link fences with metal detectors. Drive-by shootings were rare, but they happened, sometimes only a block away from a schoolyard. I went to a massive, "under-performing" Latino public high school. It was overenrolled and had a dropout rate that was much higher than average. Students who acted out were sent to the school police unit, sometimes in restraints. You learned what colors not to wear, what signs never to show, what streets not to claim, and how to turn your head and keep safe. Still, it was there where I benefited from the care of incredibly generous teachers who nurtured my love of reading, talked to me about college, and even let me use their computers to write the applications that would eventually lead me out of the neighborhood. These women told me to dream beyond the gates that enclosed us, beyond the secondhand textbooks that limited us, and beyond the social narratives that kept us all segregated on the Eastside.

This is context that fundamentally shaped my experience. My neighborhood was under-resourced, hypersegregated, and over-policed. Yet it was also a community of laborers—factory workers, gardeners, and house cleaners—of Catholic families that led processions to honor Latin American saints, of cousins and aunts and uncles, of family parties with piñatas, and of carne asadas on Christmas Day. It was violence and beauty, danger and comfort, poverty and riches, love and loss. And, in some ways, that hypersegregation sheltered me. At a high school that was virtually all Latino, there was, after all, room for Latina honor students, Latina school presidents, and Latina social justice dreamers.

Still, this part of Los Angeles was a stark contrast to the stylized depictions of the city of beaches, palm trees, Mediterranean weather, and White families. Those newspaper and television images seemed to ignore my neighborhood and its dynamics, and signaled to me that somehow I, and the world I lived in, was not the real Los Angeles, not the true California, or even the real America. The contradiction communicated to me that maybe I was part of some segregated secret, one that had to live in the shadows. A community kept in a corner, whose pictures would never be displayed on the family wall.

Proposition 187, a California-voter-approved measure to deny undocumented immigrants education and other services, and the subsequent anti-immigrant political rhetoric of the early 1990s, cemented this sense in me. This political context even seeped its way into LA Latino teenage culture at the time. I remember that pagers were popular in East Los Angeles back then. My friends had them, and I remember our excitement at learning how to page coded messages. "1-4-3" meant "I love you," and "187," well, that always meant danger and emergency. Even as middle schoolers, we knew that California, or at least Governor Pete Wilson's California, did not want us. Much later, as a scholar, I would read that this era also spurred discussions about repealing birthright citizenship for the children of the undocumented. The sense that I did not belong was always in the air. I grew up breathing it.

It was not until I moved to the San Francisco Bay Area for college that I began to read the books and take the courses that would help me make sense of my place in the state and the nation. I entered the University of California, Berkeley, as part of the first class of freshman admitted after the repeal of affirmative action because of the passage of the anti-affirmative-action Proposition 209. Talk of race was all over campus. Though Latinos represented over 40 percent of the state's under-eighteen population at the time, we made up less than 15 percent of the student body. This trend in underrepresentation would continue throughout my time at the university and for the next twenty-five years. It felt odd to be in a place where almost no professors, and only very few students, looked like me or related to my story. I felt so lonely, so often. Yet many told me that I had made it—that I had "beaten the odds" by getting out of the "hood," going to college, and creating a path toward middle-class economic freedom. But as they spoke these words, I often felt that I had lost something, something deep, in "winning."

College in the East Bay, followed by graduate school in the ivy halls of the East Coast, would finally introduce me to a more diverse array of communities and inspire new and exhilarating intellectual pursuits that would fuel me until my return to the Golden State in 2011. I am now raising my children, not in the immigrant community that sustained me in my youth—though we visit there very often—but in the broader, more diverse metropolitan area connected to this college town. As my children grow up here, I work hard to find the spaces that can nurture them, that celebrate rather than hide or neglect their immigrant background. These places are not always easy to find, even here, as we navigate middle-class environments in a state where not much of the middle class looks like us.

As I work and build a life here, I cannot help but reflect on the beauty and hardships around me. Today, Los Angeles, and Pacoima particularly, feels like an immigrant city under siege, a major target of masked homeland security efforts. The vibrant city parks, which have long served as a respite for immigrant children and families, are desolate; the Latino grocery stores that contribute mightily to the local economy are half empty; and lone parishioners sit in empty pews in churches that once seemed to burst at the seams every Sunday morning. Across the state, public school teachers and social workers, many of them Latinas, find themselves on the front lines of an immigration battle bent on separating families, deporting long-standing community members, and punishing an imperfect state. While we do not know how long these intense federal actions will last, I do think they will have social, moral, and economic ripple effects for generations to come. Today's children who fear that their parents might not come home could very likely be tomorrow's adults who question whether they have ever belonged.

And to me, the contemporary immigration assault on California's families feels worse than the assault in the 1990s during the era of Governor Wilson, if only because it makes me realize that I too had wanted to believe that in California, the past could remain history. Of course, there are many differences between then and now, especially in the way the federal government is now orchestrating much of the anti-immigrant fervor. But still, the masked agents, the guns, the need for red cards, the unmarked vehicles, and the birthright citizenship discourse together recreate that pungent scent in the air of disbelonging, un-belonging, non-belonging, perhaps-never-belonged. And every breath seems to make me wonder how long California, with its diverse groups and leaders, will keep resisting and seek to protect all its residents.

Still, I know that there are organizations, public officials, students, and everyday people that are working hard, every minute, to combat the current moment. Some are putting their bodies on the line, others are using art to articulate new forms of citizenship, and many more are taking to the streets to demand a different, more inclusive, dream for the state and nation more generally. And beyond the issue of immigration, there are many more groups and organizations working hard to make California a place worthy of its progressive discourse and its dreams of diversity. They are working to close the housing, wealth, representation, and political gaps that keep inequality so entrenched. They are proposing new, community-focused solutions to violence, homelessness, and working poverty. And they are doing this with fierce imagination, unwavering resolve, and a deep commitment to a different future.

At the same time, the contradictions of this place, and this time, still weigh heavily. It still enrages me that farmworkers in the Central Valley live and work under exploitative conditions, that the Los Angeles Unified School District is among the most racially segregated districts in the country, and that people from communities of color in the state often work more than full-time and still fall short of making ends meet. It still cuts deep to hear news about how powerful California's economy is as I drive past camps of the unhoused on my way to my campus office. And in some ways, we are all part of what recreates these contradictions repeatedly, whether we are conscious of it or not.

Still, this is a place of dreams, including my own. And it is my hope that the stories we tell here will have us all pause . . . and reflect . . . on how our everyday thoughts and actions reproduce the inequalities that affect us all. It is my hope that we can use the insights on the following pages to spark new conversations, new forms of resistance, and new dreams—ones that carry with them the necessary integrity and vision for true change.

Tianna S. Paschel

I grew up mostly in California, in the parts that most people don't care to know about and don't know to care about. Between Fresno, Bakersfield, and Sacramento, I grew up in the forgotten part, the not-so-progressive parts, even parts that—at least for now—might be called Trump country. My childhood was solid working class inching toward the middle class by the time my single mom got promoted from prison guard to correctional counselor at a prison in one of those in-between places—Folsom, Delano, or Chowchilla, sometimes known as Prison Alley. This was the California that tourists don't come to visit, the one that doesn't appear in the movies where there always seems to be a coastline nearby.

I remember when I was a kid I would run ragged in apartment buildings occupied almost exclusively by people of color, but not so many Black folks. My friends' parents spoke English, Tagalog, Punjabi, and many different kinds of Spanish. They smiled at me and welcomed me into their small apartments, which were often identical to our own, sometimes only with gestures because of language barriers. It was exactly the kind of childhood from which working-class multicultural narratives about California might be woven. Diverse and integrated, a place where kids hang on to their biculturalism with few social repercussions, a place where junior high school boy bands included Filipino kids, African American kids, Chicano kids, and that one kid who was half Japanese and half White. There were only a few White kids anywhere in sight, and they tended to acquiesce to the majority-minority culture.

My childhood was also one marked by race in distinct ways. It was one where my friends told me that, while their immigrant parents loved *me*, they had warned their children to stay away from all the other Black kids at our school because they were "trouble." It was one where after middle school, we dispersed to different parts of Sacramento, many of us bussed to different places that all felt like the other end of the earth.

I spent my freshman year of high school at a predominantly White school on the other side of Sacramento, near a private airport. Instead of tiny apartments in huge apartment complexes, I was met with huge homes, some with literal airplanes in the driveway. Stonebridge, Park City, Smoke Tree, and Discovery Park—the large apartment complexes in which we were raised—were entire worlds unto themselves. However, we would discover a much different world once we got off those buses—one that was much whiter and much wealthier.

So my upbringing was one of both extreme integration and extreme segregation. It was one of class homogeneity and viscerally felt class inequalities. And I felt these differences in my bones as one of the few Black students and one of the few bussed students in the International Baccalaureate (IB), GATE, College Prep, Honors, and Advanced Placement programs. I was told by many teachers and guidance counselors throughout my school years that being in advanced classes was inappropriately ambitious for me. It was a similar kind of alienation I would experience when I went to the University of California, Los Angeles, for college, where I walked over chalk-filled sidewalks that sprawled the message to Black and Brown students: "Go home, you don't deserve to be here!" This was to be expected. Proposition 209 passed my senior year of high school; I was part of the last class to benefit from affirmative action. Years later, I would find myself detained along with dozens of others for occupying UCLA's Royce Hall in an effort to reinstate it.

This is only one of the many kinds of dis-belonging one feels in this place when you live in this skin. Let us not forget that California is the land of some of the most infamous cases of racist state violence—from the beating of Rodney King to the police killings of Tyisha Miller, Oscar Grant, and Stefon Clark, among many, many others. It is not a fluke that California, and Oakland specifically, was the birthplace of the Black Panther Party.

Despite all of this, I have been known to quietly romanticize my own upbringing. It still happens when I see groups of youth in Oakland, where I live now, who are usually all some shade of non-White but with different racialized experiences, "smeezing" or dancing to Mac Dre. I smile and think: this is a unique place. At other times, though, I am reminded of the many intimate experiences I have had with anti-Blackness in this progressive state that markets itself as a place for everyone but sometimes feels like it's not for Black folks, especially Black girls and women. It is a place where, when I was fifteen years old, I was banned, along with my shy and bookish thirteen-year-old sister, from entering Target because the security guards swore that my sister had previously stolen from the store. We had just moved to Fresno that week and lived in an apartment complex across the street. We had been so excited to be off on our own, but for years afterwards, our hearts would beat fast any time a friend suggested we go there. Even though we both knew that sister had not stolen anything from that store—she had never even been there—we still always felt a bit of shame about the incident.

These kinds of racial aggressions varied by degree and type but were as commonplace as the tender moments I had in those blocks and blocks of apartment complexes. I remember sneaking through holes in fences that our parents didn't know about, back and forth between the buildings. These memories of belonging are just as acute as those many instances in which my multiracial friends translated from their native languages the anti-Black racial slurs they heard their parents use when talking about Black people—but not about me of course. It was not always overt, that feeling of dis-belonging. I recently looked back at a handwritten card from my best friend in a program for gifted students that was far away from home. She was White, kind, and had an airplane and a large glass atrium in the entryway of her house. The card was sweet if you could just look past the four times she said some version of "you're so different."

I grew up in those places only thought of as rest stops on the way to the California that is sold to the world. When I lived in Bakersfield, country music was often blasting from pickup trucks, and in Fresno, the rich kids weren't the children of famous actors or tech executives but of industrial farm owners. When I moved to Los Angeles for college, my Angeleno friends never got tired of asking me why I spent so many weekends there. I got the clear message that these places were not considered really California, and they weren't desirable either. Even if your family lived there, why would you ever go back if you didn't have to? After all, those places in between Los Angeles and the Bay have a kind of stink to them, you know, the scent of cows and manure that you smell when driving between Tracey and the Grapevine, that smell of boringness, backwardness, bigotry.

As I began living outside of California—in Washington, DC; Rio de Janeiro; and later in Chicago—I began to reflect on my experiences in

California. I thought about my identity as both a woman of color and a Black woman—identities that seemed to flow directly from being raised in majority-minority places that didn't have a significant Black population. My trajectory from these working-class, mostly minority places to the primarily White, middle- to upper-class spaces that characterize my life today has been dizzying.

I've also reflected on why I was in California in the first place. I was born in Flint, Michigan, a place notorious for neglect and disrepair. I was born only a year after the auto plant at the center of the movie *Roger & Me* closed, resulting in the loss of tens of thousands of jobs and in generations of hurt. My life in California started when, all of a sudden, my family packed ourselves into a U-Haul truck with all of our belongings and made our way to California. Other than my mother and my sister, everyone else in that truck was a near stranger to me. I was seven years old, and my mom had just married my stepfather after knowing him for only two weeks. Over the next few years, I would learn that he was an incredibly violent man, both physically and emotionally. And until very recently, I had assumed that he had spared my mother such violence until after he moved her two thousand miles away from everyone she knew and loved to keep her isolated, vulnerable, and docile. But this was not the case. When we embarked on that life-changing trip across the country, my mom knew exactly who she had married.

Despite the protests of her family, she left with him because she saw it as her only chance to get out of Flint. She knew what lay ahead in a town where everyone she knew seemed to have a job at General Motors—until they didn't. Besides, she wasn't a factory girl anyway, she would tell me. My mom risked everything and endured irreparable abuse for one reason: she wanted a better life for me and my sister. This was her way of pursuing the California Dream, the American Dream. When the three of us finally broke free of her abusive husband with only the clothes on our backs, my mother accepted a job as a prison guard—among the highest paying jobs in California for someone who had completed a GED and some college coursework. Being locked in a prison every day, having coworkers who sometimes saw little difference between her and those incarcerated, and working constant back-to-back eight-hour shifts were a small price to pay for her newfound security in the lower-middle class.

For her, California is the dream, one that is likely impossible to accomplish for someone like her in today's economy. When I gave the commencement speech at my doctoral graduation, I remember confessing to her through tears that I thought it had all been worth it. I was surprised to find out that she agreed. And whenever I've questioned if that was actually true, typically through more tears and on my therapist's couch, a trip back home to Flint always clears things up. During one such trip, my witty and hilarious cousin, just a little older than me and no less extraordinary, showed me obituaries of people we grew up with instead of yearbooks. While writing this book I went back home to Flint a lot, burying cousins who died violently and prematurely, and visiting my three uncles, all of whom have been laid off at some point, and all of whom were in nursing homes because of preventable strokes. So much illness and premature death. It was also back in Flint where I would bury my grandmother—a migrant from a rural area outside of Pine Bluff, Arkansas. She installed spark plugs in cars for over twenty years and once told me that she had the most important job at the factory. Anytime I called her and alluded to being too busy at work, she would remind me "having too much work is better than having no work at all." This was something she knew intimately as she financially supported her children, grandchildren, and great-grandchildren until she passed away. You see, my grandmama was one of the rare ones who survived the massive layoffs and eventually retired from General Motors—no small feat.

Each trip back to Flint, I'd leave California with cash and gifts in hand, knowing I would be called on to help. Even as a struggling college student, I remember my cousins telling me, "We know y'all are livin' large in California" as they hit me up for money. It felt similar to what my friends with parents from Mexico, El Salvador, Vietnam, and the Philippines told me about their epic trips back home with suitcases filled with expected gifts. Each trip back home to California, I would leave feeling lucky, feeling spared. The growing up with no family nearby, the beatings, and the great escape from my stepfather's tyranny can sometimes feel like a small price to pay for the lives we now have in this sunny place. I'm a professor after all, and my sister is a star middle-school teacher and mentor. If I suspend my critical analysis, at my core, I feel gratitude.

We share these stories with you because, if nothing else, they place us on the pages of this book, not only as researchers but as daughters, as mothers, as people who have experienced a great deal of social mobility in a place where doing so has become less and less common. We recognize that, while our stories are unique, we have both achieved a level of privilege far beyond those whom we interviewed—though not in every way. We also understand that we live in a state, in a country, and in a world where we must wrestle and contend with inequalities in one way or another. Like all of the participants in this book, we are implicated in inequality, no matter what our backgrounds or where we are situated. In this way, we are calling for more critical thinking about the kinds of experiences that inform how we, as differently situated people, make sense of our lives here, and ultimately how we see the promise and precarity in California and beyond.

We also share this window into our lives as a guide for how we read the stories of those at the center of this book—with nuance and grace. We believe that we will never fully understand the inequalities around class, race, and immigration if we restrict our research to those experiencing their most disastrous effects: the impoverished, immigrants, and those experiencing the worst forms of systemic racism. Nor will we fully understand the reproduction of inequalities by exclusively studying the structures that give rise to them, nor by studying those who benefit the most from inequality: the wealthy, non-immigrants, and racially dominant groups. We must also study the middle and, in so doing, we must study the meaning-making processes that undergird the ways we see inequality. We are particularly interested in those understandings of the world that come from personal experience and from the cultural logics and narratives that we marshal to interpret our lives as well as the world around us. This can help us better understand why we act in the ways that we do, and more often, why we refuse to act. We believe this work is urgent and necessary, and that it calls for deep understanding rather than superficial judgment. We hope that you will read this book through this lens.

ACKNOWLEDGMENTS

A project of this scope incurs much debt. We are grateful to the many who contributed their time, energy, and brilliance to make this project possible, including our amazing team of research assistants—Jessica Law, Reubén Pérez, Amy Vasconcellos, Olivia Alvarez, Houa Vang, Cory Mengual, Barbara Truc Pham, Vianney Gomez, and Sheena Cabal—who collected interview data and refined the interview guide. We would also like to thank our undergraduate research students—des Jackson, Danko Betzhold, and Sophia Montesinos. A special thank-you to Dominic Cedillo is merited. He worked tirelessly and painstakingly to help us tie up many loose ends at a critical stage in the development of this book. Graduate student researchers also contributed greatly to our data analysis. Thank you Kerby Lynch, Diego Holguin, Sarah Payne, Robert Pickett, Nora Broege, and Chelsea Daniels. Each of you lent your unique perspective and expertise to the project, which made a difference in everything from our research design to data collection to the unpleasant phase of data cleaning so that we could begin our analysis. We are also incredibly grateful to the project managers, Teresa Kabba and Bernadette Blashill, who helped move this multi-sited and mixed-methods beast of a project along, getting us through the coding stage. They both performed smartly, skillfully, and attentive to detail, and remained dedicated to the project even through the COVID-19 pandemic. Tanya Golash-Boza, Whitney Pirtle, and Matthew Jendian at the University of California, Merced, deserve thanks for connecting us to research assistants early in the process and lending us space to meet with our research team.

This project would have taken much longer to complete and would not have its current shape without the generous support of the Russell Sage Foundation and its Presidential Authority grant. Critical funding at the home stretch also came from the Abigail Reynolds Hodgen Publication Fund at the University of California, Berkeley, as well as the Social Science Dean's Office. A special thanks to Lisa García Bedolla, then director of UCB's Institute of Governmental Studies, who consulted with us many times as we refined our methodology and was gracious enough to allow us to field our own survey through the institute for this project.

We are also indebted to a long list of colleagues across the country and in California especially, each of whom took the time to read our work, informally discuss our arguments, and help shepherd our book through various stages. They include Nikki Jones, Leigh Raiford, Michael Burawoy, Mara Loveman, Kris Gutiérrez, Ula Taylor, Cybelle Fox, and David Harding at the University of California, Berkeley, as well as Hana Brown, Dina Okamoto, Shannon Gleeson, and Lorrie Frasure. In the spring of 2024, we held a generative book workshop, where we received critical feedback on every page of the manuscript. We are extremely grateful for the generosity of Jennifer A. Jones, Natalie Masuoka, Anthony Ocampo, Vilma Ortiz, Christian Paíz, Michael Rodríguez-Muñiz, Brandi Summers, and Nicholas Vargas. Special thanks also to Raka Ray for the many years of encouragement, for her sage advice, and for her firm belief that we would produce a manuscript to be proud of. Over the years, there were many times that we thought: "what would Michael Burawoy say?" Though he passed before he could read final versions of this work, we are indebted to him for inspiring us to think about precarity and complicity, just as he has guided our vision of a life in the academy.

Holly Le, Tamar Young, and Michael Schneider worked the bureaucracy at the University of California, Berkeley, in our favor to get research assistants hired and paid, our interviews transcribed, and our travel reimbursed. They also made certain that our book workshop went off without a hitch. That kind of behind-the-scenes work is often invisibilized, and yet it is so vital to any project like this one. It is much appreciated.

We were able to present earlier versions of this research project at many universities and workshops around the country. We would like to thank all of those that invited us to share the work and who took our work seriously. They gave us much to consider during the development of the project. In that vein, a special thank you goes out to the participants of the Black Politics/Theory/History and its organizers—Juliet Hooker,

Shateema Threadcraft, and Deva Woodly—for offering a supportive and rigorous interdisciplinary space for sharing this work.

We are also grateful for the support of Leslie Wang, who helped us think through the project at a critical juncture. Her feedback was substantive and her insights on everything from the writing process to the book's audience were transformative. Jane Elliott helped shift our thinking about ourselves as scholars during the difficult final phase of preparing this book.

Additionally, we had the great pleasure of working with Suzanne Nichols at Russell Sage Foundation Press. Not only did she bet on our project, she also pushed us to recognize its greater significance. We believe that this final version of the work is much more ambitious and because of that, we hope it will reach even more people. Many thanks to Jennifer Rappaport for shepherding this book to completion. This work also benefited greatly from the caring and thoughtful editing assistance provided by Karen Villegas. Anonymous reviewers were also generous and rigorous in their analysis of the manuscript and pushed us toward writing a book that was more expansive in its framing and theoretical contributions.

Cristina—My greatest debt goes to my family, especially my parents, Maria and Cresencio, whose support and encouragement has allowed me to believe the next step was always possible. To my brothers, Albert and Jesus, thank you for having my back and for reminding me that I have never been alone. I feel so very lucky to be in family with you both. To my sister Maria, our early conversations helped get this book off the ground. Then, like today, you have inspired me, loved me, and guided me in so many ways. To my nieces and nephews, Alex, Sergio, Aidan, Johnny, and Dani, as well as Priscilla and Juan, your extended support has meant more than you know. I am also deeply indebted to my aunts Julie, Kini, and Gina for all their love and encouragement throughout the years. Special thanks to the Murray family, including Mary, Jessie, and Jake. You have welcomed me into your lives, loved Adela and Camilo, and extended our definition of family. And Mike, thank you for this next phase in our lives, for all the ways that you hold us and complete us, and for all the ways that you keep me steady in the storm. You and Lola have been my greatest gifts in this chapter. Adela and Camilo: It's here! Mom and Nina Tianna are finally done. Thank you for your patience, love, laughter, and for rooting me on toward this finish line. Maybe you will read this one day and find fragments of ideas that we have long talked about over pizza and family dinners. And maybe you will read this one day and know that I have tried my best to contribute to a new dream for us all.

Tianna—I would like to thank my mom, Pamela, for the many sacrifices she made to give me a good life, from taking unimaginable risks to making sure I had the best education possible. Thank you also for allowing me to tell your story, to tell our story. As I put closure on this second major book, I am feeling so much gratitude for the many opportunities I have had that led me here. Thank you to Mark Q. Sawyer for everything. This work would not exist were it not for all of your support. I miss you every day. Thank you, also, for leading me to Eddie Telles, to whom I will always be grateful and to Cathy J. Cohen, who has been an incredible mentor and friend to me. Much thanks to Caleb Dawson, Rae Willis-Conger, Clara Pérez Medina, Darius Gordon, des Jackson, Allison Brooke, Xavier Durham, and Jessica Law for meaningfully engaging with this work and offering feedback that helped me better clarify my contributions. Thank you to Nikki Jones for being one of the first and most consistent supporters of this work and to Christen Smith for encouraging me to find my voice within this project. Leigh Raiford, thank you for all the dreaming and conspiring that coincided with the writing of this book. I am forever changed and so incredibly thankful. I also have so much gratitude for Kara Young Ponder, who listened to many pitches of the book and offered substantive feedback and, perhaps more importantly, reminded me to rest and take care of myself along the way. Thank you to Cindi Rivera for all your compassion and guidance over the years. Thanks to my stepdad, James, for your encouragement, for sharing your story with me, and for loving and supporting me despite it all. Thank you to Celia Lacayo for your work and decades-long conversations about race and racism here. Thank you also to my sister, Crystal, and my nibling Nakaiyah, for serving as sounding boards during this project, and for helping with childcare. Without you and mom, this book would not be possible. Last but not least, I would like to thank Marshawn for being patient when I worked late nights and weekend mornings. Thank you for all the laughter and levity when all the work piled up, for the spontaneous games of tag and the sweetest cuddle sessions. By the age of seven, you had already concluded that I was "famous" because I was a published author. While I know that you will inevitably grow up and gain some perspective on this, I do hope this book lives up to at least some of the hype. All the love to all of you.

INTRODUCTION

Inequality is part of our everyday lives. Whether we experience its most disastrous effects or benefit from its proliferation, it is something that is always with us. If you are part of the commuting middle class, you may have to grapple with inequality as you pass by impoverished and working-poor neighborhoods on your way to and from work. If you take the subway or bus, you may have noticed an increase in the number of people asking for help. You might scrounge around for some change to offer them, or you might feel embarrassed and avoid eye contact by looking away. If you live in a rural area, you might drive past rows of farmworkers who toil long hours, often in the blazing heat, as you make your way to a big-box store or an all-in-one entertainment district. If you are not attuned to the inequalities around you, you might focus on the immediate: the make, model, and speed of the car in front of you; the person sitting across from you on the bus; or the sounds coming from your child playing with a tablet in the back seat of the car. In autopilot mode, you might never stop to reflect on how the United States has become one of the most unequal countries in the world.

Here, in the land of the American Dream, it is much more likely that the rich get much richer than the poor climb out of poverty. Over the past few decades, the wealthy's share of income has skyrocketed while workers' wages have stagnated. Today, the top 1 percent of earners reap about 15 percent of all income earned in the country, and the top 10 percent reap almost 50 percent.[1] The picture is more dire in terms of assets, capital, and wealth inequality. In the 1980s, the wealthiest people in the United States (the top 1 percent) owned about 25–30 percent of

https://doi.org/10.7758/uybx4321.9754

the nation's wealth (an already high share), increasing to an alarming 35 percent by 2022.[2] Furthermore, over the years, the share of Americans living in middle-class households has shrunk at the same time the percentage of wealth owned by those still in the middle has decreased. Paired with ever-increasing debt, these realities have left many in today's middle class feeling unsteady and lacking the same purchasing power as earlier generations had.[3]

This growing divide has racial overtones. Black and Latino communities' share of wealth in the United States has been decreasing,[4] especially since the 2008 financial crisis,[5] and both groups earn less than their White counterparts, have higher rates of unemployment, and have lower rates of homeownership.[6] And race continues to mark their lives and life chances beyond the purely economic sphere, including the schools they can access, the likelihood they will receive quality health care, the cleanliness of their drinking water, and the safety of the neighborhoods where they raise their children. Economic opportunity and racial marginalization are deeply intertwined in this nation, which was founded on settler colonialism and powered first by slavery and later by a racialized immigration system. Wealth and disadvantage accumulate through these systems and are handed down through the generations.

Yet while we know a lot about class inequality, its patterns, how it has shifted over time, and how it is shaped by racial dynamics, we know much less about how people make sense of inequality and how they navigate through it in their daily lives. In *Normalizing Inequality*, we set out to understand how a precarious middle class understands, lives with, and navigates these pervasive inequalities. We argue that, while individuals are largely aware of the structural conditions that shape the inequalities they experience and see around them, they tend to downplay them in favor of a more individualist and optimistic understanding. We show how they do this by using three specific narrative strategies: exceptional framing, spatial comparison, and bounded blame. We contend that while such strategies are helpful in terms of allowing people to live with and navigate inequality, they also serve to passively reproduce it.

We examine these issues in the context of California, one of the most unequal states in one of the most unequal countries in the world. Drawing on a trove of interview and survey data, we tell the story of how people make sense of the inequalities they see around them and the meaning they ascribe to the ever-changing nature of opportunity, racial inequality, and social mobility. Indeed, today's California seems split in two—a wealth-driven upper class based on growing technology and an ever-expanding lower class.[7] In such a place, even for those in the middle, life can feel precarious, and the promise of the American Dream just out of reach.

Laura is an example of this increasingly precarious middle class. A Latina in her fifties, Laura had just gotten off work as an administrator at a nearby college when she sat down for an interview. Dressed in business casual attire, she explained to us that she has held two jobs at the same time for most of her adult life: "I'm a hustler, and I've always liked to work." That afternoon, Laura spoke for two hours about her life and the constant squeeze she felt because she hadn't quite achieved middle-class status. She, like many around her, had a hard time keeping up with the city's ever-increasing cost of living. Though she had over fifteen years of experience working in higher education and had recently purchased a house, she and her husband felt financially stuck. With a pained expression, she explained that, without her daughter's rent contribution, the family would probably lose their home. At times, she said, the financial pressures felt overwhelming, and in retrospect she would have liked to have raised her children in a more upwardly mobile and safe neighborhood. Even though her home was in one of LA County's more affordable working-class Latino communities, two incomes could not sustain a single household. She needed something else—a side hustle, a third paycheck, anything to keep afloat.

Laura's feeling of being economically squeezed is common among middle-class families in Los Angeles. Between 2017 and 2024, the average home value in LA County shot up by 44 percent, and home rental prices increased by 20 percent, making Los Angeles one of the most expensive places to live in the United States.[8] Economists estimate that only 17 percent of city residents can currently afford to purchase a median-priced home there.[9] Similar trends can be observed across the state, such as in major urban centers like the San Francisco Bay Area and San Diego, which also saw real estate prices jump after the Great Recession. No region has been spared from these alarming and growing inequalities. Residents in the Central Valley have also witnessed historic cost-of-living increases despite the area's history of relative affordability compared with the coastal cities.[10]

While Laura was doing relatively well, inequality still shaped the world she inhabited. The same skyrocketing housing prices that made her dependent on her daughter to make ends meet are also behind the unprecedented number of people living on the streets and in their cars in Los Angeles. During Laura's interview, a homeless woman with disheveled hair wandered onto the outdoor public patio where we were speaking. She looked for an outlet to plug her phone into and then sat on the floor, talking to herself. Laura never gestured directly at the woman but did speak about how homelessness was now evident outside the city's downtown areas, including the more suburban, Latino working-class areas on the outskirts of the city, like her own neighborhood. She declared, "It's just gotten so much worse. . . . Oh my God, it's so much worse." Laura also noted how many more families of color, especially Latinos, had fallen into homelessness. She believed the economy had something to do with the situation, especially the 2008 recession: "People just haven't recuperated. They really haven't."

Despite it all, Laura remained hopeful. Los Angeles was, after all, a place where scores of immigrants, including her Mexican parents, made a new life after fleeing poverty and its accompanying violence. Laura explained how she really appreciated Los Angeles as a place for diverse newcomers to make a fresh start. She said she especially liked how the city celebrates her "Hispanic culture." Los Angeles, she thinks, holds the capacity to let people "always find something better" if they look and work hard enough. And she thinks that she has instilled this understanding in her daughters, both of whom recently graduated from college. Laura herself had just earned a bachelor's degree online despite having dropped out of high school in her teens. She was proud that she had climbed the career ladder against the odds in a state where Latinos have historically had the lowest levels of educational attainment. She hopes to move up and work in the chancellor's office one day or even earn a graduate degree in school counseling. As Latinos begin to earn college degrees at higher rates, Laura figured, they will need more bilingual advisors, counselors, and college administrators like her.

Many of the people we met while drafting this book talked about California in this way, acknowledging the difficulties but also taking special pride in the possibilities and diversity of the place. One of them was Keej, who was born in a refugee camp in Thailand but found himself with his parents in California's Central Valley before his second birthday.

Fresno, the largest city in the country's breadbasket, is partially hidden by endless fields of grapes, almonds, and tomatoes. The over two months of one-hundred-degree days is not for the faint of heart, but it is the reason hundreds of commercial crops take root and thrive there.

It was the agricultural industry that made Fresno home to many immigrants, their children, and their grandchildren, including the second-largest Hmong community outside Southeast Asia.[11] Keej spent most of his childhood in a run-down two-bedroom apartment, his parents in one room and he and his four siblings in the other. On a typical weekday, Keej would go to school and then work in the fields with his siblings. He spent weekends helping his parents sell produce at farmers markets around the region. His mother, now a widow and nearing her would-be retirement years, was still doing this backbreaking work, day in and day out. In their Hmong community, Keej and his family heard stories of social mobility and triumph alongside cautionary tales of poverty, racial discrimination, and criminalization. With this in mind, Keej was quick to clarify that his family and other Hmong families like his were not farmers. They were farm *laborers*. To be a farmer meant *owning* the land.

After many hardships, by the time Keej got to high school, his family had left their cramped apartment and moved into a four-bedroom house purchased through a government program meant to stave off threats to US security.[12] The sacrifices of Keej's parents had paid off. All of their children attended college, and two had advanced degrees. Keej had earned a bachelor of arts in psychology—quite an accomplishment since school had never been easy for him. He had studied, but he knew that the elementary and high schools he attended in Fresno and neighboring Clovis weren't designed for people like him to succeed. Keej had a passion for making a difference in his community and was working at a local nonprofit that advocated for water rights for Hmong and other Southeast Asian farmers in the Central Valley.

Keej felt a sense of true belonging growing up in Fresno, seeped in the Hmong community but part of a diverse group of friends, which he affectionately referred to as "the four musketeers." "I had a Black friend, a White friend, and a Hispanic Mexican [friend], and I was the Asian." He could not name a time he ever felt excluded but lamented that hiring managers would more likely choose a "Johnson" over a "Dong."[13] Keej worried that he might never be able to truly provide for his family—not in the way he would like to. His dream was to buy his family home from his mother. The house was in a working-class neighborhood on the outskirts of Fresno, which had been founded nearly a century earlier by the Bible Institute of Los Angeles. His parents had moved the family there to escape a specific racialized poverty trap that befalls many farmworker families.[14]

Indeed, California's Central Valley is home to some of the poorest census tracts in the state. Despite the abundance of water available for big agriculture, some unincorporated areas still lack safe piping and running water.[15] These places of intense poverty are often tucked away behind fields where rows of Brown laborers are harvesting, hunched over for long hours, even in extreme heat. Poverty in the Central Valley is urban and rural, in plain sight and out of view, but almost always a shade of Brown. The fact that, if it were a country, California would be the fourth largest economy in the world, brings little comfort to these residents.[16]

At the time of our interview, Keej was living in his family's home with his mother, his wife, and his children. He was proud of what his parents had accomplished, although he joked that it smelled like cows where he lived. He dreamed of the day when he would feel financially secure and his mother would never again need to labor under the hot sun. His father had passed away only a few years prior, leaving him with an even-greater sense of responsibility, no doubt because he was the eldest son. Yet even though he worked well over forty hours a week, he struggled to pay for childcare. He would sometimes fantasize about moving—understandable since housing costs in Fresno rose by a staggering 100 percent over the past ten years.[17] On the day of our interview, Keej refused to order anything at the coffee shop until he learned that we would be paying. He then ordered two drinks and two croissants, saving them to share with his family later.

In the following chapters, we delve into the stories of people like Laura and Keej to better understand how the precarious middle class makes sense of intersectional inequalities. We illustrate how people rationalize inequality by minimizing structural explanations in favor of more direct and simple explanations that emphasize individual effort. Although interviewees acknowledged the structural roots of inequality and recognized them as unjust, they often downplayed their significance, instead foregrounding merit, opportunity, and the positive aspects of the places where they live.

The minimizing of structural interpretations or the backgrounding of issues such as uneven intergenerational wealth, systemic racial disparities, and government policies that favor the rich, can result in inequality being thought of as an unfortunate but inevitable reality. Our research zeros in on this practice to reveal a set of cultural processes we call normalizing inequality, which we argue have been long overlooked in larger discussions about class inequality and racial disparities in the United States. We posit that understanding how individuals make sense of inequality can tell us a great deal about how society reproduces it.

While California is the focus of much of this book, we believe that the state is emblematic of many places across the United States, where similar dynamics are unfolding but perhaps not at the same scale or speed.[18] Indeed, far from the Pacific Ocean and Sierra Nevada, folks are living with and trying to make sense of growing inequalities and the "middle-class squeeze," as well as the roles played by various groups, including immigrants, the rich, and the tech sector, in making it so difficult to maintain middle-class stability in America.

Growing Inequality in California and the Nation

People increasingly associate the Golden State with significant inequality. Public media, think tanks, and California's Legislative Analyst's Office have been warning about the state's growing inequality. In 2018, the *Economist* magazine called California the "richest and poorest state in the union," noting that it had some of the wealthiest zip codes and industries in the nation as well as some of its poorest census tracts.[19] We don't have to look too far to see evidence of both.

Consider, for example, that the Bay Area is home to the largest technology sector in the country, including some of the most important internet, social media, and "sharing economy" corporations on the planet.[20] This industry has created tech billionaires and families whose wealth has increased exponentially over the past twenty years. At the same time, Los Angeles and the Bay Area are at the center of a homelessness epidemic.[21] Today, more unhoused people live in California than in any other state, with a share that has increased dramatically in the last two decades.[22] What is more, homelessness is no longer relegated to core downtown areas in the state's largest cities. Camps of

Figure I.1 *Change in Family Incomes Since 1980 in California*

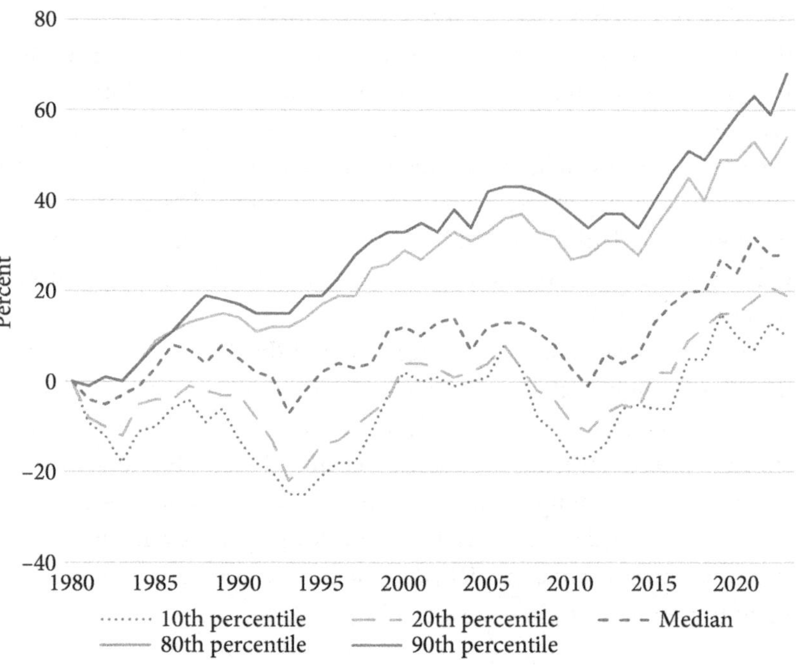

Source: Thorman and Payares-Montoya 2025. Reprinted with permission.

unhoused people now line neighborhoods in the suburbs and exurbs as well as at the perimeters of rural communities.[23]

This is not entirely new. Inequality has been growing in the state since the manufacturing decline in the 1970s, which resulted in major losses of middle-class jobs in sectors such as construction, defense, and aerospace. Throughout the 1980s and 1990s, these processes would mean that Californians in the top ten percent would witness exponential increases to their earning capacity while those at the bottom would see much more modest gains. A recent analysis by the Public Policy Institute of California, reproduced in figure I.1, clearly illustrates these trends.

Today, income inequality in California is greater than that in the United States as a whole, and overall inequality is greater than in most other states. In 2021, the Public Policy Institute of California determined that the state had the country's third-largest income gap among families.[24]

As of this writing, California has the highest rate of poverty in the nation,[25] and many of those living in poverty work full-time or close to it. The working poor often toil in jobs with unpredictable schedules, scant if any health care or retirement benefits, and little opportunity for advancement.[26] Yet California is a part of a much-larger national and global trend. Indeed, inequality is on the rise around the globe as income and wealth become increasingly concentrated.[27]

As scholars and as mothers, we are deeply invested in understanding how people interpret, normalize, and often come to accept this inequality. As Black and Brown women, this subject has significant meaning to us, if only because we come from communities that have endured the most from these economic inequalities. Indeed, African Americans and Latinos in California experience significantly higher levels of poverty, near poverty, and working poverty compared with their Asian and White counterparts. Black Californians constitute 6 percent of the state but represent 12 percent of the state's poor; and Latinos are the commanding majority in the state's poorest rural areas, including those in the Central Valley and the Imperial Valley.[28]

California's Latino school children, especially in Los Angeles, are among the most racially and class-segregated school children in the nation—attending districts where up to 80 percent of children are Latino and a majority are low income.[29] Black children often find themselves in majority-Latino public school districts and subject to many of the same resource constraints as their Latino schoolmates.

Latino and Black families also sit on the lower end of California's household income scale, and Latino and Black workers operate in labor markets that offer them retail, warehousing, and service jobs with comparatively low pay, few benefits, and unpredictable schedules.[30] In fact, in 2023 the state's Civil Rights Department estimated that about half of Latino and Black workers were in the lowest pay range in the state, compared to less than one-third of their White counterparts. Almost half of California's Latino workers and one-third of its Black workers have minimum-wage jobs compared with just 20 percent of White workers.[31]

Such racial trends are reflected in patterns of homelessness. Today, Black residents make up an alarming 26 percent of the state's unhoused population, with Latinos among the fastest-growing unhoused group in the state.[32] While the color of poverty has changed over time, the state's most destitute communities are still Black and Brown. We therefore believe it is imperative to understand how residents across communities make sense of and perhaps take for granted these stark, often racialized inequalities.

While these trends are alarming in and of themselves, inequality takes a toll on society in other ways as well. Beyond its devastating personal impact, poverty is correlated with worse health outcomes at the broader population level.[33] Across the globe, greater income inequality is also correlated with lower civic participation and engagement as well as higher rates of violent crime.[34]

Scholars have also noted the psychological toll inequality takes on individuals and society. A sense of belonging—the feeling of being included, valued, and recognized within a society[35]—is often challenging to achieve in societies characterized by high levels of structural inequality.[36] We know, for instance, that people with lower socioeconomic status report feeling alienated and out of place at much higher rates than those with higher socioeconomic status, especially in public spaces and educational settings not historically designed for them.[37] This phenomenon of marginalized people experiencing alienation is akin to being denied what sociologist Evelyn Nakano Glenn terms "substantive citizenship."[38] As she notes: "Citizenship is not just a matter of formal legal status; it is a matter of belonging, which requires recognition by other members of the community. Community members participate in drawing the boundaries of citizenship and defining who is entitled to civil, political, and social rights by granting or withholding recognition."[39]

The intersectional inequalities that we examine around race, class, and immigration directly relate to belonging and how boundaries are drawn. We suggest that, although poverty presents significant challenges on its own, inequality can foster discontent and dis-belonging, which negatively affects individuals and society in diverse ways.

Making Sense of Inequality

Scholars have shown how capitalism, especially when left unchecked, is incapable of producing egalitarian societies, tending instead toward ever-increasing inequality.[40] We also know that hierarchies are intrinsic features of almost all modern societies. Despite constant change and evolution, contemporary societies have always been unequal, with some people and groups having more status, power, and wealth than others. It is therefore no wonder that inequality has been the center of social science research across disciplines. In the field of sociology, for example, canonical works have sought to explain the economic and cultural conditions that give rise to and intensify class inequality and have also explored how different groups experience their place in the hierarchy.[41] This research has sparked vigorous debates on the nature of class, the changing mechanics of exploitation in the labor force, and the intersecting forms of material and symbolic marginalization.[42]

Over the past few decades, much contemporary work, especially urban ethnography, has focused on how those who draw the "short end of the stick" understand and navigate the societies in which they experience systemic disadvantage.[43] This research has been crucial to understanding how inequality is lived and how it gets reproduced. It shows how institutional context, including schools, neighborhoods, and labor markets, constrain and shape the opportunities and networks that poor people have access to, making it more likely that conditions of poverty reproduce themselves across generations.[44] Studies suggest that structural conditions reproduce certain cultural attitudes and shape the way poor people perceive the world around them.[45] For example, sociologist Victor Rios shows how the over-policing of poor and working-class boys of color in schools and neighborhoods influences their ideas about masculinity and opportunities for social mobility.[46]

Another line of research has focused on how growing inequality has engendered a changing set of behaviors, especially among the middle class, who seem to display increasing levels of status anxiety.[47] These changes—for example, the increase in credentialization and dual-income families—are discernable at the population level.[48] Middle-class families are getting more educated as a way of stabilizing their class position. Scholars have documented behavioral changes within families as well, including middle-class parents becoming increasingly focused on managing their children's free time and after-school activities compared with a few decades ago, largely because they want their children to get into college and eventually be able to compete in the labor market.[49]

Yet asking people how they experience inequality is one thing. It is another to ask how they see and make sense of it. Our research shifts the focus from an examination of how people navigate the negative effects of inequality to asking how—if at all—those in the middle think about inequality more generally. This shift requires an understanding of how people conceptualize the quality, origins, scale, and even time-horizon of the social disparities around them. It requires that we ask questions such as: How do folks describe inequality (for example, economic versus racial or a combination of both)? Why do they think it exists? How do they see it affecting them personally, if at all? And how do they explain its persistence, if they think it is persisting?

Survey and public opinion research has shed critical light on the question of scale—how much inequality individuals perceive. This work reveals that, despite the growing global rise in economic inequality, many continue to underestimate its significance.[50] Americans have a particular tendency to underestimate inequality when compared to those in other Western countries.[51] And Americans significantly overestimate actual social mobility—the odds of moving up the class ladder—compared with their European counterparts.[52]

Not only do people living in the United States notice less inequality than those living in other Western countries, they are also less inclined to do something about it.[53] For example, Americans are less likely than Canadians or Europeans to support redistributive policies that address inequalities.[54] Perhaps most striking, researchers have conducted laboratory experiments showing that, when most Americans are given the opportunity to redistribute wealth, they still tend to design unequal societies.[55] Moreover, compared with others in comparable countries, Americans consistently prefer higher levels of inequality.[56] But it is also important to note that recent research may be showing that Americans no longer completely accept this state of inequality. In one of the most comprehensive sociological examination of public opinion data on inequality, sociologist Leslie McCall shows, for example, that American beliefs around inequality have varied over time and, by some measures, have actually displayed a downward trend in preference for inequality.[57] This suggests a great deal of ambivalence about the subject and the need to more deeply investigate American attitudes.

Experimental work in social psychology and stratification has taken a different approach by focusing on how people explain inequality. Following Joe Feagin's research, social psychologists and public opinion researchers have argued that society is roughly made up of those with an "individualist" and those with a "structuralist" framework for understanding the reproductive nature of inequality.[58] Individualists tend to see inequality as a product of one's behavior, while structuralists point to structural issues, such as intergenerational wealth and discrimination, to explain who gets ahead and who does not.[59] To individualists, being exposed to research showing rising inequality isn't important if they believe systems are fair and meritocratic.[60]

Although the scholarship on structuralist thinkers is comparatively limited, some studies indicate they view social mobility as shaped by both historical inequalities—like policy or wealth transfers—and present-day issues such as workplace discrimination and stereotyping.[61] While an individualist might consider whether promotion and mobility processes are fair in the immediate moment, structuralist thinkers take a broader and historically minded view to understand how the system has been "rigged."[62] A great deal of experimental work conducted in psychology laboratories also shows that people in groups with lower social status, such as women and racial minorities, tend toward structuralist interpretations of inequality at greater rates than those in higher-status groups, such as men and Whites.[63] There is also growing research positing that some groups, especially racial minorities, might be "dual systems" thinkers, with both structuralist and individualist interpretations of inequality.[64] Just how this dual framework operates is not yet fully understood, especially within and across different groups.

But why does this matter?

The most important reason it matters is that it shapes people's orientation toward inequality as well as how they think about belonging and deservingness. We know, for instance, that people with higher levels of individualist tendencies are more likely to see poor people as undeserving and are less likely to support social policies such as welfare and other social benefits,[65] while structuralist thinkers are more likely to recognize high levels of inequality and therefore support redistribution policies. In other words, the way we think about inequality in all its dimensions influences how we think about what needs to be done about it and how we make sense of who belongs, and why. Beyond this, it matters because our worldview informs how we see ourselves and others. It shapes our behavior in a myriad of ways, including how we express empathy to members of different groups and how we vote. It might even determine whether we care enough about inequality to be outraged by it, and whether we are angry enough to hit the streets in protest. Put another way, how we think about the world around us creates the cultural and political context in which high levels of inequality fester and reproduce themselves.

While research on perceptions of class inequality has contributed to our understanding, it has its shortcomings. The first is methodological. Because of its heavy reliance on survey data, research has not been sufficiently focused on why people perceive inequality in the ways that they do, the processes by which they come to understand it, or how experiences and ideologies make some forms of inequality more visible than others. Yet inequality is also a reflection of social processes and power-laden arrangements and, as such, is inherently about meaning-making. So while surveys offer key insights into how people understand inequality, they do not address important cultural processes undergirding attitudes. Similarly, while discussions about structural versus individualist understandings of inequality are helpful, they can force nuanced and complex meaning-making processes into narrow categories. Indeed, individuals make sense of things in rich and dynamic, not static, ways, making them difficult to classify into broad categories. It thus makes sense that survey researchers themselves have called for more qualitative inquiries to better understand the mechanisms that shape how inequality is understood.[66] Answering that call, we lean into the messiness of sense-making, to reveal the ways people develop complex rationalizations for ever-present inequalities.

Our work builds on the literature on stratification beliefs, which examines how individuals understand their class status and perceive broader class inequality. As such we focus on the worldviews and frames that underpin individual perceptions of inequality.[67] And this, in turn, demands that we also pay attention to how deeply institutionalized narratives about mobility, especially the American Dream, shape our sense-making processes.[68]

The issue of region or place has been largely underemphasized in the literature, but we argue that it is a core part of how people come to accept the economic and racial disparities around them. Californians live in a state with the largest immigrant population in the nation. It is also thought to be a place where some of the nation's progressive politics are incubated and nurtured. Local realities and the narratives layered on top of them are the cultural milieu in which residents develop ideas about inequality. We argue that understanding how people in the Golden State make sense of inequality can tell us a lot about how place matters in general and how it relates to a broader understanding of the nation's growing divide.

The second shortcoming of the research on perceptions of class inequality is that it rarely considers the intersectional nature of material inequalities. So much of the existing literature we have mentioned thus far has focused exclusively on class inequality in societies that are also notoriously stratified by race and immigration status. And still, having a keen sense of economic inequality does not mean that one will be clear-eyed about how racism and xenophobia underlies and intensifies growing divides. For example, research about the attitudes of White working- and middle-class individuals reveals that many have deep concerns about class inequality but are indifferent to the racialized processes underlying it.[69] Recent scholarship has found that many Americans have become increasingly colorblind over time, rarely perceiving racial inequalities as structural.[70] In one important study, researchers found that "respondents thought that the Black–White wealth gap was smaller, by around 40 percentage points in 1963 and around 80 percentage points in 2016, than its actual size."[71]

It is no surprise that the race of the respondent also matters here. African Americans, for example, are much more likely than others to acknowledge structural racial inequalities and to think that the history of oppression has shaped inequalities in the present. According to recent scholarship, White people are the least likely to acknowledge structural racial inequality, while Asian and Latino individuals tend to be somewhere between Black and White people.[72] A great deal of research has also emerged on attitudes toward immigrants in the United States, but significantly less has focused on how the material realities of immigrants, and the causes of these inequalities that they face, are perceived.[73] This suggests there may be significant ideological variation even among those with structural interpretations of inequality.[74]

The ways that race and class intersect to shape perceptions of inequality have important policy implications. We know that social welfare policies have received limited support in the United States because many White people think African Americans in particular are a kind of undeserving poor.[75] Beyond the US, countries that are more ethno-racially homogenous tend to experience less inequality and have more robust social welfare programs.[76] It is no coincidence that, as immigration increases, a once-robust social safety net is being challenged in some European countries by an alarming explosion of far-right popular movements and increasing xenophobia.[77] Race, class, and immigration are profoundly entangled with each other, and our analysis of economic inequality addresses this entanglement.

Normalizing Inequality examines how people make sense of and grapple with layered inequalities in a place where they are visible and growing—a phenomenon especially evident in California. As our focus is on sense-making, we are not as concerned with the mechanics of inequality as with how inequality is imagined. To gain insight into the reproduction of inequality, we home in on the cultural and ideological aspects of inequality, as well as the ways that a sense of place affects their articulation.

HEGEMONY AND THE NORMALIZING OF INEQUALITY

Before we continue, it is important to clarify what we mean by *normalizing*. Social theorists have long studied the relationship between power and cultural dynamics, sometimes focusing on institutionalization—the process that makes ideas or practices widely accepted and unquestioned.[78] They have also shown how certain ideas come to be understood as normal and inevitable, which then shapes behavior, including as a disciplinary mechanism.[79] Normalized understandings gain traction because they serve as shared constructs, sometimes backed by deeply held ideologies or consecrated by law, that are generally taken for granted and understood as timeless and socially true.[80] In a sense, these understandings become "common sense" as folks start to accept or consent to the stark inequalities and injustices around them.

One of the most influential thinkers in this tradition is Antonio Gramsci. About a hundred years ago, he penned a thirty-volume series from a prison cell. Thinking specifically about the conditions of Fascist Italy at the time, Gramsci asked why the working class did not engage in open revolt against the prevailing regime. Writing on any scrap of paper he could find, he posited that modern states had figured out how to exert power premised on a combination of force and coercion. Using influential institutions such as education and the media, people in power can promote their own vision of society, one that makes the status quo seem not only normal but also natural and inevitable. This, he argued, had led most people to take the social order for granted, including its ingrained inequalities, and in this way consent to it.[81]

Today, we might think of hegemony as people accepting a status quo built on large and growing inequalities of various kinds. In this vein, scholars of class inequality have argued that capitalism has become a hegemonic system where the working class has, to some extent, consented to a social order premised on its exploitation.[82] Scholars of race and immigration have also found the concept of hegemony useful for explaining the often-silent reproduction of racial inequality in contemporary US society. Notably, in their classic work, sociologists Michael Omi and Howard Winant argue that after World War II, the United States changed from a system of racial domination based on overt and legally sanctioned racism to a regime primarily based on racial hegemony premised on the idea of colorblindness, which masks and reproduces ongoing racial injustices and inequalities.[83]

Like Gramsci, these scholars argue that hegemony requires an entire cultural apparatus to sustain it,[84] which might look like normalizing the idea that a round of successful collective bargaining by workers gives them a fair share of profits, or that there is no alternative to capitalism.[85] Similarly, normalizing racial hierarchy might mean passively accepting the idea that certain racial groups are not motivated enough to succeed or that we live in a true meritocracy and therefore ongoing racial disparities are the result of individual failings, not systemic constraints. Consenting to the status quo might also look like taking for granted our current racialized immigration system, which does not offer a viable path to citizenship for people who are the backbone of the US economy, or the assumption that the immigration system itself is neutral and inevitable.[86] Cultural understanding about inequalities rooted in class, race, immigration status, or a combination of factors can become naturalized as the way things should be. The greater the cultural conditioning to accept the status quo, the less likely we are to feel enraged about it or to engage in open revolt against it.

The linkages between power, culture, and the reproduction of inequality are relevant to this work, particularly because we are interested in how people like Laura and Keej understand imbricated inequalities, including why some have more than others, why some groups cannot seem to get ahead, and who is deserving of what. We show that those in the precarious middle-class display worry and concern about their current situation but also somehow manage to be hopeful. By unpacking the link between worry and hope and between anger and resolve, we can better understand how tolerance for the status quo gets reproduced and how inequality comes to be normalized. Individuals can normalize inequality even as it grows and even though they might find it inconvenient, displeasing, or even immoral.[87]

Our Approach

A few things are important to highlight about the approach we take in this book. The first concerns how we see California in relation to the rest of the country. A case can be made for California exceptionalism. The state's particular history of layered colonialisms, its large waves of immigrants, and its increasingly infamous wealth gap make it an interesting place to examine these issues. The legacy of Western frontierism, Mexico–United States relations, and over a century of continuous immigration from Asia and Latin America make it a fitting place for thinking through questions of race and immigration. What is more, because of its history as a territory of Mexico and its long-standing Mexican population, Californians have long considered Latinos as racialized, not simply a newly arrived, group.[88] Furthermore, as the "one-drop rule" and rigid racial categories continue to dominate racial classification in the rest of the country, California has shown signs that it may be embracing a degree of racial fluidity.[89] This context provides an alternative to the mainly Black-White paradigm that has historically dominated theorizing about race and racialization in the United States.

Another interesting aspect of California is its complex relationship to the rest of the country. Scholars have shown how the Golden State is at the vanguard of social, political, and demographic changes that could soon be replicated in other parts of the country. For example, while other states are only now experiencing a dramatic "Browning" of their population, similar demographic shifts have been underway in California for over five decades. Between 1970 and 2015, the state's White population decreased from 78 to 38 percent, making it a state with one of the largest "minority" populations in the country. According to demographers' estimates, the United States will reach that status in 2040.[90] California is also at the forefront of other changes on the horizon for the rest of the country, including the racial and class diversification of the suburbs; the rise of tech hubs like Silicon Valley, which has buoyed local economies while also exacerbating inequality; and the reconfiguration of urban spaces so that workers now live in exurbs and travel longer distances to find less stable work. In other words, California might be different than the rest of the country now, but many of its social trends are a sign of what may be to come in other states.[91]

We believe that California is an interesting site to explore questions around inequality because of the ways it is different, and because of the ways it is similar to the rest of the United States. The trends in California related to demographics and inequality, while distinctive in many ways, allow us to hyperfocus on the processes that undergird the normalization of inequality.[92] Indeed, in California—unlike places where inequality may be lower or more recent—inequality is unavoidable among broad swaths of the population, making the Golden State a clear example of how individuals come to understand, process, and narrate disparities. Moreover, because California is often a harbinger of what is to come in other states, it offers opportunities for exploring what might be specific to it and what might apply to other places and times.

The second part of our approach is comparative, focused on how people in four racial groups—Asian American, Latino, Black or African American, and White—across two distinct regions of California, Los Angeles and the Central Valley, make sense of inequality. This comparative approach allows us to see differences in meaning-making around inequality across groups and geographic regions. At the outset of this project, we did not know what respondents would say about how place informed their understanding of inequality or their sense of belonging. Nevertheless, our inductive methodological design allowed us to gain a better understanding of whether, when, and how place matters.

Lastly, our approach takes meaning-making seriously while also centering on how race and immigration shape experiences with material inequality. We take this analytical approach because symbolic and material inequalities are intertwined, as people with low social status experience material disadvantages linked to symbolic forms of marginalization. Examining symbolic status can also contribute to a more comprehensive understanding of the boundaries of belonging in a place that prides itself as one where everyone can belong.

INTERVIEWS

We conducted in-depth interviews along with a team of trained research assistants who were racially matched with respondents. We limited our interviews to respondents in the upper-working and lower-middle classes—the precarious middle—for two main reasons. First was a pragmatic consideration. Because the study already had a great deal of variation related to race and region, we limited the class variation. Second, given the extensive literature on the shrinking middle class, we thought that this group might feel the promise and precarity of California most acutely. The California of today faces significant challenges as housing prices escalate. The effects of gentrification, along with the influx of new wealth from Hollywood and the technology sector, have contributed to the displacement of many in the lower-middle and upper-working classes.[93] In today's California, social workers, teachers, and professional managers with college degrees moonlight as Uber and Lyft drivers, babysitters, or delivery app service workers to make ends meet. Still, for many, a college degree is worthwhile even if it comes with debilitating debt.

Our focus was on people making 80–120 percent of the average median income in their county. People in this group live with promise and precarity, engaged in practices to "make it" but often lacking much savings.[94] Some have two jobs; others work side gigs. Some work full-time jobs in government or in education, while others work for nonprofit organizations, own small businesses, or engage in freelance work. About two-thirds of respondents have college degrees but still did not believe that they were firmly in the middle class or feared slipping downward.

We focus on how these individuals in the middle, who do not experience the most disastrous consequences of a society premised on extreme economic inequalities, make sense of inequality. We ask: How salient is economic and racial inequality to their lives? What are their perceptions of the social world around them and of the future? How do they build middle-class dreams in a land of great inequality? And what might their experiences and ways of understanding inequality tell us about their own sense of belonging, and about who they believe belongs here?

Importantly, we supplemented our interview data with data from a cross-sectional online survey of California residents we conducted in 2018. The questions covered a range of issues concerning inequality, politics and ideology, economic outlook, and immigration. We contextualized interview findings with the broader survey findings. The methodological appendix at the end of this book offers more insight into our interview and coding strategy, as well as information on our sampling approach and survey.

LOS ANGELES AND THE CENTRAL VALLEY IN FOCUS

Our research focuses on the broader Los Angeles metro area and the Central Valley region. We chose Los Angeles because it is the most populous region in the state and because Latinos constitute 50 percent of the population in Los Angeles and 34 percent in Orange County.[95] At the same time, continual waves of Asian immigrants have created sizable communities there, along with their children, grandchildren, and great-grandchildren. For example, the LA region is currently home to the largest community of Filipinos in America, many of whom work and live alongside Mexican, Central American, Vietnamese, and Chinese immigrants and their descendants.[96] Moreover, immigration and the transnational ties that often come with it are part of the greater social fabric of this region. Beyond the typical areas of Thai Town, Chinatown, Koreatown, Olvera Street, and East Los, those with immigrant roots have spread out to the suburbs in many directions. Today, many look to Los Angeles because of its large multiracial and multiethnic population and the many interracial coalition efforts and organizations that have transformed local politics there.[97]

Los Angeles is also a region experiencing dramatic demographic changes at the neighborhood level, where race relations are the subject of heated political and academic debate.[98] The Watts Riots of the 1960s, the Zoot-Suit Riots of the 1920s, and the racist torching of the city's

Chinatown in the nineteenth century are all reminders that the city has long sat on simmering racial embers. Los Angeles today is among the most diverse and most segregated cities in the country, with the Los Angeles Unified School District ranking as one of the most segregated school districts in history.[99] Here, South and Eastside schools tend to enroll mostly Black and Latino students, while schools in West Los Angeles tend to be wealthier and Whiter.

These trends related to racial diversity and segregation have emerged as Los Angeles has become an economic powerhouse. A magnet for high-skilled labor in technology, finance, and entertainment, the region has kept pace, with luxury living units transforming vacant downtown streets that had once been a landscape of single-family homes.[100] However, despite its impressive economic and global clout, Los Angeles, like the rest of the country, has experienced recessions, inflation, and most recently a decrease in middle-class jobs. According to US Census Bureau data, the middle class in LA County has shrunk since the 1990s, while poverty rates have increased.[101] Today, Los Angeles ranks as one of the most economically unequal cities in the nation, trailing New York and New Orleans.[102] These disturbing dynamics came to a head in January 2025 when an unprecedented wave of wildfires swept through Southern California, killing hundreds and leaving uneven devastation in its wake, underscoring the racial dimensions of economic inequality in the region.[103]

While Latinos have among the lowest unemployment rates of any group in Los Angeles, they also have the lowest median wages, earning about half of what White residents earn and two-thirds of what employed Black and Asian residents earn per hour. Black and Latino communities have the highest poverty rates in the city, and Latinos are about twice as likely as other city residents to be considered working poor. Additionally, Black residents are more likely to be unemployed than any other group.[104] At every educational level, Latinos, Asians, and Black people earn less per hour than their White counterparts.[105] Relatedly, people in these communities, especially Latino and Black residents, report spending the largest proportion of their income on housing.[106] In the LA area, a clear racial hierarchy has developed, one that we believed might shape how people understood class inequality.

However, we knew that we could not tell the story of California by simply focusing on Los Angeles. Therefore, at the onset of this project, we included the Central Valley as an important site for examining meaning-making around inequality in California. Most earlier studies that focused on a city or region in California had bypassed the Central Valley entirely, letting Los Angeles or the Bay Area stand in for the entire state. Yet the Central Valley of California is crucial to understanding the state. Most foundationally, it has served as the breadbasket of both the state and the nation since at least the 1930s, when the federally-funded Central Valley Project brought widespread irrigation to the region.[107] Today, 40 percent of the nation's fruits, vegetables, and nuts are grown in the Central Valley, which includes two of the highest-producing agricultural counties in the country.[108] There are other industries in this region, including health care and logistics, but agriculture plays a foundational role economically and socially. In 2018, agriculture supplied one-fifth of the region's revenue, some $24 billion, and employed around 340,000 people.[109] Yet despite its importance to the social reproduction of the state and country, dominant narratives about California often leave out the Central Valley. The area is not a well-known metropole like San Francisco or Los Angeles, and it is not associated with the sweeping beauty of wine country, Yosemite, or California's endless coastlines. Instead, the Central Valley sits between these areas, literally and figuratively. It is large in size but small in the popular imagination of this state. The Central Valley is a place that feeds the state and country but is often forgotten or dismissed.

Our research focuses on the San Joaquin Valley—the lower half of the Central Valley—which spans 250 miles and includes hundreds of small towns, some of which are unincorporated, as well as a few mid-sized cities. Fresno is the largest city in this part of the region, and it is a diverse metropolis. Latinos constitute 55 percent of Fresno's population, followed by Whites (27 percent), Asians (12 percent), and Blacks (6 percent). Fresno has grown rapidly in recent decades, from a population of just under half a million in 1993 to about 800,000 in 2023.[110] Even during the COVID-19 pandemic and California's so-called exodus, Fresno still experienced population growth. Commentators argue that the relatively cheaper cost of living compared with Los Angeles and the Bay Area could be drawing people to this region, even though it is still very expensive by national standards.[111]

Yet Fresno is far from livable for all. It has the fastest-growing unhoused population in the state, and 46 percent of its children live in poverty.[112] The racial gaps in homeownership rates are large, second only to the Bay Area. Only 27 percent of Black people in Fresno own a home.[113] Life expectancy among those living in wealthier and Whiter parts of the city is almost twenty years greater than those living in the Browner and Blacker, poorer parts of town.[114]

If you zoom out from Fresno, the region's livability is even more questionable. Scattered throughout the Central Valley are towns like Planada, Seville, and Mendota, all over 90 percent Latino and among the poorest places in the state. These often-forgotten places have long acted as labor reserves for agricultural operations typically housed in neighboring towns and cities. In this California, where poverty rates are double the state average and educational attainment is about half, inequality is palpable.[115] Its often-celebrated racial diversity is also part of a stark geography of racialized poverty that is both rural and urban.

Furthermore, while the Central Valley sits geographically between the San Francisco Bay Area and Los Angeles and between the coast and the Sierra Nevada Mountains, it is also an in-between place culturally in that it bumps up against the prominent discourse of California as a progressive haven. Rather than hippies and wellness enthusiasts, this part of California is better known as home to many Republicans, religious conservatives, and right-wing movements. A disproportionate number of people identify as conservative in this area, even Democrats,[116] which was evident in the 2024 presidential election. While Donald J. Trump won only 38 percent of the popular vote in the State of California, he won many counties in the Central Valley, including Kern and Tulare, where he garnered about 60 percent of the vote.[117] The tendency of the Central Valley and other inland counties to be conservative is also evident in residents' views on political issues tied to the demographic and political economy of these places. Yet aggregate pictures of California often obscure this variation.

We conducted this study with this context in mind, offering one of the only comparative studies of California featuring the Central Valley. This inclusion allows us to analyze multiple levels of meaning and place-making at once. For instance, we asked people in different regions what it meant to be a Californian, a question that required respondents in the Central Valley to reconcile local realities with mainstream narratives about the state overall.

This book is also comparative in a second sense. It compares how race and place function across four racial groups in these different regions in the state.[118] In this way, the research moves beyond most qualitative case studies, which tend to focus on singular groups or which are stuck in the Black-White paradigm. Our framework provides analytic leverage to think systematically about localized racial and economic dynamics and reveal what, if anything, binds Californians in terms of experiences with and perceptions of race, class, and immigration.

The Argument: Normalizing Inequality

This book reveals how people living in one of the nation's most diverse and unequal states make sense of inequality and even come to see it as normal and inevitable. We find that Californians are keenly aware of the extent of inequality and its root causes. Many also see class disparities as intertwined with ethno-racial inequalities and the challenges faced by certain immigrants. Several respondents also understood and spoke eloquently about the structural and systemic inequalities that come from histories of oppression and their aftermath, as well as ongoing policies and practices that further exacerbate disparities. They noted that immigrants are often exploited and do not get paid fair wages, that police brutality is disproportionately targeted at Black communities, and that White economic and racial privilege shapes everything from what neighborhoods and schools are considered more desirable to the stories Hollywood tells.

Despite this understanding, respondents often backgrounded this structural analysis in favor of a more individualist and optimistic account of this place and their prospects there, even if they had personal experience with stunted social mobility, racism, or xenophobia. By minimizing the importance of structures, they leaned into individual ideas of possibility and foregrounded more optimistic narratives about individual mobility and belonging. In effect, we found that respondents displayed a kind of discursive "wokeness" alongside an adherence to individualist personal beliefs and compliance with a racially stratified social order. They were aware of inequality but not incensed about it, especially as it exists in California.

Yet it would be a mistake to see the people at the center of this book as dupes of the system who blindly believe in the American Dream, or in the California Dream in particular. Like Laura and Keej, many respondents said they understood that the world around them was not designed for everyone to thrive, and that decisions out of one's control, such as the cost of housing, tax policy, or the open-mindedness of a potential employer, can profoundly shape a person's circumstances. This is, therefore, not a book about false consciousness. Instead, we show that people simultaneously hold structural and individualist understandings of the world, and we reveal the processes by which they choose to minimize the former and emphasize the agency and optimism of the latter.

How exactly does the process of minimizing structural interpretations unfold? How are people able to lean on individual and meritocratic interpretations of inequality despite acknowledging the serious structural aspects of it? To answer this, we must first consider the broader cultural milieu, especially the narratives about rugged individualism inherent in the American Dream narrative. Alexis de Tocqueville famously asserted that individualism and the constant striving of a man to differentiate himself were defining markers of American life.[119] Americans, he posited, seemed to have a restless energy to seek more, build more, and forge a country led by an ethos of individual striving.[120] Ideas of individualism and self-actualization are also rooted in the discourse of the "Founding Fathers" of the United States, who wrote of a man's ability to create his own destiny and pursue happiness. For many of them, America represented a new land, a place where a man could break free from the status and cultural hierarchies of Europe, pursue the religious doctrine of his choice, and pick himself up by his very own bootstraps.[121] Other commentators shared this perspective, seeing the United States as an opportunity to build a meritocratic society that rewarded (nearly) all men, including immigrants, with opportunities unattainable in the "Old World."[122] For these thinkers, a man was his own agent of change, only inhibited by individual action and thought. The question of whether he would achieve economic comforts would be answered by his individual efforts.

Many consider California to be a prime example, even the epitome, of the American Dream.[123] Perhaps more than any other state, California has marketed a localized version of such discourse to the country and to the world. The "California Dreaming" slogan conjures the natural beauty of the state in addition to ideas about opportunity and new beginnings. This ideal has a long history tied to American frontier ideology, which coupled the move west with ideologies of Manifest Destiny, replete with settler-colonialist fantasies premised on racial domination and notions of rugged individualism.[124] Even today, countless songs, films, and books continue to popularize an understanding of California as a place where the American Dream comes true.[125]

The cultural context of the nation, and California in particular, has also been marked by select imaginings about immigration that bolster the American Dream narrative. These renditions construct the United States as a place built by immigrant "hard work" and ingenuity. It is a story of immigrants reaping the fruits of their hard work across generations, as second-generation children exceed the social status of their parents, and third-generation grandchildren follow this upward pattern.[126] These imaginings, though, rest largely on the experience of European immigrants who would eventually achieve White privilege.[127] In California, this rosy narrative overlooks the anti-immigrant systems and discourses focused primarily on Latino and some Asian communities. Nonetheless, we argue that these stories about immigration and upward mobility provide a powerful backdrop for the normalization of inequality because they reinforce individual, rather than structural, narratives of social progress, while also embracing diversity superficially. We identify three discursive practices that help individuals normalize inequality: exceptional framing, spatial comparison, and bounded blame.

Exceptional framing is the tendency to see one's personal trajectory as distinct from the statistical average. This kind of thinking involves separating the particular or the immediate from abstract trends and, in this way, perceiving oneself as an exception to the norm. The outlook includes a personal sense of optimism, which researchers have long tied to the American understanding of economic mobility and perceptions of meritocracy. Indeed, most US residents consistently overstate their chances of moving up the class ladder and exaggerate the meritocratic nature of inequality.[128] Exceptional framing draws on this optimism.

However, exceptional framing is more than just positive thinking. It also rests on a somber understanding of structural forces. A person can only be exceptional if they can see how the odds are stacked against them and against others. Many respondents in this study expressed a clearheaded and somewhat pessimistic understanding of economic opportunity in the United States and California but could still see their own path as exceptional. The separation of the individual from the social allows people to understand that others face obstacles that make social inequality inevitable. But in shifting their framing from the societal to the individual, or personal, level, respondents could feel like they were more in charge of their destiny and thus more able to overcome social obstacles. In this way, they could downplay the same structural forces they readily acknowledged in the abstract.

Time and agency play key roles in exceptional framing because the practice relies on optimism about one's personal future but not necessarily about the present. Such future-oriented thoughts provide a salve for the daily inequalities people experience and witness. Even during difficult times, with the middle class being squeezed and racial discrimination abounding in California and across the nation, many respondents, including those from Black and Latino communities, felt positively about their own personal trajectories and futures. They believe that they only need to bide their time until the future arrives. This practice echoes existing scholarship showing that ideas about the future can shape the way people see the world today.[129]

Exceptional framing allows individuals to feel like the agentic drivers of their destinies. In the same way that broad arguments about the American Dream and select imaginings of immigration celebrate the man who chooses his destiny and moves to the United States for a better life, exceptional framing allows people to believe that the future is moldable with sufficient hard work. Respondents expressed the belief that they would eventually experience social mobility, even as they bemoaned how middle-class salaries were hard to come by. They were able to de-emphasize the inequality they saw around them so they could maintain a sense of individual optimism alongside their social pessimism.

We also heard respondents relying on forms of exceptional framing when they spoke about racial inequality. Many of the people we interviewed, particularly African Americans and Latinos, recognized that structural racism shaped class disparities but also downplayed their experiences with racism by claiming these were fleeting and insignificant rather than severe and systematic. Most believed they would still get ahead despite the racialized trends and difficulties. Racism might rear its ugly head sometimes, they reasoned, but it had not really affected them in ways that mattered too much, at least not in California.

Spatial comparison is another strategy that allows people to normalize inequality. It involves seeing one's own reality through a comparative lens even if the contrast is unclear or abstract. Scholars have long argued that comparison "is an important, if not central, characteristic of human social life," allowing individuals to make sense of their place in the world.[130] Research suggests a biological basis for the human tendency to compare things, and many scholars have explored the social cognition undergirding the behavior as well as the way it affects groups.[131] Still other scholars have focused on social comparison and emotions, arguing that unhappy people tend to compare themselves to those they perceive as worse off in an attempt to "enhance their subjective well-being."[132] "Downward social comparison," they suggest, is natural, perhaps even biologically based, and functions as an adaptive strategy to make a person feel better about their own life.

While the work on the psychology of social comparison is useful, we suggest that social comparison also occurs at a spatial level. In addition to thinking they are more fortunate than others because of their personal attributes or life trajectories, many people find comfort in the idea that the place they live in is "better" than other places that they perceive as "worse." Such spatial comparisons, as social psychology research on social comparison has long established, helps individuals define "key aspects of the self, abilities, opinions, emotions, and traits, and it has central relevance for self-esteem."[133] We observed this tendency whether respondents were comparing California to Texas or to a village in Vietnam. Place is embedded in these comparisons as a set of understandings that define economic, cultural, and other possibilities.

Abstraction plays an important role in spatial comparison. We found that the ability of respondents to make sense of inequality in their communities hinged on their capacity to assess whether "things," as an abstract whole, were better for them in California or in other symbolically bounded or imagined places, such as the "US South" or "Mexico."

They did not really need to closely evaluate the contrast between areas—they didn't even need firsthand experience of the other place. In fact, it is the abstract quality of the comparisons that makes the strategy powerful and enduring. It allows people to think of California and inequality relationally, in ways they believe are not merely their individual assessment but a social truism. Comparisons took many forms in our study, including constructing the South as a racial hell (chapter 3) and imagining what immigrants' lives would have been like if they had remained in their home countries (chapter 4). Respondents often made these comparisons to paint inequality in California in a positive light—the scarcity of economic opportunities was not as bad as in El Salvador, the Golden State was not as racist as Texas, and so on. The practice allowed them to overlook the difficulties they saw around them.

Bounded blame is the third narrative strategy people use to minimize the structural nature of inequality. This practice allows individuals to translate poor people's present structural difficulties into perceived problematic future behaviors. In this way, blame is softly and abstractly placed on a group, such as "the poor," "the homeless," or "the undocumented," in a way that assumes they are at fault for continuing to reproduce structural difficulties. In other words, many see the indigent and downtrodden as living in problematic social conditions that result in their "becoming a problem in time." We heard this often throughout our interviews—for example, when respondents lamented the difficult structural conditions of exploitation that undocumented immigrants found themselves in, but then suggested that some might turn to crime or become dependent on welfare to overcome their situation.

Bounded blame rests on a few schematic moves. The first requires the construction of symbolic boundaries that sort people into abstract categories that can be easily imbued with moral judgment.[134] Respondents in this study put the strongest boundaries around the unhoused and the undocumented, subjecting them to intense but vague forms of blame. This practice also projects a sense of pessimism into the future in a manner that homogenizes the perceived behaviors of those at the bottom of the economic structure. We saw this tendency even among our Black and Brown respondents, reminding us that these communities are not immune to reinforcing the ideologies that undergird racial subjugation.

Intuitive readers might see familiar and well-documented processes at play in bounded blame. Indeed, scholars of poverty have long written about how certain racialized communities—including African Americans, Puerto Ricans, and Mexicans—are responsible for reproducing their own subjugated positions.[135] While this idea, often referred to as the culture of poverty, has been critiqued by scholars and activists alike, it is one that continues to persist, not just among conservatives but also in moderate and even progressive circles.[136] We suggest that bounded blame is a soft way of pathologizing those negatively affected by structural conditions (compared with twentieth-century debates about poverty) because critiques are often couched in empathetic discourses that elevate the cruelty of structural conditions and then ambiguously tie them to future behaviors. Nevertheless, bounded blame narratives are an integral aspect of the way inequality becomes normalized and gets reproduced.

We theorize that people downplay structural explanations of inequality through processes that involve exceptional framing, spatial comparisons, and bounded blame. Relying on exceptional framing, respondents could see their trajectories as special and apart from the structural issues that beset others in California and the nation, giving them a sense of personal agency alongside social pessimism. Bounded blame embeds agency within structures, allowing people to see poor people as vulnerable to social forces but also as reproducers of their own conditions. Spatial comparison then allows individuals to see the inequalities around them as "not as bad" as what exists in other places, whether in the United States or elsewhere, making it easier for them to overlook structural conditions. They instead focus on agency, merit, and place-based imaginaries.

Each of these strategies affects how inequality becomes accepted and how boundaries of belonging are imagined for oneself and for others. When people acknowledge but then background structural inequalities, they still need to make sense of why some get ahead and why others struggle, including the undocumented, the homeless, and many Black and Brown people. As such, issues of agency and individual action and inaction often come to the fore, which can also help individuals understand their own trajectories. Upper-working and lower-middle class respondents expressed optimism for themselves and social pessimism for select others, reinforcing the idea that belonging can be achieved with hard work. Despite believing they were being economically squeezed, most said they felt they belonged in the place they lived. Even so, their worldviews suggest that some categories of people might never share that status with them.

It is important to note that a minority of respondents did resist these discursive practices that served to minimize inequalities. Despite being in similar economic positions as the rest of the sample, this small group had more poignant critiques of the economic and racial structures of the state and tended to see themselves as excluded from the promises of its future. They refused to minimize the structural roots of problems and were pessimistic about the future. This group was racially heterogeneous but with a higher proportion of Black people and to a lesser extent Latinos. Many of them felt left behind or locked out of mainstream discourses about belonging in California and the United States. While we also expected to see major differences between the attitudes and worldviews of respondents in the Central Valley and Los Angeles, we mostly found variations on the same themes. We discuss these nuances in greater depth in later chapters.

Chapter Overviews

The following chapters examine the various ways that individuals make sense of inequality. In chapter 1, we situate the study in the broader cultural milieu that has framed inequality in the United States, and particularly in California. We dive deeply into the tropes and narratives about American individualism, including how imaginings about European migration west have fed into these understandings and, by extension, into broader narratives about inequality. We specifically look at how these cultural dynamics have played out in California, how they have shaped how the Golden State is depicted by Hollywood, by political pundits, and by the broader media. For readers particularly interested in California historiography, we posit that a set of narratives about the Golden State—as a land of racial liberalism, immigrant sanctuary, and economic abundance—set the stage for how people think about inequality in the state today. In this chapter we turn to contemporary practices of normalizing inequality and show how they are rooted in a mythologized understanding of the United States and the people it attracts, shaping narratives about place. Readers less interested in the particularities of California but piqued by the idea that inequality is rooted in place can still learn about how inequality manifests itself today.

In chapter 2, we examine how respondents make sense of economic inequality. Almost all the people we spoke to understood that the middle class was being squeezed as the "rich get richer." Some even had sophisticated arguments about how government policies and generational wealth reproduce the conditions we see today. Even so, most expressed a belief that they would personally make it, perhaps because they believe that their family legacy, whether as migrants from Mexico or Arkansas, compels them to. This perspective often coexisted with doubts about a future for the middle class and about their immediate economic improvement. However, to avoid sinking into despair, many rely on exceptional framing, bounded blame, spatial comparison, or a combination of these strategies. These perspectives allow them to imagine the world as a place where hard work pays off and where, ultimately, they will be rewarded for their frugality and patience.

Chapter 3 examines perceptions about race, racism, and racial inequality. Many respondents downplayed the scale and severity of the racism and racial inequality around them, even if they had experienced racial discrimination themselves and despite recognizing patterns of racialized segregation and opportunity. Many espoused narratives of California that emphasized diversity and multiracial belonging and de-emphasized negative experiences with race and racism, even in their own lives. Spatial comparison played a large role in glossing over racialized experiences and upholding colorblind narratives of inequality. In such discourses, "The South," "Middle America," and an unspecified "rural America" were commonly mentioned as places where racism and racial inequality were much worse than they were in California. This comparison, however abstract, helped them substantiate the idea of California, and thus their own experiences, as relatively free of inequality.

Chapter 4 looks more squarely at attitudes about immigration to understand how residents make sense of the inequality experienced by immigrants, most of whom are from Latin America or Asia. While many respondents could tell us about the exploitation that immigrants faced, they downplayed the issue and emphasized the idea that immigrants are the embodiment of the American Dream. They were able to do this partly by employing spatial comparison, which allowed them to rationalize that immigrants, despite their difficulties, were better off here than in "some other developing country" or "Latin America." Moreover, we found that while respondents expressed pro-immigration attitudes, below the surface, a significant number were deeply ambivalent about the costs associated with immigrants, especially the undocumented, and used bounded blame to describe their views and minimize the structural roots of inequality.

In chapter 5, we widen our lens to examine how people imagine belonging and inequality in the future. We show how most respondents expressed a belief that the economic future of California will be booming, but they had different ideas about who the beneficiaries would be. While White and Asian respondents had a tendency to imagine a diverse and prosperous future fueled by Big Tech, Latinos and especially Black folks were more likely to talk about California's future as one that will be increasingly unlivable and decidedly Whiter. This chapter underscores how discussions about the future can offer key insights about belonging in the present, including by revealing the contradictions of present-day inequalities.

Throughout this book, we reveal how people take for granted and normalize the inequality around them. We show how some forms of inequality, such as class and racial inequality, are more visible than others, even though they intersect in important ways. Our research illustrates how people can maintain an optimistic view of life and at the same time set firm boundaries that let them place blame on certain groups. We find that for many, hopefulness is bolstered by deep-rooted ideologies about California—and the United States more broadly—as a place of opportunity for all, where anyone can belong. Even the skeptical respondents, who did not believe in the American Dream, would occasionally rely on the language of individualism, even as they continued to embrace broader social pessimism. The practices of exceptional framing, bounded blame, and spatial comparison allow individuals to be structural and individualist interpreters of social mobility and inequality at the same time. It also lets them downplay the importance of structural issues and adopt an agentic and optimistic perspective.

Some might interpret our findings as strong evidence of inclusive belonging. After all, these narrative strategies did make people feel better about the world and their place in it. Still others may reduce this to a story of false consciousness. We encourage the reader to avoid either interpretation definitively. We posit that neither take seriously the nuances we noted in the stories that Californians like Keej and Laura shared with us—stories about struggle and fear as well as optimism for this place at this moment in history. In a similar vein, we caution against reading this book as a cynical take on California in particular. Indeed, we believe that the practices found here likely exist elsewhere, with any potential differences likely ones of texture and degree rather than of the nature of processes. Californians, just like people living in unequal societies around the country and world, are simply trying to make sense of the world they have largely inherited and must navigate.

A humble note about intention. We grew up in California, one of us in Los Angeles and the other in Sacramento and the Central Valley, both of us returned to California to start our families. Precisely because of this, we are painfully aware of the many contradictions of this place. Working communities like the ones we come from, whether in the Golden State or elsewhere, bear much of the brunt of rising inequality and the increasing concentration of wealth. We believe that a different course of action for a different California and a different nation will require critical policy and structural changes in addition to deep work by an engaged populace committed to the co-construction of a new vision. To make sense of the world today, we will all need to push our imaginations beyond the narratives, frames, and structures we have been given to explain the world around us. In order to do so, it is crucial that we pause and reflect on how people make sense of, tolerate, and even consent to our shared and increasingly precarious trajectory. We hope this book illuminates overlooked, commonplace processes and helps us dream of new economic possibilities, racial repair, counter-hegemonic action, and true belonging.

CHAPTER ONE

FROM THE AMERICAN DREAM TO CALIFORNIA DREAMIN'

California has been described as a land of golden opportunity, a multiracial haven, and a new beginning for immigrants. A former Spanish colony and then a Mexican state, the region's hills and possibilities once lured White settlers west to establish camps in the Sierras with the hope of striking gold—literally. Others came to California looking for new economic opportunities, sometimes fleeing violence and dire economic circumstances. In the nineteenth century, Chinese migrants came to build mining camps and separate Chinatowns, often out of necessity rather than choice. Later, the state would see a record number of African Americans migrate from the South, desperate to find a semblance of the American Dream unhindered by overt racial violence.

After 1965, the state solidified its reputation as a central immigrant gateway for the nation, sheltering generations of Asian and Latin American families pursuing economic, political, and social possibilities, and redefining the culture of California and the United States more broadly. These diverse migrations were fraught from the outset because they were premised on the dispossession of Native Americans, including the Shasta, the Ohlone, and the Tipai, among many others. This fundamental contradiction is one of many that define this place.

Today, California stands out for having the fourth largest economy in the world.[1] It is also one of the nation's first majority-minority states, marking it as an early indicator of demographic change in the country. Yet ideas about what California is, demographically, culturally, economically, and politically, are as much about material realities as they are about a kind of perpetual frontierism embedded in discourses

https://doi.org/10.7758/uybx4321.3243

about the state. California is often defined as a trailblazer, a land of multiracial promise, a place where the American Dream can be pursued not just by a select few, but by all. It is also a place that has become synonymous with technology, a place already in the future, so to speak, both in its population and politics.

We are all familiar with the idea of the American Dream—the idea of rugged individualism that holds that anyone who works hard not only can make it here but also can thrive. Although this ideology is widespread and deeply woven into the fabric of American mythology throughout the United States, the Golden State has doubled down on this narrative. Although cities, towns, and regions around the country have evoked their own specific versions of American individualism, perhaps none have held on to the language of "dream" as staunchly as California has.

In the late nineteenth century, the myth of streets paved in gold gave way to tales of agricultural and trade fortunes, all positioning the Golden State as a place where those who experienced tough times in other regions could make a fresh start. Over a century later, this idea would persist partly because of the invention of Hollywood as an industry and as an engine that would create and disseminate ideas about California as a land of glamour and reinvention. This is the idea embodied in the 1965 blockbuster hit "California Dreamin'" by The Mamas and The Papas, which describes fleeing cold winters and making a new life in a warmer climate. As the song's protagonist gets on her knees, she pretends to pray, singing "I'd be safe and warm (I'd be safe and warm)/if I was in LA (if I was in LA)/California Dreaming."[2] In some ways, the song can be read as not merely a draw to a better climate, but also as an escape from the traditional and outdated social norms of the East. After all, the protagonist in the song doesn't actually pray, she only pretends to.

The idea of a fresh start was still alive in 2018, when we embarked on this project, as it likely had been for countless (im)migrants, including our own parents, who came from Flint, Michigan, and Michoacán, Mexico, respectively, in search of better lives. Discourse and imagery around "dreaming" still seemed inescapable in scholarly and popular works alike with some buying into the idea of the California Dream. Even those who were skeptical of this narrative still engaged with it, seeing it more as a myth than a reality.

California's relationship to the American Dream has also been the center of media attention that alternates between proclaiming its vitality and its demise. In 2021, for example, *The Atlantic* ran a long essay titled "The California Dream is Dying," which points to the high rates of outmigration among the middle class, the increase in inequality, and the way that policies have hampered economic growth and educational opportunities.[3] Some clapped back, contending that, despite its imperfections, the Golden State was still an economic powerhouse; a global leader on clean energy; and an important site of economic mobility, especially for the children of immigrants. Feeding into the dizzying debate, recent books have labeled California the "comeback state" and a state of "resistance and resilience," while others decry it as "cracked up" and a "paradise lost."[4] In these portrayals, the Golden State is either the land of innovation, diversity, and incredible opportunity or a place that is unaffordable, unequal, and ultimately unlivable. What is not contested in any of these perspectives is that California should be the place of dreams in the first place.

Yet while dreaming is one metaphor for understanding this state, another is fault lines—divisions and fractures strongly associated with past and future earthquakes. Academic volumes on conflict, uneasy tensions, and inequality in California frequently evoke seismic fault lines as a metaphor for understanding the state's complex social dynamics. This imagery is powerful because it shows how structural fissures lie just beneath the surface of seemingly smooth and sound social relations. Indigenous scholar and writer Louis Owens explains, for example, "California contains a vast meanness and a measure of infinite promise, and between these two opposed forces lies a fault line capable of generating cataclysmic stories, poems, art."[5] We don't always see or acknowledge these fault lines even though they can shake the very ground underneath us, but we always know they are there.

Rather than emphasize the promise of this place in terms of its demography, progressive record, or inherent ability to resolve problems around race and diversity, the fault line metaphor underscores how California is a place of deep contradictions and inequalities. From this view, the image of abundant economic opportunities and unrivaled racial diversity butts up against the more sobering reality of increasing economic inequality, rising poverty, and a pernicious racial hierarchy where Black, Brown, and some Asian groups often reside at the bottom.

The contradictions abound in the here and now. There are more people living in sanctuary cities and counties in California than any other state,[6] yet California is also the place where the controversial Proposition 187 passed, prohibiting undocumented persons, including children, from accessing education and health care.[7] The state houses seven of the country's top-ten least racially segregated cities, but 50 percent of its population still lives in racially segregated communities.[8] Even though California has a very high rate of interracial marriage and is home to the largest number of people who identify as multiracial, it is also home to some of the most segregated school districts in the country.[9] We also cannot ignore the fact that the state has become notorious for highly publicized cases of racialized state violence, epitomized by the violent beating of Rodney King,[10] and more recently by the police killings of Oscar Grant,[11] Sean Monterrosa,[12] and Stephon Clark.[13]

In this chapter, we examine the cultural backdrop that undergirds how residents make sense of inequality in California. Our broader argument is that inequality becomes normalized as individuals develop narrative practices—exceptional framing, spatial comparison, and bounded blame—that minimize structural explanations of the growing divide. Here we seek to contextualize these practices historically and culturally. In so doing, we explore how ideas about California and its relationship to racial and economic inequality set the stage for how folks make sense of disparities today. But first we focus on the role of national ideology—specifically the American Dream and its relationship to racialized migrations, individualism, and meritocracy—to understand California's relationship to the rest of the nation.

Dreams and Fissures

What is the American Dream? The answer is not straightforward, in large part because the concept has shifted over time. The idea has consistently involved ideological tensions between individualism and equal opportunity, on the one hand, and material expectations on the other.[14] With the former comes the idealized understanding that hard work can lead to gains for all, regardless of origin. Yet even when he coined the phrase in 1931, J. T. Adams warned that the concept should not be reduced to material comforts such as "motors cars" and "high wages" at the expense of overshadowing the ideal of a social order that when developed to its highest standard would allow all men to work hard, reap just rewards, become civically engaged, and witness progress across generations.[15]

Still, the concept remains broad, allowing political commentators on the left and the right to bend it toward their political goals. Politicians have long described this sort of meritocratic social contract as fleeting and fragile, as something that can be rescued or resuscitated during election cycles. Barack Obama wrote of the need to "recover" the American Dream right before running for presidential office.[16] And Donald Trump, when launching his candidacy for president in 2016, warned that the American Dream was in peril but could be brought back "bigger and stronger" if he were to be elected.[17]

Yet instead of inspiring aversion, national polls suggest that Americans have, for the most part, bought into the concept. For example, in a poll conducted in the mid-1980s, which simply asked Americans whether the "American Dream" was alive and well, 86 percent answered in the affirmative.[18] Since then, surveys have been mixed on the issue, sometimes showing high support, upwards of 80 percent in the 1990s, and sometimes indicating much lower support, just under 50 percent in the early 2000s.[19] The different outcomes are partly the result of the formatting of questions because Americans are more likely to say that the American Dream is attainable than they are to say that they have achieved it.[20] The varying trends also speak to the importance of historical context and periodization.[21] With rising inequality, many are feeling more ambivalent about the American Dream, seeing it as an important part of national sentiment but something that, while still possible, will be harder for future generations to achieve.[22]

Today, national polls show that about 75 percent of Americans believe that they have "achieved the American Dream," or are "on their way towards doing so."[23] Only about one-third believe that their children will have similar opportunities. Many seem to believe fiercely in the American Dream concept, however defined, but live with a present uncertainty about what the economic future holds for their children.

Among Californians, we see similar trends. While the wording of survey questions differs, today a significant majority of people in the state, about 60 percent, claim to believe in the American Dream. However, 60 percent of them also believe it is less attainable in California than elsewhere in America.[24] State residents seem to be of two minds on the issue: a majority embrace the American Dream and see it alive and well but also believe it is harder to achieve now than it was previously, and that it will be even harder for their children to achieve. And for an important minority, the American Dream in California seems completely unattainable, an idea, in the famous words of comedian George Carlin, that "you have to be asleep to believe in."[25]

For the most part, people today define the American Dream as achieving middle-class status, which includes homeownership and the image of a "white picket fence," which they relate to ideas about freedom and individualism.[26] Historically, these ideas have fueled internal and international migration.[27] The image of the Statue of Liberty, for example, has long helped to uphold idealized understandings of the United States as a nation of immigrants seeking better material and political futures.[28] Once here, migrants and their descendants have been imagined as free to move to find new opportunities in an ever-expanding and changing United States.

It is important to consider the ways that these early ideals are clearly linked to the broader US settler colonial project, through which ideas about meritocracy and diversity have also been shaped. Writing about the racist historical structures underlying ideas of US citizenship, political theorist Cristina Beltrán reminds us that the freedom to work hard and gain rewards has historically been premised on limiting the freedom and mobility of others, especially Native American and Black communities. The restless energy underlying the individual pursuit of happiness and the eventual building of the nation was originally understood to be the providence of White men, she argues. And while other non-White residents certainly worked hard, the returns on their labor were often expropriated, exploited, or stolen for the benefit of White communities.[29]

Moreover, scholars have revealed how frontier ideology, the sense that American White men were free to move west and build, motivated much of the nation's settler colonial efforts. Freedom in the United States, and freedom to move toward the Pacific Ocean, historian Greg Grandin contends, was linked to a White racial project intent on displacing, exploiting, and even terrorizing communities of color. Frontier ideology romanticized the idea of the White American pioneer who had risked it all to work hard and reap the fruits of his labor west of the Mississippi.[30] Western racial hierarchies emerged out of the violent displacement of Indigenous people as well as Mexican, Asian, and non-White others. Eugenicists and nationalist politicians at the time characterized these inequalities as the natural and patriotic consequences of the broader effort to colonize the West, on the one hand, and European-American enlightenment on the other.[31] In this way, historian Natalia Molina reminds us, the ideals and energy underlying the American Dream have long reflected built-in racial inequalities, or what we might think of as dream fissures, in the West and the nation more broadly.[32]

This history has led many to criticize the idea of the American Dream, pointing to how the ideology has long had conflicts and tensions embedded within it. Perhaps most famously, Dr. Martin Luther King spoke of the "schizophrenic personality" of the American Dream, contending that it obscured the systemic aspects of racial inequality while emphasizing the ideals of equal opportunity.[33] Scholars have also found that some communities of color, but especially African Americans, are critical of the concept of the American Dream today, many seeing it as an ideological façade that glosses over racism, discrimination, and institutionalized inequalities.[34] Still, abstract ideals of meritocracy and the understanding that hard work should lead to gains receive a great deal of multiracial support, including within immigrant communities.[35] The difference, we posit, is that some can believe in meritocratic individualism while also understanding the American Dream to be imperfect and a tool for the reproduction of racial inequalities. Others tether "colorblind" interpretations of present inequalities to their understanding of the American Dream,[36] which, of course, has important implications for how folks make sense of inequality more broadly.

Toward the California Dream

Ideas about place, especially the American Dream, provide the cultural architecture for making sense of inequality. We suggest that these understandings of the American Dream and the nation's growing divide are also filtered through localized narratives. In this way, inequality is something understood as near and obvious on the one hand and far and abstract on the other. It is understood, for example, through observations operating at an immediate spatial level, such as the unhoused on the street; the stark contrast between communities on different sides of the railroad tracks; and the racial politics that define one's neighborhood. We argue that people often see a kind of geography of opportunity, however abstract, that filters their understandings of poverty and opportunity, belonging and exclusion, the possible and the impossible.

To gain a deeper understanding of how Californians perceive inequality, it is essential to first analyze the prevailing narratives that shape their conception of the Golden State. These narratives—or place-based tropes—contribute to the cultural backdrop rooted in that broader US ideology, especially the American Dream and its emphasis on individualism. This is because such narratives shape their understanding of the immediate. In other words, we argue that folks make sense of inequality partly by thinking about how it operates in California, and this thinking is often tied to narratives about the kind of place the Golden State is and which forms of inequalities and opportunities are endemic to this place. For example, Keej and Laura, introduced in the previous chapter, view their opportunities through the lens of California's reputation as a place where hardworking immigrants can achieve social mobility. Other narratives about California that shape their understanding of inequality today reflect on its diversity, the nature of its strong but uneven economy, and its future. In what follows, we describe three broad narratives and their historical significance, as well as recognize the ways that they are all deeply connected.

NARRATIVE 1: CALIFORNIA AS A SANCTUARY FOR MIGRANTS

The first narrative is that California is, perhaps more than any other region, a magnet for migrants, a place where domestic and international migration took place on overdrive. This trope is not new but instead has a long history imbued with its own racial and political contradictions.

Early-nineteenth-century commentators described California as a region where abundant land with access to trade with the Pacific would help ensure prosperity and opportunity for those Americans who dared leave the overcrowded cities of the East to venture west.[37] And while California's natural geography had already made it attractive to settlers, the official discovery of gold in 1848 sealed its position as the destination of various settler colonial projects. Within a year, the Constitution of California was adopted, and the Gold Rush was in full swing. It is against this backdrop that the state would come to be seen not as a far-off, backwater, Spanish colonial acquisition, but as a place of a golden opportunity for settlers of every variety.

Between 1850 and 1860, the population of the state tripled, as settlers of all colors made their way West in search of riches.[38] Among them were White migrants from the Midwest and the East, Mexican nationals from farther South who were now considered immigrants,[39] and Chinese immigrants—who constituted a substantial percentage of those coming in seek of good fortune.[40] Yet even as the Gold Rush seemed to be a manifestation of the American Dream in its most quintessential form, the reality for most was far from a rags-to-riches story. While some 750,000 pounds of gold were extracted in California between 1848 and 1855, very few people actually got rich. In this way, the Gold Rush serves as a metaphor for subsequent waves of migrants to the Golden State, a place for migrant dreamers, although often with dreams deferred.

After the Gold Rush, the promise of land and economic opportunity continued to draw White men and families to California. The White migrants who made up this great population movement were economically diverse, including farmers, businessmen, and laborers, all seeking fortunes. These migrants also had diverse origins and dreams. Many were fleeing from a dream they felt had expired in the overcrowded big cities of the East, which some of them now saw as overrun with newer Southern and Eastern European immigrants.[41]

For some, this increase in White western migration provided a political opportunity to shape California into a particular type of migrant destination. For nativists, eugenicists, and others who helped shape California's early statehood, White migration was an opportunity to reboot, a chance to create a White man's paradise unsullied by "indigestible" or "unredeemable" immigrants—those not-quite-White, White people.[42] Historian David Wrobel notes that despite its racial diversity, the state was sold as a "wonderland of Whiteness," "where cultural diversity was nothing more than an attractive background to the main stage where a narrative of White economic and social opportunity and dominance played out."[43] In addition to the assurance that California was the land of milk and honey (for White people), many likely also found appealing that the number of "undesirables"—such as Native Americans, African-Americans, Mexicans, and unassimilable

European immigrants—was large enough to constitute a necessary underclass but too small to dominate the culture or to get in their way.[44]

Of course, to non-White people, the state was far from a place of equal opportunity.[45] After three decades of steady immigration, particularly from China, the Chinese Exclusion Act of 1882 in addition to local-level ordinances restricted the access and movement of Chinese people in California. Beyond xenophobia, Chinese exclusion was fueled by concerns over labor market competition, which had been somewhat quelled previously by the large state revenues accrued by taxing Chinese mining companies and workers.[46] In addition to anti-Chinese policies, anti-Chinese racial terror reached a peak at the end of the nineteenth century as angry White mobs burned down dozens of Chinatowns, organized anti-Chinese clubs, and drove Chinese and suspected Chinese workers and families from their homes.[47] This pendulum swing from a level of tacit acceptance of a group to their overt exclusion would happen to other newcomers as well.

African Americans began to migrate to California in great numbers in the late nineteenth century, many seeing the chance to escape racial terror in the US South. This promise was particularly appealing because many were only one generation out of slavery. But they would learn quickly that the promises of formal freedom meant little in the South in terms of their freedom from terror and their quest toward peace, dignity, and economic mobility. In San Francisco, Black migrants would amass considerable wealth, helping establish the Fillmore district, often referred to as the "Harlem of the West" because of its wealth and cultural vibrance.[48] Los Angeles was also a hub for Black uplift. In writing about the history of Black Angelenos, Douglas Flamming notes that the West "occupied a meaningful place in Black Americans' hearts and minds. Through newspapers, magazines, art, political speeches, and dime novels, the Western Ideal had already assumed a powerful position in mainstream American mythology. The ideal held that the American West was a singularly egalitarian place, where opportunity was open to all citizens, regardless of background, lineage, or wealth."[49]

The message that conditions were objectively better in California compared with the South rippled through Black America via newspapers and letters. Historian Josh Sides notes that there was a "common perception among Black Angelenos that Los Angeles was a kind of racial paradise for African Americans." He notes that even W. E. B. Du Bois had bought into this idea. In a 1913 article in *The Crisis*, Du Bois noted, "Los Angeles was wonderful. The air was scented with orange blossoms, and the beautiful homes lay low crouching on the earth as though they loved its scents and flowers. Nowhere in the United States is the Negro so well and beautifully housed, nor the average efficiency and intelligence in the colored population so high. Here is an aggressive, hopeful group—with some wealth, large industrial opportunity and a buoyant spirit."[50] Du Bois was far from alone in this sentiment.

In some ways, the idea of California as a migration frontier and a possible site of racial reinvention fulfilled its promise. Los Angeles seemed exceptional to these new migrants, with its higher Black homeownership rates than any other city in the nation, racially integrated neighborhoods, and decent public schools.[51] Perhaps most importantly, "they lived, for the most part, free from fear of physical violence."[52] Indeed, while anti-Black violence was not completely absent in Los Angeles or California more generally, given its numerous Ku Klux Klan chapters and racial lynching campaigns, Black migrants seemed to be experiencing less overt racial violence in this context.[53]

Yet while many Black migrants came to California hoping for unbridled opportunity, their early social mobility was often thwarted, and in some cases undone, as a racial topography began to crystalize in the Golden State, especially in the post-World War II period. Many faced the harsh reality of housing segregation, labor market discrimination, redlining, and social restrictions such as segregated pools, which would complicate the notion that this was the land of equal opportunity for Black migrants.[54] These migrants and their descendants would also subsequently find themselves on the wrong side of police violence and later the state's prison boom.[55]

The trajectory of Japanese migrants was also dizzying. At the turn of the twentieth century, hundreds of thousands of Japanese migrants were recruited to establish themselves in California, where some would find social mobility, mostly in agricultural endeavors and small businesses. Yet this period was also followed by one of extreme backlash, beginning with a series of policies at the state and local level that made it virtually impossible for the foreign-born, or "aliens," to own land, culminating in geopolitical dynamics that would lead to mass internment. During World War II, the majority of the approximately 120,000 Japanese Americans who were incarcerated found themselves in internment camps in California; and about two-thirds of those interned were US citizens, some of whom lost their freedom as well as their land and property.[56] This violence left scars across generations around citizenship and belonging, which were layered on top of long-standing practices of gendered racial discrimination in labor markets that disfavored Japanese American women.[57]

Though just as the earth began to shift under the Japanese migrants and their descendants, others were still contributing to the endless cycle of hopeful newcomers to California.[58] In addition to the previously noted Black migration, Mexican migration increased between 1910 and 1930 as nearly one million people fled the country during the Mexican Revolution.[59] While this wave of migrants found economic opportunity and growing agricultural infrastructure, they also found a vicious nativism aimed at them, which would take the form of racist violence and proliferating Ku Klux Klan chapters, forced deportations that affected citizens and noncitizens alike, raids, and legal and extrajudicial exclusion from social spaces. Scholars estimate that hundreds of people of Mexican descent were killed by extrajudicial police lynchings and at the hands of angry White mobs.[60] This violence echoed that of the Gold Rush period, during which White nativism, aided by competition over resources, led to anti-Mexican mob violence and the lynching of many people of Mexican, Asian, and Native American descent.[61] Among the many ironies of such nativism are the fact that California had once been a territory of Mexico, that the majority White population had been there for less than a generation, and that these were all stolen lands in the first place.

By the 1940s, despite the dynamics of racialized violence and exclusion, Mexican migrants were settling in California, sometimes as seasonal workers but more often as permanent residents. During World War II, the shifting geopolitics and racial attitudes that had disadvantaged Japanese Americans had opened up some opportunities for Mexican migrants engaged in low-wage labor. The war effort combined with Japanese internment had left California's farms desolate and in desperate need of laborers, to feed not only California but also the nation. Through bilateral agreements between Mexico and the United States, over four million workers would come as contract laborers to California and Texas between 1942 and 1964 as part of the Mexican Farm Labor Program. While these "braceros" were temporary workers, many returned

Figure 1.1 *California Population by Race as Percentage of Total Population*

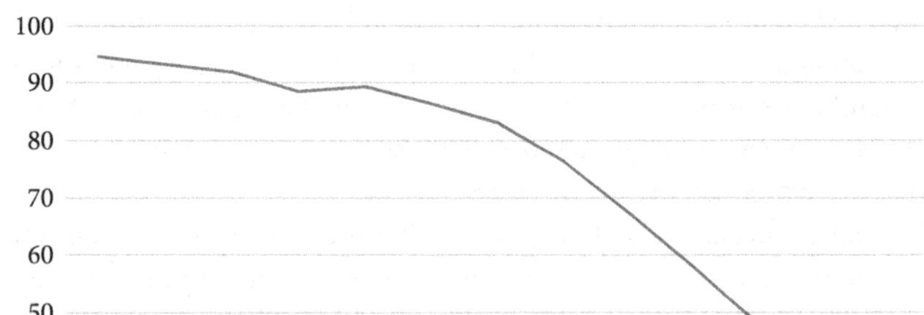

Source: Authors' calculations using US Census Bureau decennial censuses and American Community Survey and the California Department of Finance Population Estimates and Population Projections.

numerous times, and their presence would forever change the state's culture as well as its labor and citizenship regimes.[62]

Immigration from Mexico would ultimately constitute a much larger demographic revolution in the state and in the country. By 1970, California was well on its way to becoming a majority-Latino state, partly because of changes to immigration laws after 1965, and partly because of changes in the labor market, especially in the agricultural sector. The proportion of California residents who were born outside of the United States grew from 10 to 30 percent of the total population between 1960 and 2010. This group included a sizable number from Korea and the Philippines, although the overwhelming majority came from Mexico and later from Central American countries. In a few decades, California went from having one of the country's highest White population rates in the 1940s to having one of the lowest. We outline these demographic trends in figure 1.1.[63]

These waves of immigration fundamentally changed the demographics of the state as well as its cultural and social fabric. They also helped reinforce overt anti-Mexican and generalized anti-immigrant sentiment at the local and state level.[64] As migrants and their children began to create communities, especially in Central and Southern California, they also began to experience increasing segregation in housing and education. For them, like other non-European migrants before them, California's discourse of dreams and exceptionalism soured like spoiled milk. Rather than limitless opportunity, many were met with ghettoization. Rather than boundless economic uplift, many found that they would not have the same opportunities as their White counterparts to advance at their jobs. Some minority communities were excluded from entire industries altogether.[65] Furthermore, the continual migration from Mexico and Central America would expand a racialized underclass of perpetual, precarious labor.[66] This was a far cry from the privileges of citizenship promised to those of "Spanish blood" during the official founding of the state of California.[67]

By the 1980s, just as the state reached a tipping point in which racial "minorities" would outnumber the White population, it was also clear to many that the dream of unhampered economic success for a multiracial California was foreclosed. These limits were laid bare through the intense social mobilization that would start in prior decades, including the Watts Riots, the Chicano movement, the Farmworkers movement, the establishment of the first chapter of the Black Panther Party, the Occupation of Alcatraz, and the East Los Angeles Walkouts.[68] Moreover, an increasingly non-White majority would be at the forefront of other important mass mobilizations, from the Free Speech Movement to the resurgence of a labor movement in the 1980s that was decidedly Browner than previously. These social movements made plain the contradictions around race and class in California that were baked into the very founding of the state.

Still, the original understanding of California as a place *of* and possibly *for* immigrants echoes loudly. It can be heard in political speeches, in which immigrants are hailed as the "backbone of our communities, a driving force behind our economy, and an essential part of our history as a state."[69] Even conservatives recognize the importance of immigrants to the state's social and economic infrastructure.[70] Today, California leads the nation in terms of pro-immigrant local and state-level policies, reinforcing its reputation as a welcoming place for newcomers.[71] Yet this reality sits alongside currently persisting disparities, including the fact that immigrants in the state are much less likely than those born in the United States to have job protections, fair pay, affordable housing, health insurance, and access to quality schools.[72] It is precisely these historically embedded contradictions that people have to navigate as they make sense of this place.

NARRATIVE 2: CALIFORNIA AS THE LAND OF MULTIRACIAL PROMISE

The second narrative that shapes understandings of promise and precarity in California is the idea that the state is an exceptional place when it comes to race and multiculturalism. This idea has emerged at various moments in the state's history, beginning with the founding of California as a "free" or non-slavery" state. As early as the late nineteenth century, elite White settlers to California began to articulate what might be called a proto-racial liberal position, which was similar to *mestizaje* ideologies developing in Latin American countries over the same period.[73] Scholars have argued that it was during this period that common discourses about California in other parts of the country highlighted its status as a "new" territory in multiple senses of the word. This frontier, blank-slate version of California was projected onto the economic potential embodied in the Gold Rush from 1848 to 1855 as well as the state's racial or social potential. Later, in the early twentieth century, California was thought to be a place unburdened by a history of slavery and entrenched racism, where the potential for harmony and mobility was infinite.

This branding of California can be at least partly traced to prominent White settlers and frontiersmen, including Charles Lummis, who famously walked from Ohio to California and claimed that western migration would allow Americans to transcend from "little, narrow, prejudiced, intolerant Yankee[s] into more liberal westerners who appreciated Hispanic and American Indian cultures."[74] [White] "westerners," he argued, were exceptional in their racial politics and dispositions. Over the course of decades, Charles Lummis, as editor of the *Los Angeles Times*, would become a strong spokesperson for the vision of California as a land of racial tolerance.[75]

The image of California as a place best positioned to shed the history of prejudice in the United States would also permeate academia. Writing about Harvard historian Frederick Jackson Turner, Greg Grandin notes, "The kind of Americanism Turner represented took all the unbounded optimism that went into the founding of the United States and bet that the country's progress, moving forward on the frontier and into the world, would reduce racism to a remnant and leave it behind a residue. It would dilute other social problems as well, including poverty, inequality, and extremism, teaching diverse people how to live together in peace."[76] To Turner and others, as the place where frontierism met the constraint of running out of land, California offered the possibility of positive racial and other relations. Similar portrayals of California as a place that transcended the narrow-mindedness of the rest of the nation can be found in more recent work such as that of California historian Kevin Starr, who once described the state as "the interplay of traditional cultures and frontier innovation in the creation of a distinctive California society." What made California distinctive for Starr was the "importance and legacy of ethnic and cultural diversity."[77]

But this idea of California as exceptional was built on more than dreams alone. It was also born of policies developed in the mid-twentieth century. Historian Mark Brilliant outlines how the state led the nation in antidiscrimination legislation and litigation, making it a pioneer in what he calls "racial liberalism."[78] For Brilliant, such an orientation was premised on equal opportunity legislation that aspired to a kind of expansion of the social safety net for all men, regardless of color. These efforts, he posits, eventually seeped into the cultural fabric of the state.[79] In 1937, "the state created a committee on race relations in California whose charge was to disseminate "educational material" to promote "voluntary acceptance of the anti-discrimination principle."[80] Such principles of California as an exemplar of racial liberalism even became central to the campaigns of local and state-level politicians during this period and ever since.[81] In 1944, LA Mayor Fletcher Bowron famously declared that in Los Angeles, "we have no master race . . . our freedoms are for all people." The irony was the same year, tens of thousands of Japanese Americans, many from Los Angeles, were experiencing unimaginable loss in internment camps throughout the state.

Thus, while California's distinctive origin is evident in the names of its cities and streets and in its built environment, which includes forts and Spanish missions, it is not entirely culturally distinct from the long-lasting American tradition of racial exclusion and violence. What instead gave the state its exceptional flavor was what some would call its "racial ambivalence," or the oscillation between acceptance and exclusion of communities of color.[82] The historic racial and economic justice movements in California, beginning in the 1970s, would reveal fault lines, exposing visible damage to the façade of racial liberalism.

Today, newcomers continue to establish themselves in California, which oscillates between being a land of inclusion and radical exclusion. In the 2010s, after a turbulent history of anti-immigrant and racially conservative legislation such as Proposition 187 and Proposition 209, the state reinvented itself once again as a diverse and liberal bubble, a sanctuary state in an increasingly conservative outside world. Indeed, in 2016, as the nation elected Donald Trump, California legalized marijuana; expanded parole for those with nonviolent convictions; overturned restrictions in bilingual education; and, in some counties, allowed noncitizen parents to vote in school board elections. In 2018, the state elected Kamala Harris, its first Black woman senator, who would go on to be Vice President. And in 2020, Alex Padilla became the state's first Latino US senator. Still, California's largest school districts remain highly segregated, as do its largest cities, and poverty trends undeniably reveal a racial hierarchy with Black and Latino residents at the bottom.

The deep racial contradictions we see today must be understood as part of a long legacy. This includes the emergence of the idea of California as a non-slavery state and a place where a multiracial group of migrants could make their home, in part because it was not burdened by a racial past in the same way as other parts of the country were. If nothing else, this early history sets the stage for a more complex system of inequalities and race relations. Instead of a racial order premised on a Black-White binary or a Black-White-Indigenous triad, California has been a place characterized by what historian Daniel Hosang calls "variegated racial domination." A kind of multifocal White supremacy emerged in which Whites occupied a high status over a diverse group of non-Whites. As historian Kelly Lytle Hernández reminds us, efforts to eliminate Native Americans and exclude and expel non-White people have long been baked into California's history.[83]

Although non-White groups in California encountered various systemic disadvantages, they also experienced significant periods of social and economic integration at different times. This material fact likely served to keep middle-class dreams afloat for future cycles of diverse newcomers. Despite the challenges and complications, the idea of California as racially liberal persisted. The image remains powerful, even as it is perpetually resisted, because enough people either find some truth in it or have to believe that it must be so. It persists despite the very real racial hierarchies in the state and even as the state has historically swung back and forth from progressive to conservative on racial politics compared with the rest of the nation.

NARRATIVE 3: CALIFORNIA AS THE LAND OF PLENTY

We have already told tales of streets paved with gold and diverse populations coming to find their versions of that economic promise. But what of social mobility and the dreams of economic stability in the Golden State? While frontier ideology undergirded nineteenth-century settlement projects and the search for riches west of the Mississippi, the notion of a middle class in California and the nation was popularized after World War II when the middle class witnessed its most significant growth to date, buoyed by the efforts of veterans eager to use their GI Bill benefits and to start families.[84] As soldiers returned stateside and the US economy grew, a new sense of freedom would be found in the suburban landscape with its single-family homes promising more space and a feeling that one had achieved the American Dream.[85] By the late 1950s, the idea of the American Dream as an ideological source of motivation was tightly linked to concrete ideas of homeownership, job stability, and economic movement into the middle class.[86]

In the postwar era and following decades, Hollywood helped project the notion of California as the land of middle-class dreams. Producing movies such as American Graffiti and television shows showcasing a vision of middle-class life amid California sunshine and suburbs, the industry helped raise the Golden State's national profile.[87] A booming postwar economy in the state also helped make the celluloid dreams a reality for many young families. Cities like Los Angeles and San Diego soon witnessed unprecedented population growth and joined San Francisco as major economic powerhouses whose industrial capacities could rival their Eastern counterparts.[88] By the late 1950s, the state had capitalized on its agricultural prowess and also became a leader in the energy and defense sectors, as well as tourism, cultural production, and even manufacturing. Soon thereafter, the state would pioneer an innovative tech economy that would result in exponential growth, cementing California as the nation's largest economy.

Of course, this economic success made the state attractive to people living elsewhere. Between 1950 and 1975, California doubled its population, signaling to many that it was a formidable player in the nation's economic and political landscape.[89] Even small-town newspapers in the Midwest, from Kansas to Ohio, reported on the outmigration of citizens to the Golden State, positioning it as a move toward upward mobility for the young, the ambitious, and the restless.[90] California was a destination state, a place where everyone was "from somewhere else" and where new dreams could be pursued.[91]

As international migration grew in California, media reports quickly seized on the notion that the American Dream was pliable enough to extend to the newer stream of Asian and Latin American newcomers. National and international news outlets featured stories of "new immigrants" searching for the American Dream in California.[92] Although these headlines often ran alongside pieces linking immigration to fears of a demographic takeover, the more positive stories focused on how the Golden State offered immigrants from the Global South opportunities to "work hard" and get ahead.[93] This was the promise of a good life for all who would dare to move far westward or cross perilous borders to create new lives in California.

In several ways, California's economy seemed to deliver for many of its new residents. By the 1970s, California developed more jobs in trade, industry, and technology combined than almost any other state in the nation. Historian Gerald Nash notes that, even then, California was an economic harbinger, boasting the most diversified and efficient agricultural economy in the country, a nascent, but innovative technology sector, and a new type of service-oriented economy that outpaced the nation. During this period, it was common to read articles on the state's economy claiming, "California's today is America's tomorrow."[94]

Much of this economic success lifted the middle class in the state. California's Legislative Analyst's Office reported that "from 1975 to 1990, the average annual personal income growth was a full percentage point higher in California than the nation," while at the same time noting that the "average annual growth" in wages was significantly greater for

Californian workers than for American laborers in other states.[95] By the dawn of the twenty-first century, California had become a destination where, despite exclusionary practices and in some cases exclusionary legislation, international and internal migrants alike fled with hopes of securing middle-class homes, jobs, and lifestyles. Whether from Muncie, Memphis, Michoacán, or Manila, migrants came at a record pace, and by 2020, the state's population had reached forty million, doubling since 1970.

But this is not simply a linear economic story. Economic progress in the state has never offered equal opportunity or trickle-down riches to all residents. While average middle-class wages trended upward in the postwar era, these figures obscure other patterns. Indeed, alongside economic growth, the state witnessed rapidly increasing economic inequality, which exacerbated long-standing segregation patterns in housing and labor markets. Inequality was on the rise across the nation, but it was especially acute in the Golden State. The 1970s rise in technology and service occupations coincided with a downturn in manufacturing, leading to severe cuts in middle-class jobs such as those in construction, banking, and aerospace. Throughout the 1980s and 1990s, these trends would result in income inequality in the state surpassing that of many other states.[96]

Furthermore, inequality in the state went hand in hand with the racial diversification of the population. Rather than the orange-scented streets that Du Bois would encounter, contemporary analysts would see extreme wealth and extreme segregation, with a disproportionate number of African Americans and Latinos among the impoverished and the incarcerated. Writing about Los Angeles in this same period, urban planning and Black studies scholar Clyde Woods notes "as the homeless population increased, its demographics shifted from transient White males to recently unemployed African Americans and Latinos, particularly from resource-deprived South-Central Los Angeles."[97] By 1982, that population was about 30,000, and in 2023, it was over 75,000.

Conclusion

Long established ideologies and narratives about migration, racial liberalism, and economic opportunity shape how people perceive and discuss inequality. These ideas are abstract at the national level, such as when folks believe that the United States is a place of dreaming and opportunity, but sometimes more specific at the level of state and region, like understanding California as being more liberal and more diverse than other states or Los Angeles as a melting pot of different people. These narratives shape how people make sense of inequality as well as their practices. As we will see in the chapters that follow, ideas about who historically belongs here and what kind of place California and the nation are creep into commonplace understandings of inequality.

We now turn to our empirical data—which were mainly drawn from our interviews—to better understand how California's precarious middle class makes sense of the inequality they experience and observe. Over the next three chapters, we first focus on economic inequality, then on racial inequality, and finally on the inequality experienced by immigrants, to better understand these sense-making processes. Throughout our analyses, we recognize the deep interconnections of race, class, and immigration that make it impossible to discuss them in silos. Indeed, as we see with the three narratives about California explored earlier, there is a great deal of entanglement. The notion of the state as a sanctuary for migrants, for instance, is tied to assumptions about economic mobility and belonging, just as the idea of California as a land of economic possibility draws heavily on the image of migrants and immigrants making it here. We recognize that rather than existing in isolation, race, class, and immigration are profoundly entwined. Even so, we believe that by disentangling these different dimensions of inequality, however imperfectly, we can learn more about the specific logic underpinning each as well as their interrelationships.

CHAPTER TWO

CLASS INEQUALITY IN THE LAND OF PLENTY

Craig showed up to the Coffee Bean in Burbank sporting a shirt that read "Wakanda Forever." He was a transplant in his fifties raised by a single mother in Pittsburgh, Pennsylvania. Craig's parents had divorced before he could even remember, and his mother, a music teacher, was able to provide a solid middle-class life for his brother and him. She had nurtured Craig's love of music from a young age, and he was selected to go to a prestigious magnet high school with an International Baccalaureate program. Craig recounted how hard it was to be one of the few magnet kids that did not come from a well-off neighborhood, but he also felt a kind of freedom at this school, which he described as diverse and focused on the arts. Craig had always thought of himself and his upbringing as middle class, not as wealthy as his classmates but not struggling like some of the people he knew growing up. During his senior year of high school, he was accepted into a university with a conservatory to major in musical theater, but after a couple of years, he felt he had made the wrong decision. His father had been a software engineer, and Craig hoped he might follow in his footsteps. Craig shared that while his father had not been very active in his life, he had taught him something: coding. By his third year of college, as Craig pivoted to a focus on a career in computers, he decided that a college focused on the arts would not adequately prepare him. Besides, his girlfriend was pregnant—at twenty-one years old, he was going to be a father. Craig dropped out of college and later moved to Los Angeles, hoping to find much-needed success in the West.

https://doi.org/10.7758/uybx4321.6756

When Craig arrived in California, he found it was not as easy to break into computer work as he thought it would be. As many newcomers these days do, he drove for Uber and Lyft, day and night, to make ends meet. Gradually, he began working with small businesses to help them develop their websites, including a cannabis delivery service in the early days of legalization. At the time of the interview, Craig had lived in Los Angeles for ten years, and while he did not have a college degree, he had amassed many years of experience in web design and programming. And he knew those skills were highly marketable. Craig ran a business with his brother developing websites, mostly for floral shops, which was successful enough that he was able to pay off his remaining college loans. Craig felt proud of his accomplishments, but making $90,000 a year was not enough to support the lifestyle he really wanted. When asked about his class status at the time, he lamented: "Nationally, I would be considered middle class based on how much I make. But . . . um . . . maybe not so much in California." Later he confided that he was deeply frustrated with how expensive life was in Los Angeles specifically. Homeownership seemed completely out of the question, and he explained that things "just don't match. I mean, from what I do at my level of expertise and my . . . my salary, like, I should be just live a very . . . I should be able to live a very comfortable life in a house." Instead, Craig rented an apartment in a region where homeownership had become increasingly inaccessible.[1] His disappointment was palpable. Like many others, he wondered if he would ever become solidly middle class in the Golden State. Rather than complain, however, he embraced the "beautiful struggle" mentality, believing that things would ultimately work themselves out.

In this chapter, we draw on rich interview and survey data to better understand how the precarious middle—the upper-working class and lower-middle class—in California live with and even consent to the broad inequalities around them. We show that, on the one hand, many residents perceive California's economy as increasingly unequal and devolving into a two-class structure that squeezes out the middle. In this understanding, structural conditions, like the location of "good" schools and neighborhoods, or tax and corporate loopholes for the rich, create a society that rigs the system for the wealthy and narrows opportunity for everyone else. Across all racial groups, and across the Los Angeles and Central Valley regions, we found that respondents had a keen understanding of the variety of local and regional issues that made it difficult to achieve middle-class status in the land of plenty.

We found that spatial comparison helped people sort out just how severe and untenable California's cost of living was. By contrasting the Golden State's relatively high prices and unaffordable homes with sticker prices in other, lower-cost states, such as Kansas, Arizona, and Texas, respondents could signal that the middle was getting left out of California prosperity. Respondents evoked spatial comparison as a way of inferring that something might be tarnished here in the Golden State, to suggest that even when one does everything right to get ahead, it was still impossible compared to other places in the United States.

Ultimately, though, respondents downplayed the structural inequalities they saw around them while expressing optimism about their personal upward mobility. To imagine a more golden-colored picture of their future trajectory, many engaged in exceptional framing—the practice of seeing oneself as distinct from the norm or as an exception to the prevailing structural trends. Hence, we were told that through hard work, smart practices, and patience, they could beat the odds that seemed to be stacked against so many others in the middle. In doing so, respondents could minimize the structural conditions of inequality and adopt a more individualistic understanding, replete with bootstraps, of who gets ahead and why.

Finally, we found that respondents minimized the inequalities around them through bounded blame. This cultural strategy involves viewing poor people as bound by and subject to their structural circumstances. In this, poor people are thought to engage in behaviors that reproduce their economic condition. This version of "blame the poor" is nuanced and includes the recognition that structural conditions create inequalities. Yet it also entails drawing a causal link between conditions and behavior to suggest that individual actions help keep poor people poor. Respondents told us that they empathized with poor people and could see how conditions such as unfair economic starts or bad luck contributed to their situation while at the same time positing, in subtle and nuanced ways, that they likely remained poor because they held alternative values and engaged in unproductive and even criminal behaviors.

The ability to recognize inequalities in California and then downplay structural understandings allows many to interpret the expanding divide through a more optimistic and individualistic perspective. With this attitude, broad challenges, such as reaching middle-class status in an increasingly unequal economy, are less about the dire need for wide-scale structural change and more about motivation or one's ability to simply "want it" more than others. In this way, many respondents focus on individual agency in their narratives about why some people "make it" and thereby create understandings that emphasize choice and behavior over abstract, systemic dynamics. We suggest this tendency leads to complacency and compliance, which aids in the reproduction of inequality. In the following pages, we describe how respondents discussed the subject of inequality in the state, revealing how spatial comparison helped them contextualize their own experiences with economic opportunities and setbacks. We then examine in more depth how respondents used exceptional framing and bounded blame as strategies for downplaying the structural nature of the inequalities they perceived.

California, a Place for the Rich and Poor

Christian is an immigrant from the Philippines in his late thirties. He has lived in the Los Angeles area for over fifteen years. He migrated soon after obtaining his bachelor's degree and immediately set out to complete a training course in medical billing at a local community college. He had been working in that industry for many years, and although he had rarely been unemployed, he did not yet own a home and wondered how he could afford to do so in LA's current housing market. He is a registered Democrat but bemoaned the political partisanship of the current moment and said his politics were more "middle of the road."

During his interview, Christian told us unequivocally that California is a good place to get ahead economically because "in the Philippines there is no opportunity, unless you work for the government or are an influential person." He admired his aunt, who migrated to Southern California decades ago with "only two luggage bags and ended up owning a small business." In his mind, she came with only a pipe dream and was able to achieve her entrepreneurial goals through hard work.

While this narrative might have led Christian to see ample paths toward middle-class stability, when asked what he thought of the economy, he noted: "Uh, this economy is doing good but doesn't really . . .

doesn't feel like [it's] in a good way. Are we really growing the economy, or are we living in another bubble? [*laughs*], you know, a bubble bursts later on. And, basic[ally] the economy is good, but I see a lot of people homeless. . . . [In] today's economy . . . um . . . the rich are getting richer. The poor are getting poorer. The middle class are declining. We're now getting one—or only two—two categories—you are rich, or you are poor."

To him, the present economic moment felt unsteady, more and more like an hourglass, with a growing number of rich and poor and an increasingly untenable life for the middle class. His aunt was probably able to succeed because she came at a time when wages were more likely to keep up with inflation. Christian believes that things are tougher for his generation.

Many others in our study had the same deep feeling in their gut as Christian that California and the entire nation was squeezing out its middle. Even respondents claiming to have scant information about the actual health of the economy and a superficial understanding of the political debates around the issue had a nagging sense that the growing wealth gap was disappearing the middle class. For example, Jerry, an Asian American who works as a consultant in Los Angeles told us, "Like I said, the rich are getting richer, and the poor are getting poorer. . . . I have no other—no data to support that it is increasing or not . . . but, I mean, I just feel like I've noticed it more." Similarly, when asked who she thought was getting ahead in today's economy, one respondent in Los Angeles shared, "Um, well . . . I guess it kind of seems like the rich are getting richer, the poor are getting poorer, and the middle class are getting poorer too, again with them losing their jobs . . . um. . . . Yeah, I . . . I don't know." In these examples, respondents admitted having little information, relying instead on strong gut feelings about the matter, perhaps based on everyday experiences or social media. Whatever the case, it felt true to them even if not factually verified.

Of course, others felt they had a clear sense of what was happening with the economy, which often aligned with their political worldviews. For example, John is an academic specialist in Los Angeles and a registered Democrat. He told us he closely follows the economy, noting: "Your rich get richer. We understand that. And the gap it's just widening. It's not really lessened. I think that certainly . . . but what we need to do is certainly more government subsidy. And the reason why I say that is, the more the bottom is raised up, the better it is for everyone."

Other respondents that leaned Democrat suggested that more middle-class opportunities would emerge in California if it instituted a fairer tax system that did not favor the rich, and if the legislature created additional social safety net programs. They had a keen understanding of the economy's hourglass shape and that more progressive policies could best improve the situation.

Those on the right, while fewer in number in our sample, also tended to think the state was becoming a dual economy and were alarmed by the purported middle-class squeeze in the state. Yet unlike the more progressive respondents, the more conservative ones lamented the "handouts" that they felt fed into a seemingly corrupt social welfare system and increased the number of impoverished people. Dave, a military veteran in his late fifties who volunteers as a lay preacher in his Central Valley church, noted with a chuckle: "Oh, without a doubt, the middle . . . yeah . . . the . . . the . . . it is . . . it is . . . the middle class has almost gone away. Now it's . . . it's becoming more and more you have the rich and you have the poor. When I was in the military, we used to laugh about that. It . . . it was a funny little thing but there's so much truth to it. We used to say the rich get richer and the poor get babies."

At another point in the interview he would explain that poor people remained poor because "welfare programs" seemed to entice them to have more children than they could afford. His thoughts on income inequality were related to his assumption that poor people had large families and a poor work ethic that made them reliant on handouts. But Dave also felt that the rich were gaining on their preestablished advantage, with generational wealth creating uneven starting points.

Yet regardless of the political reasons they believed undergirded increasing income inequality, respondents thought that the middle class was being squeezed out of opportunities.[2] Moreover, this understanding of the dual economy, whether based in fact, feeling, or political ideology, was often easily transposed onto how respondents understood California as a place to live. For example, Bai, an Asian American respondent in Los Angeles, paused a bit when asked what he thought his neighborhood might look like in the future and then noted: "It's gonna be a big disbursement of rich and poor. . . . I feel like it's already that's the case right here, but I feel like it's gonna get worse. . . . Like, for people who rent out homes, it's just kind of more and more. . . . It's gonna . . . cost is gonna go up and they're gonna have to find somewhere else to live."

Later in the book, we will delve deeper into the thoughts expressed by respondents about the future of the state and its various neighborhoods. For now, we would like to underscore that respondents acknowledged that inequality had grown and that the economy had become increasingly divided, not simply between rich and poor people but between rich and poor neighborhoods.

Respondents expressed deep anguish at the inequality they observed, often finding it hard to believe just how striking the contrast was between severe poverty and great wealth in the cities in which they lived. John, a respondent in Los Angeles, described it this way:

> I was [in] downtown LA yesterday, and you're right there on Skid Row, and it's just . . . I mean, it's beyond disheartening. It was to the point where I just can't believe they actually allow people to live like that. I know they're down there for all different types of reasons. But then I go five blocks over, I see some of the tallest buildings in the world, some of the wealthiest companies in the world, just five blocks away. And not only that, you see, building in downtown LA is almost at [an] all-time high. I mean, you're talking about these hotels and the condos and the residences. I don't even want to know how much some of those are going for. And you're talking about, like I say, billion-dollar companies that are just literally, literally right down the street.

A similar sentiment was shared in the Central Valley, although folks there talked less about construction and skyscrapers and more about how inequality was quickly changing the feel of local neighborhoods. For instance, when asked about her views on the economy, Isabel, a Mexican American living in Fresno, explained, "You see it all over the place. You know people who have and those that have not. . . . I go home, and you see the homelessness, you come to Fresno State area, and you see the nice cars."

It is not as if there are no middle-class areas in California—there certainly are. Although scholars note that California's economy has become more unequal, they are unsure about how acute the middle-class shrinkage in the state has been or even how it can be measured.[3]

The most recent estimates suggest that the middle class shrunk by 7 percent between 2010 and 2020, but that is only the case when certain data parameters are considered. Debates also abound about how widespread gentrification has been and whether middle-class neighborhoods are shrinking in different parts of the state.[4] What is clear is that the *feeling* of an increasingly hourglass economy is pervasive among the upper-working-class and lower-middle-class respondents—a feeling readily transposed onto the California landscape.

Importantly, our interview results echo many of the available survey findings. In 2015, for example, the University of California, Berkeley's Institute of Governmental Studies found that most respondents in the state, across party lines and regions, thought that inequality was increasing in the nation and in the state.[5] The partisan difference lay in what people thought should be done about it. Similarly, in 2021, the Public Policy Institute of California found that close to 70 percent of respondents agreed that the "gap between the rich and the poor is getting larger."[6]

Spatial Comparison and the California Exodus

An important driver of perceptions of a dual economy among many respondents was the idea that middle-class folks were leaving for other states with lower costs of living. Many respondents talked about the issue even though they were not specifically prompted to do so. For example, when asked about the future economic condition of California, Alex, a Fresno resident, noted:

> You're gonna have three groups in California, there's the super wealthy, whether it's tech money, retirement money, or family money, however they [get it], and then the super poor, a lot of immigrants. . . . And then the government workers to redistribute the income. And the middle class, be that White, Black, Hispanic, Asian, you know, the insurance agents or whatever . . . the . . . the guy that owns a . . . a lawn mowing company . . . whatever . . . they're getting the hell out. They're going to Nevada, they're going to Texas, and . . . um . . . it's sad to me because this is . . . it's the most wonderful place in the world when you combine the . . . the climate and the fact that it's a big state, with the diverse natural resource[s], and it's in America. . . . It's . . . it's an attractive place in the world.

To Alex, California was already squeezing out small business owners and a racially diverse middle class, and the pull of neighboring states with their comparatively lower cost of living meant an acceleration of the hourglass economy processes already at play. Other respondents similarly knew individuals in their social networks, including friends and family members, who had moved out of the state to find middle-class opportunities elsewhere. We heard about family members who had moved to Texas, Kansas, Nevada, Arizona, and elsewhere to buy a home in a middle-class neighborhood.

Still, interviewees did not have to actually know anyone personally who had left the Golden State to acknowledge middle-class flight. Simply pointing out the different costs of living elsewhere was enough for many. For example, Phil is a transplant from the Midwest. Although he has been living in California for over two decades and is raising a daughter in Los Angeles, he noted that his income as a small business owner simply doesn't yield enough for homeownership. He also told us that he could not afford the many luxuries the city offers, like great restaurants and other forms of entertainment. He shared "we go when we can . . . but we just can't afford it." When reflecting on this, he said he had knowingly made a "lifestyle choice" to live a "lower-middle class" existence in Los Angeles, though he posited that his income elsewhere would make him more firmly middle class. He continued: "And I think I'm gonna be s-sociologically . . . I don't think there's any middle class left . . . in Southern California anymore. . . . Whereas I would say like in . . . let's say . . . I have some friends in Kansas City—that's like the all-American suburb. They're middle class. And they make about what I make. They have jobs and work, but they live a lot better on the same money. But they're . . . they're [out there]. . . . It's not very diverse. You know, [but] they feel comfortable in it."

In fact, the interviewees' responses reflected a contemporary public debate. At the time we collected our data, news headlines about "blue states" witnessing a mass "exodus" all pointed to California. Conservative politicians even proclaimed facetiously that California was "hemorrhaging population."[7] Yet the issue became more than simply political theater when business media outlets began to tie out-migration to the state's high cost of living. In 2018, *Market Watch* published the headline "California Exodus Gathers Strength as Home Prices Continue Upward March," and Realtor.com proclaimed soon thereafter,

"With No Letup in Home Prices, the California Exodus Grows."[8] The 2020 census count reported that California's population growth had slowed between 2010 and 2020 and fell flat in 2017, leading to the loss of a congressional seat.[9] But opinions are mixed on whether the shift amounted to an "exodus," with most researchers noting that the loss has been much more modest than reported by major news outlets.[10]

Other states have taken stock of California's demographic trends. *The Atlanta Journal-Constitution*, for example, ran a headline the year we conducted interviews titled, "For Fleeing Californians, Atlanta is a Top Destination."[11] Later, Nevada Public Radio would ask listeners rhetorically "Is California Ruining Nevada?" in a segment about California migrants driving up housing prices.[12] In Texas, where the issue of California out-migration conjured up many political imaginations, sayings like "Don't California My Texas" dotted major news outlets.[13] And while some questioned whether California out-migration was good for receiving states, others were clear that it was. Indeed, in 2020, the state of Ohio launched a $70 million campaign that purchased billboards in California and other places that encouraged residents to move to the Buckeye State. Some of the billboards tried to entice Californians with simple statements such as "Live where you can actually save for a rainy day."[14]

For some in our sample, out-migration was the only way they could ever imagine developing a rainy-day fund. For example, Kareem worked in the entertainment production field and oversaw an entrepreneurial side venture in Los Angeles. During his interview, Kareem said he felt that he and his wife were part of a missing middle class in California. When asked exactly why he thought this, he replied, "Because if I took my income and I took my wife's income and we moved to the Midwest, we'd be completely fine." Similarly, another respondent told us that homeownership would be attainable for him if only he would move. He explained: "Look, we're paying $18,000 for our rental. You go to Texas, you can buy a house for $150,000—for a brand-new house. That same house here in California . . . in our neighborhood . . . it's going to be maybe $600,000 or $700,000. I've checked the market."

Regardless of the accuracy of his figures about the current housing market, it is important to note that respondents continually stressed the comparative cost of living in other states. In other words, many understood affordability and inequality in California in spatial comparison to the imagined cost of living in other states.

Only a few respondents saw the Golden State as a place with *increasing* middle-class opportunities. Yet even they had a sense that these opportunities would only be available to those invested in certain booming sectors, such as technology and real estate. Overall, respondents from across the political spectrum tended to see uncertain or negative prospects in the state for the middle class and the aspiring middle class.

Spatial comparison, in this instance, allowed respondents to contextualize and make sense of the structural aspects of economic inequality in California. Later, we will show how spatial comparison also helps respondents to minimize inequality around race and immigration status. Here, respondents tended to see things as "bad" in California compared with other places. The Golden State stood out for its exceptionally high cost of living, contributing to a broad pessimism about upward mobility.

Why Is California Unequal?

Yet while respondents expressed that life in California was getting harder for the middle class, some questions remained: Why did they think it was getting harder? What were the causes? Combing through our interviews, we found that respondents offered three main explanations. The first centered on family wealth and social location. For example, Megan, an African American woman from Los Angeles, described her vision of a better California: "A more respectful society where [folks] know that everybody doesn't start on first base, you know what I mean? Because there's some people that are not even born anywhere near the ballpark. And they got to get to the ballpark. And there are people that are born on third base. And they're like, 'Well, why can't everybody make it. . . .' You know . . . it's just like, wait a minute . . . you were born on third base. You know what I mean? Somebody else was not even in the ballpark."

Here, Megan acknowledged that individuals start in different social locations. Some come from middle-class or upper-class neighborhoods and attend some of the state's best schools—they are born on second or third base—while others grow up struggling in poor, violent, and neglected areas, and might not even be in walking distance of the ballpark. Megan believed that starting points matter and affect life outcomes. A person who is not even born in the ballpark, she suggested, might never be able to reach the middle class—or get to home base. This metaphor underscores the fact that Megan, like many other respondents, understood that structural obstacles impacted middle-class opportunity in the state. For the most part, they could point to how factors other than one's ability, such as being born in a good neighborhood with good schools and middle-class parents, can lead to later economic advantages.[15]

In fact, respondents were so aware of these structural advantages that they told us about how they were trying to secure them for their own children. For example, Grace, one of our few Republican interviewees in our LA sample, told us plainly that she was raising her kids in the San Fernando Valley because she wanted access to better resources. She stated, "Um, if you live in LA, public school is . . . they are not very good. But if you live in the Valley where White people live, then you get a better chance, you know . . . um . . . having a better education." For Grace, Los Angeles had a particular, racialized geography of opportunity, which she believed would benefit her children over the long run.

Many other respondents pointed to how race impacted a person's economic prospects. Black respondents in particular noted that Black families in California were often deprived of good schools, good jobs, and safe neighborhoods, arguing that they were therefore closed off from middle-class opportunities. Still other respondents, especially Latinos, told us about how immigration policies kept them from getting better jobs and accessing opportunities. Immigrant communities lack resources, they argued, because immigrants themselves often cannot get the jobs, education, or credit necessary for social mobility. Importantly, these findings dovetail with state-wide research showing that about 70 percent of California residents see racial disparities as a leading cause of economic inequality.[16]

Some respondents explained the inequalities they saw around them by pointing to how social networks helped rich people stay rich. For example, when asked to elaborate on why he thought rich people were getting ahead in today's economy, Sanjay, a South Asian LA resident, told us: "Connections . . . it's all connections. I think that everything you do in life is connections. . . . I don't think anything in life comes down to talent anymore. I think it's who you know first. A lot of times, it's a White person, knowing a White person."

As a professional working in information technology (IT), he said he saw firsthand how these networks play out in his field. And when asked if it's simply that some, including people of color, are not as well connected or simply do not know that connections matter, Sanjay continued: "Yeah, I think it is. But I think they don't know the connections because the connections are not willing to talk to them. They'd rather connect their best friend's son." To Sanjay, the issue of connections worked insidiously in labor markets to help some groups, especially middle- and upper-class White people, get ahead. And once they got ahead, Sanjay saw them as able to stay ahead through favorable policies, especially those related to taxes. Later in the interview, he explained: "I just know I don't make a great amount of money, but I make a good salary. I pay a s—t load of taxes. But I also know friends who . . . don't have to pay anything and they make maybe triple what I'm making. So, I don't know, I just feel like the rich are still being favored in some way."

Sanjay saw the rich getting ahead not through one but through multiple channels. And to him, the issue was not simply about being lucky enough to take advantage of these structural imbalances. It was also about government policies that allowed the rich to accumulate advantages.

This sentiment about the rich and ultrarich paying less taxes and gaining advantages through government policy was widespread among respondents. Many described the nexus between policy and wealth as a sort of game or a system that the rich had rigged. Suleima, a Latina from Los Angeles, told us, "This year I had to pay more taxes than Jeff Bezos, and Jeff Bezos is making a ridiculous amount of money compared to me. But I'm paying more in taxes than him. So, I just, like, this system isn't working for the rest of us." Many respondents viewed tax loopholes, government contracts, and other incentives as upholding an unfair economic system.

Overall, respondents had a sense that inequality in California was linked to various structural conditions that helped the wealthy game the system. On the whole, they felt that opportunities were shrinking in the middle because one's life position—or starting base—offered fewer paths to upward mobility in today's California and because networks and economic policy helped rich people stay rich. Of course, liberals and conservatives in our sample differed on *how* the government could create more opportunities. While those on the left pointed to the need to regulate corporations, those on the right talked about policies affecting small businesses. What they shared was a sense that upward social mobility had become more difficult. Most respondents also had a sense that California residents were part of an economy that favored the wealthy at the expense of others, including the middle class.

Exceptional Framing of Class Inequality

Respondents clearly echoed the news headlines about California. Positive political proclamations about the strength of California's economy notwithstanding, even before the pandemic, interviewees forecasted negative trends that would eventually come to fruition. A 2024 report by the Public Policy Institute of California showed that California lost population at increasing rates between 2010 and 2020 and that the majority of this loss was among the middle class, especially young professionals with a bachelor of arts.[17] Later that year, the research outlet California Community Builders estimated that while high earners and low earners in the state grew by more than 30 percent between 2000 and 2020, middle-income earners decreased by 7 percent.[18] In other words, California's economy witnessed loss in the middle of the income scale and growth at the high and low ends.

How do we reconcile the strength of the state's economy—the fourth largest in the world—with respondents' feelings and the data about a middle-class squeeze in the state? Put simply, both can be true. The state can add more jobs and witness more growth—but only at the extremes rather than in the middle.[19] And the growth can be uneven, with much larger gains at the top end of the economic scale. In 2023, the state's Future of Work Commission noted that "while real wages for high-income workers have increased over the past forty years, median wages have generally stagnated, and even slightly declined for low-income workers."[20]

This sense of a squeezed middle class coincides with broader social pessimism and anxiety about the present moment. In 2023, the Public Policy Institute of California found that two out of three Californians were anxious about their economic prospects.[21] This economic pessimism was also evident in our survey data. In our statewide survey, we asked respondents: "Now thinking back three to four years, do you think your family was better or worse off three years ago?" Eighty percent of respondents told us their family was "better off," "much better off," or "about the same." Only 20 percent said they were worse off, signaling to us that a significant number of respondents were more anxious about the present than the past. More information on the survey and how it is linked to interview responses is presented in the methodological appendix.

Upon further analysis of the data, we came upon a surprising, counterintuitive finding—respondents seemed to be anxious about the present but also optimistic about the immediate future. When we asked survey and interview respondents to think forward a year and opine on whether they would be better or worse off, the majority of respondents conjectured that they would be better or much better off, signaling a sort of optimism about the years ahead. Only a small fraction of the survey sample, about 10 percent, thought they would be worse off. Here, as opposed to the question about the past, the responses about the future suggest a more upward trajectory. This finding reflects the well-documented general sense of optimism among Americans about the future, as they tend to overestimate their future social mobility compared with others in comparable countries.[22] We also found, surprisingly, that Latino and African American respondents were more optimistic about the future than their White and Asian counterparts.

How might we consider these pieces of data together, especially when we account for the fact that many of the interviewees spoke at length about a dual-class Californian economy and shrinking opportunities for the middle class in the state? Exceptional framing, or the ability to see one's future as distinct from the statistical average, explains a lot.

Interview respondents simultaneously expressed social pessimism about the general state of the middle class and individual optimism about their economic prospects because they saw themselves as exceptions to the norm. For example, Mei was born in Vietnam but raised in a housing project in Los Angeles. She never graduated from a four-year university but has held full- and part-time jobs concurrently for many years. While she said she thinks the economy is good for those that are "hustlers" and own their own businesses, she lamented the middle-class squeeze that makes her part of the lower-middle class despite how much she works. She thought it was hard for people to make it into the middle class today.

Still, when asked what her situation would look like in one to three years, she said that "it can only go up" because "I always wanna strive higher." Mei was optimistic and certain that her will and her intelligence would improve her economic position in the near future, even as she acknowledged how hard this can be.

Similarly, Josué, who is in his late twenties, works full-time and lives with his parents in a house that the entire family recently purchased together. He said that it was getting more expensive to live in Los Angeles every year, and he was not sure when he would be able to purchase a home of his own. Yet Josué still believed that the future was bright for him, in large part because he simply wanted to succeed more than others did. When asked whether he would move up or down the class ladder in a few years, he responded: "I think honestly, up. One, because I look at my friends and I guess comparing myself to my friends . . . they're comfortable in their jobs. And I'm always the one that wants to do better. They're okay with their nine-to-five jobs . . . or whatever. So, I feel like in that way, not that I'm better than them, but I feel like I have more ambition to keep on making more money, to keep on doing better for myself. So then one day I don't have to struggle with money and just be okay."

For Josué, exceptional framing works through social comparison. When he contrasts his ambitions to those of his friends, he finds evidence for a more optimistic rendering of his trajectory.

Other interviewees tied their optimism to their role as parents. For example, Marisa, a Latina who regretted never finishing her college degree, told us that she believed she would move up the economic ladder even though she was currently unable to buy a house and despite feeling like the structural obstacles impeding middle-class mobility "are never going to end." She thought she would be an exception to the statistical average because her role as a parent motivates her to beat the odds. Reflecting on how difficult it was to grow up in poverty in the Central Valley, she told us: "Like . . . I know, how hard it can be, and it's just not something I want my kids to look back and, you know, say, oh, I didn't have anything, I couldn't go here or, you know, we just ate whatever we could find in the cabinet. I don't want them to ever feel or think that way, so . . . yeah, like there's no other option for us than to just keep going up [*laughs*]."

These contradictory findings of social pessimism and individual optimism bear out across distinct strands of social science research. Public opinion data, for example, show that Americans tend to underestimate the level of income inequality at the national level; and a state's economic context correlates strongly with these perceptions.[23] The proportion of Californians who perceive rising income inequality is higher than the national average, even controlling for political party and ideological factors.[24] In other words, Californians are more likely than Texans, for example, to state that economic inequality is rising across the country. To some extent, this finding likely reflects the undeniable increase in the phenomenon over the past four decades in California specifically.[25] It is likely easier to see more inequality nationally when it is also close to home and when media coverage frames California as the "poorest and richest state in America."[26]

Other social psychology studies have shown that many individuals express a personal optimism bias when thinking about the future. This research reveals that individuals minimize their personal future risk and tend to think that they are better equipped than others to weather any challenges. Decades of research have documented optimism bias with respect to future disease and general health risks, as well as crime/victimization, labor, and environmental risks.[27] Recent work has also documented a substantial amount of optimism bias in Americans' subjective expectations about their future in terms of labor market transitions, and this dovetails with many studies that show that Americans are generally much more positive about their future social mobility patterns than current data patterns imply.[28] Of course, these studies report significant variances in who is more or less likely to have an optimism bias regarding their future trajectory. Yet, overall, Americans tend to be more hopeful about their earnings, job market prospects, and savings than actual data patterns would predict.[29]

In the next section, we unpack this contradiction, focusing attention on how individuals arrive at their optimism while also perceiving a middle-class squeeze. Cultural sociologists have long shown that individuals have contradictory understandings of a wide variety of issues, including love, finances, and family.[30] Indeed, individuals do not understand issues, especially those as complex as one's prospects for social mobility, in a simple manner. Rather than see these issues in black and white, they often view them as shades of gray. And as they do so, they hold fast to a set of practices that help them make sense of contradictions and that buffer them from the resulting ambivalence.

WORK HARD AND BIDE TIME

Kevin grew up in a working-class Asian immigrant neighborhood in the suburbs of Los Angeles. His father made minimum wage working in a warehouse, and his mother worked at a nail salon. Still, they emphasized to Kevin the importance of focusing on academics and saved their money to send him and his siblings to private school. Kevin ended up majoring in chemistry in college and is now an environmental engineer working for the federal government. Although he has worked with various employers since graduating, now in his late twenties, he views his current compliance role as significantly more stable. When asked if he owned a home, he quipped that he was not "rich" and suggested that a person had to be wealthy to buy real estate in Los Angeles. Still, he considered himself to be on his way up. With regard to his economic standing, he noted: "I, well I guess, I don't own many assets, but I don't have any debt. . . . So, I'm not sure if that's considered low or middle class. I guess within like five to ten years, I would consider myself middle class, but I consider myself low[er] class as of right now."

When asked why he felt like he would probably move into the middle class within the next five years, he said: "I think it's because my current job is, I guess, respectable and it pays well. Enough to cover my bills and I don't spend a lot. So, in terms of cash flow, I have a positive cash flow monthly, and throughout my life."

Kevin said he thought the Los Angeles housing market makes homeownership out of reach. He and his girlfriend still lived with her parents. However, he thought that if he just held on and continued to work hard, save, and bide his time for a few years, he would have an opportunity to enter the middle class. Similarly, Josué saw the future with a measure of optimism because his career had opportunities for advancement that would open up as he gained more experience. A quality control manager with a degree in engineering, he had already seen an increase in his living situation since starting a new job. He explained: "I moved up a little bit, and I will keep moving up. . . . Um, because once you are getting experience, with that comes a pay increase, and . . . and if I actually get the job I am looking for, then my income will increase more."

Like Kevin and Josué, many in our sample focused on working hard and biding their time. They believed the future would be better if only they managed to keep working and wait for new opportunities to emerge. They still acknowledged that, overall, the middle class might have fewer opportunities to grow or stay economically afloat, but they were also invested in the belief that hard work would pay off in time.

Of course, Kevin and Josué have college degrees, and one might reasonably conclude that biding time only works for those that are on a steady professional path. But we found that this attitude was also common among non-college-educated respondents. For example, Mary worked full-time at a warehouse in Fresno and never graduated from college, but she still had a lot of college debt. A young grandmother in her late forties, she worked ten-hour graveyard shifts, four days a week. She had been promoted a few times in three years, and though she did not make enough money to own her own home, she believed things would get better for her. Her string of promotions, she believed, would continue if she focused on working hard and paying off her debt. "I'm hoping to only go up" she told us. For Mary, California, including the Central Valley, had become increasingly unaffordable, but she believed that her work ethic would lead to her receiving the pay raises she needed to pay off her student loans and live more comfortably.

Respondents' logic about biding time extended to their partners as well. For instance, Sergio was born and raised in a largely Mexican and African American neighborhood in Fresno. He recalled vacillating between being poor and working class, as his stepfather worked in construction and his mother stayed at home to care for him and his siblings. He went to public school and went "straight to work" after graduating high school. At the time of the interview, he lived in an apartment with his wife and son and worked a steady set of shifts at a local warehouse. He also took side jobs as a handyman when he could. He hoped to own a home one day. When asked how he planned to accomplish that, he explained, "My wife . . . she has been getting good raises." He continued: "I think from this point I can only go up. . . . The career . . . the career my wife has . . . she's . . . she just keeps going. She's an accountant, so it will go up." Sergio believed that his financial standing would change when these developments in his family took hold. Critical to this plan was the underlying assumption that his wife was working hard and waiting for opportunities to materialize.

Similarly, Sherrie was also waiting for a family development. A single mother, she lived in a Los Angeles studio apartment with her teenage daughter. She shared that she came from a highly educated, middle-class, African American, military family and, "my dad had like eight degrees." Sherrie did not finish college but had accrued many years of experience in administrative work. She explained that she did "on-call" work for production studios, handling everything from human resources to bookkeeping issues, all while also holding a full-time job as a telemarketer. Sherrie's situation left her feeling economically squeezed, and she considered herself to be "one step down from the middle class." When asked about whether she thought she would move up or down the class ladder in the near future, she said: "Um, I'm hoping to move a little up. Not too li- . . . not too much like the Jeffersons but in between. . . . Um, what would probably help me is probably . . . I don't know to be honest with you. I think . . . I think what would probably help if when my daughter isn't . . . when she turns eighteen. And then she will pursue the things that she wants to do more. It'll take a little bit of pressure off of me."

Sherrie believed that changes in her economic situation would come with a new life milestone—when her child got older and she could spend more of her time and resources on herself. Later in her interview, she explained that when her daughter moves out, she will have more flexibility and more time to search for production work in Hollywood. For now, she said she manages with her side hustles and telemarketing job, squeezing into a small apartment to make ends meet.

Finally, some saw themselves on an eventual upward trajectory because they were in entrepreneurial positions that they expected would eventually pay. Joy, for example, was born and raised in Ohio and moved to Los Angeles to pursue acting and a creative career. While she still dabbled in acting, Joy also took a job in the insurance industry to pay her bills. She explained that she would soon start her own life insurance agency and was excited about this next step. Joy noted, "It will work perfectly for me because I'm still doing what I am doing. . . . I'm still auditioning and things like that. . . . I definitely think [the future is] going to be upward."

This belief in the eventual rewards of patience and hard work are the tenets of meritocratic thinking, that one reaps what one sows. The idea is that patience and hard work will pay off. This bootstrap thinking remains pervasive in California, despite the extremely high levels of class inequality. Many of the interviewees believed they would eventually reap the rewards of hard work personally even when they were being realistic and even when they spoke at length about the increasing levels of economic inequality in California more broadly.

ABILITY TO DO MORE WITH LESS

Another way respondents engaged in exceptional framing was by focusing on frugality. Many respondents told us that they were optimistic about entering the middle class because they had learned to change their behaviors and become "money smart." They believed that being conservative with their spending could help them save enough to enter the middle class one day. For example, Megan, who earlier told us that some people in California are born outside the metaphoric ballpark, grew up in a historically African American working- and middle-class neighborhood in Los Angeles. Her father was a mechanic, and her mother was a clerical worker for a large corporation. When thinking about her family's class status growing up, she told us that her parents had sent her and her siblings to private school, although they "weren't, like, wealthy living in Beverly Hills. . . . There was never anything that I ever wanted that I couldn't get or that I didn't get no matter what the amount was."

After high school, Megan moved to Europe and tried to pursue a creative career but ended up returning to Los Angeles a few years later. She earned a bachelor's and a master's degree from a nearby state university. Currently working full-time as a freelance bookkeeper, Megan noted, "I'm making more money than I would if I was working at a company just doing bookkeeping." Yet as a single mother with a young son, she found it hard to make ends meet. And though she would love to have her own house, or at least her own apartment, she found that it was smarter to curb this desire and instead be content living with her son in her uncle's home. She longed for more independence but also recognized that housing was just "so expensive." She continued, "Even, like, in the ghetto, you know, it's for a one-bedroom, it's like the r- . . . the rent prices are just, like, outrageous." For the moment, Megan's living situation allowed her to save money for an eventual home purchase, which she expected might only happen if there was a downturn in the economy. She told us, "I'm being frugal," and though she could "buy little treats and different things now and then," she would rather just save her money. When asked for an example of how she gets by as a single mother, she shared: "I mean, just even now, like doing my hair. I mean, I . . . and you know, I'm just gonna go to the beauty school across the street because I'm like, I can't . . . I mean, I can afford to go to like a salon . . . I'm like, why would I give them $30 or $40 to wash my hair when I can go there for $5. [*laughs*] You know what I mean? So, it's just things like that w-where you just don't . . . I just live frugal."

Like Megan, many other respondents spoke of being more frugal and monitoring their needs. Those with more working-class jobs spoke of limiting their desires so they could pay all their bills or contribute to their savings. Many interviewees who had lived through difficult times, such as unemployment, credit mishaps, or health emergencies, sought to build whatever savings they could.

Some respondents thought that living frugally was a learned behavior, a sort of self-discipline that arose from their childhood experiences. For example, Diana, the daughter of undocumented immigrant parents, told us that she and her five siblings were mainly raised by a single mother. Her father was "in and out of the house a lot" and was even jailed for some time. She remembered her mother using food stamps during their weekly grocery trips, using the pawn shop for collateral, and finding creative ways to obtain food and donated clothing. She thought that her experiences growing up had shaped her spending and saving habits, noting: "Um, I'm pretty frugal and pretty . . . like this goes back to my mom being really resourceful and kinda teaching me those things. Um, that's not to say I didn't have credit card debt when I was, like, younger in college. Like . . . definitely did when I first . . . had my first credit card. I'm like, what do I do with this? Um, learned my lesson. So now . . . um . . . my only debt is student loan debt."

Frugality to Diana meant being focused on paying off her graduate student loans and forgoing things like upgrading to a nicer apartment. At the time of the interview, she was living in a "very small studio" in East LA and regularly faced an hour-long commute to her office. The money that she saved from living in a more humble apartment went toward savings and making headway on her student loans, but she still had over $50,000 to go.

Even the interviewees who did not have significant educational debt and who worked in professional careers told us of the importance of being frugal. Kevin, the environmental engineer we met earlier who said he could not afford to own a home because he was "not rich," said that he and his girlfriend rented a room in her family's home to save money. He thought of himself as a "minimalist" and noted, "I'm not a big spender." He further explained that he and his girlfriend limit eating out, spend a lot of time in nature and in public libraries, and often forgo desires like purchasing a new car, which he had yet to buy. These practices, along with the various side gigs he was engaged in at the time of the interview allowed him to save toward eventual homeownership—even if he couldn't achieve that anytime soon. Indeed, when asked if he saw himself as a homeowner in the near future, he noted, "Even if [I] save one to two thousand a month . . . that is still a long time. . . . It will take at least ten years." Still, Kevin was hopeful and believed that his frugal ethos would eventually help him stay on top of Los Angeles' increasing cost of living and enter the middle class.

Even as respondents recognized their own agency, they were aware that economic opportunities were diminishing for the middle class, and they could easily point to ways that structural issues, such as one's starting point in life and social networks, made it easier for some to get ahead than others. Respondents acknowledged how government policies, gentrification processes, and even broader generational trends buoy those who are better off, making it harder for today's aspiring middle class. They saw the economy as an hourglass, with fewer opportunities to achieve middle-class stability than there were in prior decades.

Across the political spectrum, our interview data show that respondents developed guiding tenets to help manage the angst associated with not being fully part of the middle class. Respondents indicated that working hard and finding ways to do more with less were important strategies to employ while they bided their time and waited for opportunities for upward mobility. Their belief systems gave them cultural strategies for action and, just as important, respite from the general sense that upward social mobility was beyond their reach in a state with a rapidly tightening middle.[31] These convictions offered them comfort and a sense that they can overcome any obstacles. What came to the fore in such narratives was personal hope and optimism about their futures, anchored in a sense of individual agency.

In all of this, having a sense of personal agency was important, especially because many see the economy as unpredictable and the cost of living soaring at a dizzying pace. For example, Megan, who told us earlier that she lives with her uncle and only gets her hair cut by students at beauty schools, also shared that her greatest concern was having no economic safety net in today's economy: "The economy is getting really bad because people cannot afford housing, people cannot afford the basic necessities. Jobs are becoming . . . um . . . people are getting, like, robots to do jobs for . . . for us. So pretty soon, some industries are gonna be wiped completely out. . . . And people are gonna be replaced by . . . um . . . robots or computers. Or AI doing their job."

While Megan's words might have sounded like science fiction just a few years ago, they seem increasingly plausible today. They also speak to a deeper fear that the opaque forces driving the Golden State's hourglass economy will put workers, including the aspiring middle class, in dire economic straits. In this broad pessimistic scenario, Megan held on to the one thing she felt she could control: her work and spending habits. These individualistic beliefs offered her some relief in an economy that often felt like shifting sand.

PERCEPTIONS OF THE POOR IN AN UNEQUAL CALIFORNIA

Many in the precarious middle class consider themselves to be exceptional, allowing them to feel pessimistic about social and economic conditions while staying optimistic as individuals. How exactly might such understandings help people naturalize inequality? The answer comes into better focus when we analyze how respondents spoke of people living in poverty, especially the unhoused.

Reflecting on the status of poor people, respondents simultaneously emphasized and minimized structural issues to explain why poor people remain poor. For example, Aracely, a Latina who grew up in different parts of Fresno with a single mother, shared that while she did not feel she grew up needing anything, she recognized in retrospect that her family was likely poor. After graduating high school, she attended a community college. She is now a single mother herself and lives with her mother and stepfather. At the time of the interview, she worked at a nonprofit organization that connects low-income individuals with health services. As a proud registered Democrat, she thought of herself as much more liberal than others in the area. Recall that the Central Valley is home to most of the state's red counties, including a majority of California counties that went for Trump in 2016 and 2024.[32]

Aracely felt that it was really hard for the working class to get ahead today. When asked about the economy writ large, she noted, "I definitely think that the rich are getting richer and the poor are getting poorer." She explained that while some of the rich might get ahead through "hard work," many more get ahead through favorable tax breaks, connections, and family wealth. She also felt that factors such as bad schools, substandard housing, and violence in poor neighborhoods make it hard for poor people to achieve mobility. These observations suggest that Aracely viewed economic standing as mainly linked to one's structural position. However, when she elaborated on the conditions of people living in poverty, the role of individual behaviors and values came to the fore. She explained, "Especially if you're low income, I don't think it's easy. And it's maybe with my job, maybe just growing up, you notice things more. I don't think it's easy to rise above your environment sometimes because they're just perpetuating certain behaviors, certain things, um and it's not cheap. I think everything costs. And so, it's hard to get out of being on the lower spectrum."

Here we see that Aracely perceives poor people as being mired in a difficult structural position and also "perpetuating certain behaviors" that might keep them tethered to their socioeconomic station. When asked to elaborate, she explained: "I would say actually that the poor, it's hard for them with drugs because . . . um . . . and there are drugs prevalent in some of those neighborhoods. People get addicted and then you have that coming in as a factor."

She perceived poor people as economically stuck and engaging in criminal and other behaviors that kept them mired in poverty. Her argument about behavior was subtle. Aracely, like others, did not begin her assessment of poor people with value judgments about their behavior. But the idea of behavior, and what poor people have done wrong, crept in, sandwiched between more progressive stances about the importance of structure and inequality. Aracely never used overtly disparaging names to describe poor people, which are sometimes used in public discourse and especially by conservative media. Instead, Aracely's focus on poor people's behavior and values was covert. She noted that people living in poverty seemed to be in a difficult situation and because of this, they engaged in problematic behaviors. Poor people, she said, are not themselves a problem, but their problematic situation creates opportunities for problematic behavior. In this way, Aracely emphasized structural constraints in ways that helped soften her criticism of poor people's behavior.

This type of subtle cultural criticism, or bounded blame, was shared by a majority of respondents, including those that thought of themselves as progressives. They emphasized structural issues, the effects of gentrification, the structure of debt, and the lack of social welfare resources to explain poverty. But they would sometimes also include a subtle remark about the behaviors or values that poor people exhibited, suggesting that this was what keeps them impoverished.

Aaron offers another example. A Democrat from Los Angeles, he grew up in a working-class family, the son of Mexican immigrants. He never went to college, but he had worked at a unionized construction job for over a decade. His regular work commute involved getting up at 4:30 AM, driving for more than an hour, and arriving before his 6:30 AM shift started. Since graduating high school, Aaron had never really been unemployed, although he thought that construction work was hard because it has periods of steady and intermittent work. When asked about the economy and who gets ahead, he told us that "Whites" are ahead. After all, they are the ones that lead corporations, he explained. Further, he noted that these White-led corporations are often discriminatory and try to hoard opportunities in ways that keep Latinos out. Aaron also had a sense that in Los Angeles, segregated Black and Brown neighborhoods have fewer opportunities, while neighborhoods with more White and Asian people have better schools. He also explained that policies unfairly target working families, like those that keep the undocumented undocumented, thereby limiting their earnings potential. Lastly, Aaron believed that tax policies unfairly help the rich at the expense of poor people, noting that they help "billionaires become trillionaires" at the working man's expense.

In this way, Aaron's analysis of inequality could be said to lean heavily on structural conditions. Yet when asked about who gets ahead in the economy, he told us that those who move "up" are "people who go out and actively try to better themselves. The people that are losing ground are, not in all cases but generally, lazy people. They don't have a drive." Aaron believed the economy was structurally unequal, helping some more than others, but he also thought that values and behavior were a part of the mobility process. In many ways, bounded blame is a perfect description of the narrative he constructed about poor people.

This wrestling with structural, cultural, and individualistic explanations resurfaced later in Aaron's interview when he was asked what if anything the government could do to help those losing out in the economy. He responded that the government should definitely help those that are not getting ahead but only to a certain extent because too much help could create dependency and exploitation. He noted: "When I was younger, I knew families, like, that were on assistance for thirty years. So, I'm kind of in the middle there. You need it, but there are people who . . . are taking advantage, so that's where I don't believe in helping them much."

He and other respondents easily entangled structural arguments about the economy with softer forms of bias that blamed poor people for their lack of initiative. Aaron, like others, would likely never lead an analysis of inequality by pointing to dependency behaviors, but he does leave room to ponder the role of individual values when thinking about why poor people stay poor.

Respondents had a general sense that the structure of the economy favored the rich while also believing that individual values played an important role in determining outcomes. Further, their worldviews emphasized how the presumed behavioral issues that came with poverty—including drugs, lack of education, and laziness—could be an important source of one's social standing. In this way, respondents created a cultural boundary around poor people, seeing them as having very different values than their own while at the same time recognizing that they are stuck in an unfair economy.

HOMELESS PEOPLE WITH A PROBLEM, BEHAVING PROBLEMATICALLY

Respondents most clearly linked individual cultural characteristics with poverty when discussing homelessness. By and large, respondents described this population as a distinct "other" with alternative values, behaviors, and mental conditions. For example, Jesse, a Latino from Los Angeles, told us about the unhoused people near his home: "Well, I don't know if you're familiar with this neighborhood, but there are prostitutes, there's homeless. There's a lot of family vans, like those trailer park homes, there's a lot of that stuff going on lately. Mental health and people with no concept of reality as a whole. They're self-medicated all the time. So as a result, you kind of can't differentiate who's normal anymore . . . there's a breakdown in social norms."

For him, homeless people were not "normal"—they were a group apart. When asked what could be done about the situation, Jesse mentioned the need for mental health services first and foremost but also told us that many homeless people struggle with drug and alcohol addiction. These representations of homeless people as mentally ill and as drug addicts mirror stereotypes found in broader media suggesting that homelessness is largely the result of individual mental, cultural, and behavioral conditions.[33] In other words, the unhoused are also exceptional but not because they double down on positive individual practices that lead to mobility. Instead, according to many respondents, the homeless are exceptional because they succumb to traits that reproduce the worst of their structural conditions.

Still, respondents had a keen sense that the economy was also at play here. They explained how gentrification, the high cost of living, and a lack of mobility opportunities contributed to poverty. But homelessness was often cited as a special case, where structural issues collided with individual shortcomings. For example, when asked why she thought homelessness was increasing, Rose, a respondent from Los Angeles, noted:

> I . . . um . . . I think I justify it in my mind . . . um . . . that a lot of them are probably . . . um . . . mentally not able to cope with society expectations . . . you know? I think that . . . uh . . . a lot of the sad stories, you know, where you lose your job and then you can't afford to pay rent, and then you have to live in your car, and then, I don't know, can you afford a cellphone? You don't have an address, you know? Like how do you start to look for another job when you don't even have an address? . . . Um, yeah. I think it's . . . it's a . . . it's a real . . . it's a real struggle. I think people find themselves in a situation that they just don't know how to . . . to . . . to get out of. . . . And then I think, yeah, it's starts to make people crazy.

Rose is suggesting that homelessness can "make people crazy," by either exacerbating their preexisting conditions or driving them toward cognitive instability. What is important to our research is not that she referenced mental health but that she perceives behaviors (e.g., "not able to cope," "don't know how to get out of . . .") as drivers behind people being locked in poverty. By positioning unhoused people as a group that cannot cope with social expectations, Rose, like others, was drawing on cultural boundaries to position the homeless as inferior or even as not belonging.

For some respondents, though, homelessness was not an abstract phenomenon, but a condition felt close to home. At the extreme, some, including Megan, feared themselves to be dangerously close to facing housing insecurity. Megan explained that she thought this risk was inherent to the working and lower-middle class in Los Angeles: "Well, I mean, at this rate, you know, like they say, like, everyone in LA is like two or three paychecks away from or . . . or pay decreases from sleeping in their cars or either, you know, being homeless . . . being in a situation to where they're going to have to take in a renter or, you know, something like that."

Here Megan makes a large leap between conditions of the working class and the unhoused, noting the precarity of her own position in the middle while underscoring how homelessness haunts discussions of social mobility and social stagnation in California. Other respondents echoed these precarious feelings. For example, Laura, the woman who works in higher education whom we first met in the introduction told us:

> I don't think I consider myself poor only because I have a house, and whether it's through help of my daughter, we've been able to . . . to maintain the house, you know, I think that . . . but I definitely wouldn't consider myself, you know, on the upper end. Because I have no savings. . . . So right now, if I . . . if ever lose it . . . if I would have lost my job, I could not live number one, off unemployment. . . . Of course you know, there's family that can help me but, you know, I would then . . . I would probably become homeless at that point in time.

Respondents characterized the homeless as a daily example of what could happen to them if they were not careful. This underlying fear festered in part because the structural conditions that lead to homelessness—an incredibly high cost of living, an uncertain labor market, and simply bad luck—were clearly on the minds of respondents, leaving many with feelings of instability—even if their becoming unhoused was somewhat far-fetched. Indeed, Laura and Megan may have exaggerated the odds of becoming unhoused, but what matters is that disturbing trends in the economy have made people in the middle feel steps away from being homeless. In this way, the unhoused represented a cautionary tale that spoke directly to their fears around being in the middle in an increasingly hourglass economy, with alarmingly rising costs year after year. It is no wonder then why respondents would hold fast to their individualistic tenets and invest in ideas about hard work and sacrifice. Such beliefs provide a cognitive safeguard from nearby unhoused dangers for people like Megan and Laura.

While not all respondents drew a strong link between homelessness and cultural values, those that did repeated harmful stereotypes and characterized individual behaviors and morals as somehow derivative of the unfair structural conditions that kept people in California in poverty. Despite this nuance, the unhoused were ultimately seen as engaging in behaviors that kept them unhoused.

Conclusion

In this chapter, we have focused on how people in California adjust to and come to understand the economic inequality around them. We found that interviewees largely believed that in California, "the rich get richer, and the poor get poorer." Their own opportunities for reaching the middle class seemed to be shrinking by the year, as housing costs and homelessness rose at alarming rates. In this context, respondents could readily identify a variety of structural issues, like the racialized geography of opportunity, the role of social networks, and government policies that benefit the rich and squeeze the middle. As they developed these ideas, we found that they also relied heavily on spatial comparison. In comparing the cost of housing, food, and goods in California to elsewhere, respondents signaled that opportunities had shrunk in the state and that they had not entirely bought into the notion that the state was a land of plenty for all. Many seemed to have heard such stories or knew someone that was better off in a state with a lower cost of living. But here in California, some felt that only those who were born "rich" or who somehow had lucky breaks or connections could get ahead.

Ultimately, though, we found that respondents downplayed structural understandings, as well as their concerns about the cost of living in the state, emphasizing that hard work and frugality would eventually pay off and help them beat the economic odds. Many framed their own trajectories as exceptional and thus focused on how their own efforts would help them get ahead. And while some of the respondents, especially those in professional fields, clearly had more access than others to career opportunities, we found that many less-educated respondents were also invested in exceptional framing. They often pointed to how individual efforts would ultimately be rewarded and how they would prevail. Respondents engaged in this practice across all racial groups and in both of the regions where we conducted interviews.

Of course, respondents' modes of exceptional framing varied. Some wholeheartedly leaned into narratives premised on individualism while others engaged in deep structural analyses and bootstrap thinking in equal measures. Yet even those with the most sophisticated structural analyses occasionally fell back on narratives of "hard work" to explain their mobility trajectory and their own future projects. This focus on individual behavior may also have allowed many respondents to form boundaries around "the poor," especially "the homeless," seeing them as a group not only with particular conditions but also with distinct behaviors and values. While respondents told us about the myriad ways that structural conditions—including one's class origin and neighborhood—kept people in poverty, they also suggested that poor people held a different set of values and made personal choices that kept them poor. In this way, they often blamed poor people, even if indirectly, for their conditions. Even many of our liberal respondents engaged in this kind of bounded blame, especially when talking about unhoused people.

What does this all mean? In some ways, the research points to a quintessentially Californian story. Respondents are building their middle-class dreams on top of an increasingly shaky economic foundation that leaves them grasping for a sense of agency and control in earthquake territory. LA respondents in particular see the city growing with new billion-dollar developments and million-dollar housing that is out of their economic reach, while they also see camps of unhoused communities lining even wider swaths of the urban landscape. Central Valley respondents see neighborhoods becoming richer or poorer, and the cost of living increasing by the year. In this context, making sense of inequality involves acknowledging societal-level conditions, including gentrification and tax policy, while also leaning into explanations that center on choices, behaviors, and values—the things that respondents can control. For many, exceptional framing and bounded blame provide an important sense of agency.

We thought we might find differences across regions, such as respondents in the Central Valley displaying less anxiety about the present, but this was not the case. Respondents in the Central Valley were as cynical about the contemporary economy as those in Los Angeles despite living in an area with a comparatively lower cost of living. And perhaps because of the alarming rise of homelessness in places like Fresno and Bakersfield, many Central Valley respondents talked about homelessness in similar ways as LA respondents. In the following chapters, we explore these geographic differences further, uncovering when they matter and when they do not.

Beyond California, inequality is growing across the United States. What we find in the Golden State is therefore likely already at play elsewhere. Understood in this light, the findings in this chapter provide an inside look into how the growing divide becomes normalized more broadly. This normalization involves prioritizing agency while acknowledging structure, yet only in ways that allow for personal hope through processes like exceptional framing and bounded blame. Interestingly, our Black and Latino respondents were among the more optimistic in our sample, telling us that their hard work would eventually pay off, even if believing this meant that they also thought poor and unhoused people simply did not "want it" or did not work hard enough.

These contradictions fascinate us and explain how respondents could come to see inequality as a problem, an annoyance, and something to be remedied, while also accepting it as a fact of life, as a byproduct of structural conditions meeting individual choices. Our findings also show how people end up consenting to inequality even while understanding how nefarious and structurally determined it can be. Respondents recognized all the contradictions of the economy around them but stopped short of developing a story centered on structural change. Respondents understand and take serious issue with the growing divide but also seem lured and comforted by explanations that emphasize individual agency. In this way, they can see the downtrodden and their own future through a bootstrap lens, ultimately reproducing the cultural hegemony that sustains the status quo.

In general, interviewees found life in California complex and rife with economic insecurity and uncertainty for many, including the aspiring middle class. Still, many found ways to make sense of and accept the situation, taking comfort where they could. In the next chapter, we zero in on how respondents make sense of racial inequality more specifically. By taking a deeper look at how people come to understand racial disparities, and the role of racism, we can make better sense of how Californians understand inequality, especially since increasingly in the land of plenty, there seem to be opportunities for fewer and fewer.

CHAPTER THREE

RACIAL INEQUALITY IN THE LAND OF MULTIRACIAL PROMISE

Pam had managed to get a job as a correctional officer at North Kern, a newly built medium-security state prison in Chowchilla, California. In great part owing to the prison boom, which began in the 1980s and disproportionately incarcerated Blacks and Latinos, Pam had stable employment.[1] She had worked in small towns up and down inland California, but her new job required her to relocate to Bakersfield, the largest city in the area, which is located just forty miles south of the prison. She had two less-than-happy teenage daughters in tow, and the work wasn't ideal, but it paid well and didn't require a college degree. Plus, the job offered Pam and her family a means of survival even if it meant she has to be scanned and locked into a secure facility where she looked more like the people behind bars than the ones guarding them. Working in these in-between places, which quietly helped fuel California's economy, also meant living near and often driving through "sundown towns"—segregated White enclaves that use legal and extra-legal racial terror to keep non-White people out.

Being one of the first workers on North Kern's payroll put Pam high on the seniority list, which meant she might not have to work nights. She might even have a shot at getting a Saturday or Sunday off, something she hadn't had in years. Importantly, transferring to this prison in the Central Valley also meant she'd be among the first to be called for overtime, and working extra shifts would allow her to save the money she needed to fulfill her dream of buying a home.

The first order of business in this place, so far away from the Midwest where she was raised, was to buy new uniforms. And she had a lead.

https://doi.org/10.7758/uybx4321.9689

A White co-worker had raved about a nice shop where she had gotten her own uniforms in a town called Oildale just a few miles up the road from the prison. Not knowing the area, Pam planned to take her advice. However, when she mentioned the shop to one of her Black co-workers they were extremely concerned: "Oildale? You don't want to get caught there! Don't even stop for gas!" Needless to say, Pam ultimately chose a different shop and also passed on the warning to her children, who were on the cusp of independence—a scary prospect for any parent but especially for a Black parent, and especially in a place like Bakersfield.

Over the next few years, Pam would learn that everyone close to her had more direct encounters with California's sundown towns. For example, her stepson's high school basketball team had to be escorted out of the stadium by police after winning against an Oildale team flanked by fans in Ku Klux Klan hoods. Pam's second husband, James Wallace, also had stories to tell. He had come to California in August 1980 to attend college in Taft, a small town in the area. Growing up in Newport News, Virginia, he was accustomed to seeing a vibrant Black middle class. After all, he lived just down the road from Hampton University, one of the nation's first historically Black universities. But Taft College, on the other side of the country, had offered James a full scholarship to join their track and field team. When he arrived at Taft, he was "welcomed" by an infamous sign that read "N—don't let the sun go down on you in Taft."[2] James saw the irony in leaving the South only to find this kind of overt racism in California. He would soon learn that he had been recruited, in part, to replenish the college's track team after the last group of Black athletes had been literally run out of town by the violence of a racist White mob.[3] James never got the chance to experience that quintessentially Californian college experience he had dreamed of, nor did he end up finishing college at all. He, like Pam, would eventually find his path to the middle class by working in prisons.

In some ways, stories like these run counter to what we might imagine California to be. Decades before the Paschels would make a home in California, would-be African American migrants in the US South would receive news of a freer place with better race relations, where people of color had an easier path to economic mobility and stability.[4] Those messages, partly fiction and partly based on the experiences of earlier waves of migrants, reached James in Newport News. They also found their way to Pam in Flint, Michigan. It didn't matter that the actual experiences of African Americans in California were much more complicated or that Los Angeles was a poor stand-in for the entire state. They both found themselves westbound.

James's and Pam's stories are also reminiscent of those of many immigrants from Latin American and Asian countries who found themselves California-bound in the latter part of the twentieth century. They also likely received messages about California being a place where people like them could settle and make lives for themselves that would be better than what they could achieve if they had remained in their home countries. As the state grew to house the largest immigrant population in the country, it also came to host several of the most diverse cities in America. And though California has never been a place easily defined by a simple Black-White binary, this new demographic reality would add new layers of complexity to the state's racial landscape. It would mean, among other things, that questions of race and immigration would be intrinsically entangled, making it impossible to talk about one without the other. It would also further underscore the multidimensional, rather than binary, nature of race relations in the state.

California might also be understood as a place like any other in America where racial inequalities continue to loom large. In 2016, for example, the wealth held by the White population in California was about seven times that of the Black and Latino populations.[5] The Black-White wealth gap is almost identical to what it was prior to the Civil Rights Act and persists across educational levels.[6] California is a place where more diversity typically means more segregation, as we see so clearly in the case of Latino children who are more likely to live in neighborhoods with high levels of concentrated poverty and attend more racially segregated schools today than in prior decades.[7] It is also worth noting that while California's Asian population as a whole has higher levels of education, higher household incomes, and more wealth than average, this is not the case when data are broken down by country of origin or parents' country of origin. For example, the socioeconomic status of Southeast Asians is closer to that of Black and Hispanic populations than it is to the socioeconomic status of White people or other Asian Americans.[8] Perhaps surprisingly, California has also been an incubator for racially regressive policies at the national level that seek to criminalize immigrants and unravel affirmative action in education and employment.[9]

Despite these present-day disparities and the state's troubled past, politicians still often talk about California as a kind of sanctuary state for immigrants and for people of color. California Governor Gavin Newsom invoked this exceptionalism while conducting the state's roll call at the 2024 Democratic National Convention to the song "They Not Like Us" by LA-raised rapper Kendrick Lamar.[10] The idea of California as being different from the nation was also particularly pronounced during the various phases of this book project. We began data collection in 2018 during Donald Trump's first administration, when California may have felt more like a bubble, a reprieve from Trump's America. The commander in chief had already become infamous for his overt and incendiary brand of racism spewed from the perch of the highest office in the land. Beyond discourse, it was then that the Trump administration put forward policies like the Muslim travel ban and the inhumane separation of families at the United States–Mexico border, and the president incited racist rhetoric against immigrants, particularly Mexicans.

A few years later, when we sat down to write the final version of this book, Trump was in the White House again, and again the political differences between his administration and mainstream politics in California were on full display. These tensions bubbled up to a point of crisis when masked men nominally representing the federal government began to storm the streets of Los Angeles in full riot gear and military-grade tanks and weapons, ready for war. We mention this political context because it likely shaped how people in California talked about race and racism.

We now turn to an examination of how Californians in the middle make sense of race, racism, and racial inequality in their own lives and in the world around them. We found that respondents grappled with contradictions between the ideal of California as a racially egalitarian place and their lived experiences, which often reveal a different story about how race operates here. Even so, when faced with these contradictions, many respondents minimize the racial inequalities they see around them, backgrounding racism and foregrounding a more progressive and inclusive version of California. From this perspective, California is not a perfect multiracial paradise but is a place where you do not have to worry much about racism. Belonging in this place, then, means recognizing patterns of racial inequality while also espousing exceptional narratives about California as a place of diversity, multiracial belonging, and equal opportunity. This involved respondents relying heavily on two narrative strategies, both of which reify the symbolic and physical boundaries around the state of California and ultimately articulate who belongs here.

The first discursive move involved leaning into spatial comparison by drawing a geographic and cultural boundary around the state, invoking places like "Texas," "the South," and "Middle America" as worse off in terms of race relations. It was against this often abstracted and flattened idea of these other places—typically imagined as less diverse and more racially intolerant—that California became coherent as a place. In order for this to work, respondents had to render the red parts of California invisible to sustain the idea of California solely as a progressive, diversity-loving sanctuary state.

The second and related discursive move, also premised on abstraction, involved talking about California through the lens of exceptionalism. Unlike the kind of merit-based, individual exceptionalism discussed in the previous chapter, this was a kind of place-based, abstract exceptionalism that involved the celebration of a vague multiculturalism that often bracketed more overt instances of racism and extreme racialized inequality. For people of color, this discursive maneuver often meant naming experiences with racism in their own lives but usually downplaying them in favor of a neater and more positive account of race relations in this seemingly exceptional state.

Multiracial Belonging and the California Dream

Both the idea of California as a place rife with racial inequalities and the idea of it as a place of easy race relations, were present in the minds of the Californians with whom we spoke. At some point in their interviews, nearly all respondents talked about patterns of racial inequality, typically as they thought about racial geographies. They were not colorblind: they saw how race and class coalesced in ways that structured their social realities. Most respondents casually mentioned these inequalities in passing, usually as they navigated the racialized and classed geographies of the cities where they lived. Across the ideological spectrum, respondents talked about the "good" parts of town, which were almost always White or possibly Asian neighborhoods, and the "bad" or "rough" part of town, which were usually Black and Brown neighborhoods. Often in a matter-of-fact tone, respondents explained how their families navigated the class-based and racialized landscape of education, pointing out and sometimes naturalizing the differences between different schools. Rather than engaging in critical analysis, most the many respondents who discussed racialized patterns of inequality expressed them as taken-for-granted social facts.

Yet when asked if they thought racism was an issue in California, many respondents replied with some version of "racism is not so bad *here*." In so doing, they sometimes highlighted the overall progressive ethos of the state that shielded Californians from the worst of racial violence and hatred. As Ang, a Chinese American man raised in Los Angeles noted, "People in LA, I don't think they really care too much. Everybody's very relaxed here. And there's like, such a melting pot of all kinds of different groups." Much of the logic we heard was about the inherent diversity of California, which many thought had led to racial tolerance and even an embrace of diversity as a point of pride and identity.[11] In this way, California was thought to be a place that was extremely diverse because it was welcoming to all kinds of people, and simultaneously welcoming to all kinds of people because it was diverse.

Kareem had a similar response. He grew up middle class in a town about thirty miles east of LA County and had moved to Los Angeles right after college. When asked if he thought that racial discrimination existed in Los Angeles, he responded: "Oh, absolutely. It exists everywhere. . . . LA is, aside from SF, probably [one of] the most liberal places in the world—in the United States, I should say. I can't speak to all the other countries. Um, but, you know, it's very liberal in the sense that, you know, you can . . . everyone has the opportunity to go . . . to go get after however they see fit . . . um, so LA is very, you know, receptive to all walks of life."

Kareem talked about structural racism and how it had created a racial wealth gap that inhibited social mobility for Black residents, but he also shared that he had not experienced any kind of discrimination that he could recall. Kareem, like many others, attributed his experiences to the state's progressive culture and its demographics. This theme was particularly prominent in our interviews with Asian and Latino respondents. They found comfort in being a sizable minority and sometimes a majority in their cities or neighborhoods.

SAFETY IN NUMBERS

We have known for decades that having a critical mass of people with whom minoritized people share similar experiences can lead to positive outcomes in schools or the workplace.[12] This feeling of safety in numbers is likely also important at broader scales, including the neighborhood, city, and even state level. What made California special and different from other places to many of our Asian and Latino respondents was its population. While the Asian and Latino populations in California are radically different in size—with Asians making up 15 percent of the population and Latinos close to 40 percent—they did have similar narratives about how these demographics insulated them from certain kinds of racial marginalization. Having a critical mass of a particular population also meant that for some respondents, race was not a salient feature of their daily lives. And just beneath the surface of their experiences was also the fact that both groups tend to be associated with immigration, which in other parts of the country might lead to their nationality being questioned. However, in the context of California, because of the size of these communities, interviewees explained that they rarely have to explain why they are here.

For example, Mary, a respondent in her forties who grew up in Fresno with a mother from Colorado and a father from Mexico, explained that race did not play "any kind of role" in her life other than when she studied abroad in Spain and grew frustrated with people labeling her "Mexican" when she understood herself to be "American." She grew up speaking English and living in mostly White neighborhoods but was painfully aware that others saw her as Mexican or Mexican American. She recounted how offended she felt when people would assume that she spoke Spanish when she did not. When asked if she thought racial discrimination happened in Fresno, she responded: "No, because you've got so many people that [are], you know, the same. Yeah, there's too many of us." While Mary wished that the world saw her the way she saw herself, not as Mexican or Spanish but just as American, her experiences also catalogue the fact that there are many Mexicans and Mexican Americans in Fresno, and California, more generally.

And this reality led Mary to the idea of there being "too many" Latinos to be discriminated against, which came up in other interviews as well. For many respondents, comfort with racial diversity was a pragmatic consequence of California being a majority-minority state. Keej explained: "California, you know, is so diverse that people hate you but they're gonna see you. People can hate the Hmong, but they're gonna see them every day in Fresno. So, I just feel like in other parts of the country, [there] may be less population, less diverse [populations]."

These dynamics matter considering that social scientists have argued that one of the primary tenets of Asian racialization in the United States is related to their presumed "perpetual foreigner" status.[13] Whether your great grandparents had migrated in the nineteenth century from Japan or you had recently arrived from Vietnam, you could be subject to the same question: "Where are you from?" However, the people that we spoke with for this book felt protected from that type of othering, that kind of ignorance, in California, home to nearly half of all people of Asian descent in the country.

This othering was also clearly expressed during our interview with Sen, who noted that race did not play a large role in his life growing up in Los Angeles: "Um, obviously, I . . . I think you're always still aware to a certain extent, but I think . . . uh . . . out here not as much because . . . people that grew up here and live here are so used to seeing Asian representation. . . . Uh, honestly, for the most part, I don't really feel like it matters too much out here."

He added, however, that he felt like a "minority" when he travels to different parts of the country. He recalled going to Wyoming on a business trip:

> And, uh, I mean, again, it was . . . it wasn't anything malicious, but I was actually stopped a lot of times when I was just walking around. Because some of these people had never actually even met an Asian American person outside of television. . . . I was literally the first Asian person they'd ever even saw in person. So did they stop you just to, like, talk to you and ask you like . . . um . . . sometimes it was kind of silly, like they would ask if I knew karate, that kind of stuff. But again, it wasn't from a place of . . . of . . . of maliciousness. It was just out

> of just curiosity and that's what people have to realize, is a lot of the intent is positive or just curious.

Sen emphasized that these experiences were based on curiosity rather than malice. But they still made him feel like he did not quite belong in that part of the United States. In California, by contrast, race had not marked his daily life very much and therefore did not matter much to him.

As diverse Asian interviewees discussed their experiences in California, they often emphasized how the demographics of California—the fact that there are large Asian and Latino foreign-born populations—helped insulate them from what Claire Kim calls "civic ostracism."[14] The sheer size of these populations helped normalize their presence and shielded them from people who would insinuate that they should not be here. Many Asian respondents who did recall negative experiences of being seen as perpetual foreigners often reasoned that it would be worse in other states. In other words, spatial comparison helped them minimize instances of racial dis-belonging in California.

This was the case with Jennifer, who, as the youngest child in her family, was born in the United States and grew up in a household where everyone else had been born in Vietnam. While she was well aware of how race shaped the way individuals and groups engaged with each other in the Central Valley, she did not feel like it shaped her own life much: "I'm just in a little bubble of California, so I feel like we're pretty diverse and mixed, and usually going to other states is not as mixed, so I just felt like, oh, we're already . . . from my viewpoint that will see . . . I don't really see discrimination, like, in real life that much to me, but I know it's there, but I don't really think about it."

This was one of many instances when an Asian respondent said that they did not think about race or that they did not see race as a factor in their daily lives.

These experiences led some respondents to think of California not just as a multicultural paradise but as a kind of Asian haven. For instance, Kevin, who was raised in Los Angeles by Vietnamese parents, often shook off stereotypes about being good at math. He said that being Asian was a "major benefit" in his life. When asked to clarify, he said "Yeah, it never hurt me, so I don't see any downside to being Asian. Or at least how it affected my life." Unprompted, he, like many others, understood his experiences as specific to California. "But also like, because I'm in California, so . . . there's a big racial diversity here."

Ang also painted a picture of California as a haven for Asians—but not necessarily for African Americans or Latinos. Having grown up in parts of Los Angeles where African Americans made up 90 percent of the public schools, Ang was aware that race still factored into some people's daily lives. Yet while he recognized that there was real racial resentment against "Hispanics" and "Blacks" in Los Angeles, he felt that these racial divisions were made worse because people in those groups had a chip on their shoulder.

> I feel like, I always felt like Latinos, they feel like . . . uh . . . I feel that they feel like they're kinda looked down on a bit. You know, treated like lower or something like that. So, you wanna like . . . uh . . . kind of stand up and fight. They have that kind of aggression. Um, I mean, yes, they can be very nice. I mean, they are very nice people and stuff like that, but they always have this fighting mentality, like they wanna fight for everything. And I see that in a lot of other cultures too. Probably African Americans too. And lots of time, I find African American people . . . I find . . . I feel bad . . . I feel kinda sad about the whole thing with them because, I mean, it feels like they really . . . they're taught to be really aggressive and really, like, being kind [of] mean, like, really fight, you know, for every little thing.

Ang acknowledged that this "shield," this being "defensive" as he put it, likely developed as a reaction to experiences of racism and mistreatment. Still, he asserted that Asians had also experienced a history of racial violence that could have but hadn't hardened them in the same way. He noted, "I feel like Asians, they kinda like . . . uh . . . of course, obviously in the past, you know, Chinese people, they were the railroad slaves, whatever. But I feel . . . and even Japanese, you know, during World War II or whatever, they were like treated real bad. But I feel like, today, Asians, they're almost like Canada. . . . Everyone always kinda likes them. They're neutral."

In a classic model minority maneuver, Ang implied that while the Chinese and Japanese were able to overcome a past of racial persecution in California, Black and Latino communities were not.[15] In such a view, ongoing racial issues and divisions were less about continuing racism and more about the "aggression" of Black and Latino people choosing to be defined by that history. And yet, at times during the interview, Ang expressed sympathy with these groups; he understood that they had been "put down" and maybe because of that "really have to fight for [their] position"; Nevertheless, he also confessed that he still kept "a distance" especially, from African Americans. Ang's denial of a reality of racism in contemporary California was premised on bounded blame. He reasoned that Latinos and African Americans made their own predicaments worse with their behavior. Also, perhaps ironically, he did this while also admitting to behavior that could very well be interpreted as discriminatory. For example, what might it mean for Ang to keep his distance from African Americans if he is ever in a position to hire or rent an apartment to one or if his child wants to marry someone from these groups?

Some Latino respondents shared similar experiences where race was not salient because they were the majority population in California. Gina, for example, talked about her life growing up in predominantly Mexican and Mexican American neighborhoods in Fresno:

> Uh, I think we're pretty progressive. I mean, I don't know if it's just because of, you know, I'm kind of in my little bubble and you know, I . . . my family's all Mexican, and my husband's family is all Mexican, and where I work is an incredibly diverse location, literally diversity is one of our, you know, mottoes. Um, so I feel like we're doing really well. I mean, it's probably not as great as it might be in a bigger city just because there's more people and different kinds of people . . . people are just . . . um . . . they don't see the different races. I think that's the biggest part of it. Here there's [many Mexicans], you're so used to it, like that's why I say being Latina to me doesn't . . . I just don't see myself [as different], I forget I'm a different color. When I walk into a place, I don't think about it.

Gina contrasted this experience with that of her adult son and his family, who had moved to Kentucky. When he called home, he would complain about how he always stood out and was stared at by a lot of people in Kentucky. In that context, Gina shared, being Latino was a novelty at best and a threat at worst, leading her son and his family to feel, othered, isolated, and that they did not belong.

Yet this demographic reality of Latinos being the majority population in major cities as well as in some rural areas in California may have led some of our Latino interviewees to minimize what seemed to be run-ins with racism and racial barriers. Like Asian respondents, more often than not, they leaned into more harmonious narratives about race in the Golden State. Michael, for example, a Latino man from Fresno, when asked if racism existed there, responded: "I don't really know how to answer. I mean, I know in California there's a lot of Hispanic influence like everywhere you go, it doesn't, you know, it doesn't matter where you go. So yeah. And, uh, you know, in other cities too. I mean, you know like . . . uh . . . like in the Bay Area, there . . . there's like . . . it's like just like a big melting pot of cultures really, you know?"

However, just like many Asian and other Latino respondents, Michael's colorblind narrative fell apart when we probed deeper, revealing numerous experiences he had faced related to racism and classism. For example, Michael told us that there tends to be a lot of discrimination in the construction industry: "I used to deal with those owners of companies, a head of architecture, stuff like that. Really affluent, rich, White, and they don't talk to you, they talk down to you. I would believe yes in that specific group, like in that group. I don't know what you would call it, but they're affluent upper class."

Michael viewed these experiences as a kind of social closure that was about both race and class. Nevertheless, these experiences felt rare to him. His social networks mostly comprised Latinos, and he only occasionally encountered non-Latinos at his job. As such, he did not feel that race and racism were particularly determining factors in his life.

Aaron, a Latino from Los Angeles, also had a tendency to minimize racism despite acknowledging it. When asked about racial discrimination in Los Angeles, he said that it absolutely existed: "Because I think it's harder for some people to basically get ahead in what they're doing because of their ethnicity, and I believe that, basically, some people still believe that they're more superior to other people. I'd say White people, I believe that . . . not all of them, but there's a lot of them out there that think that they're better because they're White."

But then he added the caveat that California is not as bad as other places: "Well, I believe there's less discrimination here in California than in other parts, because right here we have a lot of different ethnic groups, so basically California's one of the ones that is the melting pot like they say." This view of racism in California was likely informed by his own experiences as a self-described person to whom race "doesn't really matter . . . 90 percent of the time, it doesn't matter. If people ask me, I'll tell you I'm Latin."

Taken out of context, such moments in our interviews with Latino respondents might signal a sort of colorblindness on their part. Indeed, scholars have found that Latinos are less likely than other minoritized groups to perceive racial discrimination even when they face significant forms of it in their daily lives.[16] Yet while some of the Latino interviewees may have been expressing their own ease at fading into a kind of rainbow nation, context matters. California is home to over fifteen million Latinos—the largest number in any US state and the largest share of the state's population. Our interviews were conducted in two regions with relatively significant Latino populations in a state known for its significant Latino population. In both Los Angeles and Fresno counties, Latinos comprise about half of the population. A strength in numbers emerges from such contexts, easing many Latinos' concerns about race relations.

Yet Los Angeles in particular is both extremely diverse and extremely segregated.[17] A 2021 study found that among 221 metropolitan areas, Los Angeles was the sixth most segregated.[18] The high concentration of Latinos in certain neighborhoods is mirrored in Southern California's public school system, where Latino children are more segregated today than they were decades ago. As Gary Orfield and Jongyeon Ee note in their 2014 study, "California has had an extremely dramatic increase in the segregation of Latinos, who on average attended schools that were 54 percent White in 1970, but now attend schools that are 84 percent non-White."[19] This means that for many Latinos in this area, apart from work, they often find themselves surrounded only by other Latinos.

Indeed, some of our Latino interviewees were insulated from daily interactions with non-Latinos[20] as a consequence of this "segregated diversity."[21] It therefore makes sense that some did not carry the burden of thinking about themselves as "other," "ethnic," or different from the norm. In this sense, race did not always seem salient to these respondents or, at the very least, they did not feel marked as a racialized other in their daily lives. Nevertheless, living in segregated neighborhoods that were likely underserved in a variety of ways meant that these respondents were not entirely insulated from the structural effects of racism, even if it was harder to see.

There also seemed to be a desire to see race relations in their communities in a particular light, which sometimes made it difficult for respondents to see racism even when they had experienced it directly. Some Asian American respondents, for example, despite feeling relatively protected from racism in California, recounted numerous experiences with it. For instance, Harpreet had grown up mostly in Fresno but moved with his family to New York when he was in high school. While he did believe that racism existed in California in a general sense, he initially said that he had not personally experienced it. As the interview progressed, however, Harpreet recalled how kids would call him racist names and constantly tell him to go back to "his country," something he admitted was both painful and confusing since he was born in the United States. This experience with racism lay just beneath the surface and may not have come out without some careful probing. Sharing these memories then opened up a conversation about how race might be impacting his life as an adult. Harpreet admitted to being a bit on edge with Trump in office, although he also felt somewhat safe in a region with a high concentration of Indians—particularly those from his Punjabi ethnic group.[22] He concluded that despite a grim national context defined by racism and growing anti-immigrant sentiment, racism was not "prevalent" in Fresno anymore.

Jerry, a second-generation Cambodian American, also had a tendency to see the bright side of race relations. He lamented that "race comes into play when [he's] reading the news, watching the news," and that the "social climate" of the country was particularly divisive. But he felt that race was not a salient factor in his own life: "I don't really think about race a whole lot. I mean, it's nice living in LA where it's pretty diverse." He said he had never been discriminated against other than a couple of times when people called him "Asian slurs, like cheeky slurs." There had also been incidents when he didn't feel welcome at country clubs when playing golf as a guest of a member. With a lot of stuttering and pauses, Jerry explained, "I've seen some, like, looks and stares of, like . . . um, you know, this . . . this country club should only have White males here, or something like that." However, Jerry dismissed these experiences because they were not, in his mind, that serious. After all, they did not lead to him losing a job or something else he felt to be really consequential. "Um, uh, I can't remember a time where I . . . in my career though, where I've, like, not got a promotion or anything . . . uh . . . like that. Um, I guess maybe it's more subtly." Despite these kinds of "inconveniences," many Asian interviewees emphasized how little race mattered in their daily lives, in part because they were a sizable group and recognized as part of the state's social fabric.

This type of dismissive maneuvering was also evident with Sanjay, who was born in India but moved to the United States at the age of four. He grew up in a Christian household in mostly White neighborhoods and strongly identified culturally as American. When asked what role race played in his life, he did not seem to understand the question and seemed uncomfortable in general with our questions about race. When asked if he thought racial discrimination existed in Los Angeles, he said "I would say, I feel like it's pretty diverse here. I don't feel like there's any sort of . . . I think there's cultural barriers, but I don't think there's really racial barriers. But I know I've been to other parts of the country where I can see it. I see the racial barriers." However, as we dived deeper into the interview, Sanjay talked about the gap he felt between his own self-identification and how people see him. He explained: "I don't even think of myself as Indian, I think of myself as American. But when it comes up, when I'm feeling insecure or uncomfortable, I use it as sort of like a crutch. . . . I mostly hang out with White people, so I always sort of . . . I feel like I make it a point a lot, which is really stupid, I know it shouldn't be a point. But you kind of feel it sometimes, you feel, like yeah, I'm the only one who doesn't look like the rest."

Beyond differentiation, Sanjay shared that his friends often made "racial jokes" about him, usually related to the September 11 attacks. While he tensed up when talking about this, he also shrugged it off as benign. He even said that he sometimes makes the jokes himself to address the "elephant in the room."

> It just sort of feels like, I don't know, most of my friends are White. So, it's always sort of like a joke that I kind of bring on as like a self-deprecation of, like yeah, I'm the Brown guy. I don't know, it just sort of feels like you have to put yourself into it, you don't already belong here. . . . I definitely felt like anytime I was around White people, I was going to get a racist comment, like a terrorist comment all the time, always. I don't feel it as much anymore, especially living in LA. . . . I don't know, I feel like living in LA it's not as big of a deal. People are very progressive here; they don't really care.

Sanjay thought this progressiveness was part of the larger culture of the West Coast. He explained: "I grew up in Seattle, and I've always lived on the West Coast, pretty progressive. So, I've never really seen too many racial barriers. We've seen racist stuff, obviously. But no, I wouldn't say." Similarly, Christian, another Asian American respondent, could not recall a single instance of being discriminated against when asked. Yet earlier in the interview he shared that where he worked White people "always have a good deal and they get promoted easily." This phrase, uttered in a matter-of-fact tone, was simply true rather than something to get riled up about. What was implied but left unsaid was that if White people were getting easily promoted, others were not. In this way, Christian's words were as much about privilege as they were about disadvantage, and they stood in tension with the idea that race did not matter much in his life or in the world he inhabited. The minimizing of racism in all these cases was premised on the downplaying of racist incidents they had personally experienced.[23]

More generally, and across all racial groups, we found that narratives of racial progressiveness in California were often premised on the idea that the state was not like other parts of the country—where race was more consequential.

Spatial Comparison: "This Ain't Texas"

In making sense of race and racial inequality in their own communities and state, respondents often conjured up and deployed ideas about other places, like Texas, as a counternarrative that allowed them to see California more clearly. Indeed, when we asked about racism in Los Angeles or the Central Valley, interviewees often compared the area to the South or less frequently to the Midwest. In what follows, we show how this imagining of racial hells was very important in the construction of the narrative of California as a multiracial paradise or—at the very least—a not-so-bad place for racism and racial inequality.[24]

Katie, a White woman living in Los Angeles explained: "I feel like LA is pretty progressive in terms of like . . . compared to like the South or something. But I feel like race plays a role here, like for sure." Similarly, Xochitl, a Latina born and raised in LA County, held that racism existed in California but not at levels found outside the state. She had spent some time on the East Coast and thought it was much less racially tolerant than California. She said:

> I think we're more accepting of different racial . . . um . . . um . . . s- . . . the scope that we're in . . . um . . . we're yeah . . . we're very much kind of open to them, not like in the East Coast. . . . They're really [*laughs*] . . . they're really like very rac- racially . . . you don't . . . uh . . . they're . . . they're really prejudiced out there. They really are. 'We don't like Blacks, we don't like Hispanics or it's the White community. Y-yeah. Especially if you go down to the real South, which I've been to, and it's, yeah. They will give you dirty looks and they'll, they'll just size you up.

Xochitl had not felt that kind of racial division or tension in Southern California. In a similar vein, Ang, whom we discussed earlier, was aware that racial discrimination happened "here and there" in California. However, the stories about racism in other states were the ones more deeply etched in his brain. After having a hard time recalling any way that race mattered in the context of Los Angeles, he said, "But I do hear stories about other states that are still very racist. And . . . um . . . I haven't been there yet, so I don't know [*laughs*]." People often noted that race relations were notably worse elsewhere, especially in the South. For instance, when asked about racial discrimination in Los Angeles, John, an African American man who grew up in South Central LA, responded: "I think it's not as prevalent. I mean, it's not as obvious here in Los Angeles as it is in other parts of the country. I really haven't traveled much but from what I hear, down South it's more obvious and more overt than it is here in Los Angeles. It definitely exists here as well, but you have a smorgasbord of races and nationalities here, and they're able to try to mix and get along." John later admitted that he sometimes saw racism "rear its ugly head" in California but emphasized that it was rare.

Similarly, Harpreet talked about the current political climate outside California. He had friends completing their medical residencies across the country, including in Alabama, and while they did not seem to be experiencing a great deal of overt racism, he was leery: "To be honest, I would personally be hesitant to be going in those regions now than I was before [interrupted] in the southern, like in middle America or southern region. One hundred percent honest, I would be [much more] hesitant now than I was maybe five to six years ago."

The idea of California as a bubble was perhaps more pronounced at this time than it had ever been, as Californians turned on their televisions and opened their computers to see increasing polarization and the mainstreaming of overt racism. Harpreet suspected that this Trumpian moment had exaggerated the differences between California and the rest of the country. He explained: "It's the huge influence of the political climate that we are in right now, so I think maybe I'm biased."

While many respondents had not spent much or any time in the South, Howard was one of the few with tangible experiences in that region. He had been raised between Houston and New Orleans but moved to California six months before Hurricane Katrina. Like many others, Howard invoked the South—specifically Texas—when talking about what California was *not*. He recounted a time when he and his wife went on a road trip right after their wedding.

> You can take the 10 freeway all the way there or you can go up a little bit, and it turns into the 20 freeway where it comes down through Texas, and you pass through a lot more rural towns. So, my wife and I decided to take a route, and we made a stop at this really small town and by a Dairy Queen—we wanted some ice cream. So, we walk into the place, we push the door, it's got the little cowbell up there that tells everybody that you walked in. And so, we walk in and everybody in there is White. Everybody there was having conversations and they all stopped and looked at us. Nobody there was talking, they all stopped and looked as if an alien would walk in right now, we'd all stop and look and that's what they did. And I mean, it went on for . . . [it was] really uncomfortable. And so, it was to the point where my wife grabbed my hand and she's like, "What are we going to do?" I said, "We're going to get our ice cream and we're going to walk out," because I'm from Houston and I'm used to . . . there was a huge Confederate flag hanging on the wall. It wasn't where you wanted to be. And that's racism in the South. Nobody was literally racist towards us. Was a bit of a racist vortex, but you could feel that in the air like it was humidity.

This experience was similar to what Pam might have experienced if she actually had stopped in Oildale to order her uniforms and to James's experience attending college in a sundown town. Though, for Howard, this was a quintessentially Texas experience, one that, as a Southerner himself, he felt better equipped to deal with than his California-raised wife. The irony is that this could have also happened, and does, in California, even if it was not the experience that most of the interviewees lived daily. Migrants like Howard had not typically settled in places like Oildale or Taft. Instead, they more often chose the larger cities in the Golden State, where the air felt lighter, less suffocating. Howard's use of weather as a metaphor for his experience is brilliant, articulating the unspoken but very real weight of racism, which sometimes is harder to name than to feel. He also invoked "humidity," perhaps unwittingly, which is typically higher in the US South than it is in the West.

The ideas that animate such spatial comparisons have many origins, including media reports of actual racist and anti-immigrant legislation unfolding in other states. Laws such as the "Show me your papers" bill, or SB1070 of Arizona and many other copycat laws passed in Georgia, Alabama, and Tennessee, lay just beneath the surface of our interviews. Among other things, SB1070 required immigrants to carry their immigration documents with them at all times, thereby exposing immigrants and perceived immigrants to having their citizenship status investigated by the police. So, while interviewees did not always explicitly name these laws or federal policies, such as the Muslim travel ban, they were clearly thinking about race relations in California against a regional and national political backdrop.

Jessica, for instance, did not have extensive experience outside California but, like Howard, had heard talk of anti-immigrant legislation in other states. Besides, she felt that her few experiences outside of the state had made it clear that California was a safer place for her to be given her background. Jessica was born in the United States to parents from Mexico and Guatemala and was working as a pharmacy technician at the time of the interview. She explained:

> You hear, what is it Arizona? It was really racist and then, you know what? I experienced it over his phone. I had to call a client in Mississippi, and I had to let them know that their medication wasn't covered. And the lady was giving me such a hard time, and she passed me to her husband. And her husband was really, really racist. He was like, "Can you pass me someone that speaks better English?" And I'm just . . . I thought my English was okay. It made me wonder, do I have that much of an accent? And it made me wonder . . . people like my mom and my dad that have a little thicker accent, the kind of things they have to go through and the discrimination that they have to go

> through. Me that . . . I've been here my whole life. And I felt I talked English right, correctly. I think that to me really . . . I was like "wow, there [are] really racist people out there." And it just . . . it really did open up my eyes, and it kind of brought me down, and I asked my coworkers, "Do I have an accent?"

Jessica's fears seem valid considering the draconian anti-immigrant legislation that had opened the door to the widespread racial targeting of Latinos regardless of their actual citizenship status. Compared with such examples from across the country broadcast in English and Spanish on national television news and radio stations, contemporary California looked like an immigrant dreamland to Jessica and others. In this context, many interviewees from Los Angeles and the Central Valley felt that race did not play a prominent role in their daily lives.

This perception of would-be dis-belonging in the South, highlighted here because of one's accent, was a common theme, especially among Latino and Asian respondents—many themselves either immigrants or the children of immigrants. Often, these interviewees were able to explain what California was *not*. It was not the South, or the Midwest, or middle America, or any other place—real or imagined—where there are many more White people and where racism is much worse. When asked about racism in California, Lisa, whose parents had immigrated to California from El Salvador, volunteered, "It could be worse in other parts because it's not like here where it's so mixed." Similarly, Kevin recounted a time when his parents went on a road trip to Louisiana and experienced a great deal of discomfort and sense of not belonging: "And so, there's not too many Asian people there [in Louisiana]. So, they didn't get like racially profiled or anything, but they did get some of these weird looks. They didn't feel comfortable. Maybe they can see the discomfort in other people. In a way. So, it wasn't . . . there was no . . . nothing bad happened but it was . . . they can tell the tense . . . intensity . . . or just, you know, the social pressures when they went there."

He added that rather than fear of racism or overt racial violence, there was just a sense of discomfort that he felt was commonplace in states with a smaller or nonexistent Asian population. Among Asian respondents in particular, their real and imagined experiences in places like the South stood in stark contrast with their experiences around race in California.

Yet while some of the interviewees based their ideas of California as a comparative racial sanctuary on personal experiences, others built them on much shakier ground. As they stumbled over the names of states and botched the demographics and histories of those places, they did remain certain of one thing: Race relations must be better in the Golden State. Maybe they have to be. Ideas of other places were readily available in the minds of respondents, even among those who had little experience traveling outside California. Isabel, for example, shared, "Okay . . . um . . . what about other parts of the United States other than here? I feel this might be better. [*laughs*]. More accepting, more diverse." When asked why she thought this, she responded: "Cause of the news. I'm like, you know, I don't know how come people like to keep going to the South or, you know, having these certain conversations with certain people is that, you know, aren't here. But then I've never been outside California so I wouldn't know [*laughs*]."

Even when interviewees had no direct experience with other places, they still had vivid imaginings about what life might be like elsewhere. As one interviewee put it: "I mean, like *definitely* compared to Texas, yes. We're more [*laughs*] like racially tolerant." The laugh—shared between interviewee and interviewer—suggests that we are all in on the joke: whatever California *is*, it is definitely *not* Texas. Central to this inside joke is the idea that California is not merely different than Texas but also morally superior to it where matters of race were concerned.

Yet California's relative racial tolerance requires both the naturalizing of racism outside California and the obscuring of racism and racial inequality within it. Our interview with Grace offers a clear example of this phenomenon. An Asian American woman married to a Mexican American man, Grace described "Hispanics" and "Blacks" as "lazy" and felt strongly that she did not want her kids, who were half Latino, to hang out with "Hispanic" kids. Despite this, she did not think that race was a problem in Los Angeles. When we asked her if she felt that some people were treated like they're less American than others, she first asked for clarification: "Treated by whom?" The interviewer clarified, "By other Americans." Grace responded quickly and emphatically, "In . . . in California? No, I don't think so. Probably in the South maybe. Uh, it always goes back to discrimination—but I've never seen anybody treated less American than, you know, I don't know . . . by any other. I don't know. No, I don't think so. Not here though."

Grace's perceptions of race in Los Angeles were largely influenced by her brother, who lived in Georgia and often shared stories about the segregation of Blacks and Whites. When asked if she thought there was racism in Los Angeles, she said "I don't think so. LA is like a melting pot from everywhere. Um, Hispanics are more now than Asian . . . and . . . um . . . um . . . there's no . . . I don't think there . . . maybe in the South, yeah, but not in LA." When asked why she thought racial discrimination might be different in the South, she said:

> Because I think . . . um . . . I think from the past, you know, the . . . they are more into Confederate ways of thinking, you know? Slavery, they all studied in the South, while we are here, we don't really care. You know, so I think there are more conservative . . . uh . . . conservatives in the South, and then they . . . they . . . the way they think is . . . um . . . Whites have to have more rights than the rest of the races. That's how I think. Until now, I . . . we can't change the way of their thinking because it's been in their heart, in their blood.

The South's history of racial violence, particularly slavery, profoundly shapes racial attitudes in the present, both in California and elsewhere. As Karen, an African American respondent put it, "Um, you know, I . . . I mean, I . . . I feel like it's probably worse in the South just because they have that reputation. Um, but I don't know, that's just kind of conjecture, rumor." In her book *South to America* (2023), Imani Perry contends that in discussions about the nation's racial past, "there is a consensus that the South is supposed to bear the brunt of the shame, and that the nation's sins are disposed upon it."[25]

In this vein, many interviewees rendered the South uniquely racist in contrast with an exceptional California, which they saw as somehow outside of the nation's violent racial history. In so doing, they regurgitated discourses about the region as a blank racial slate, where race relations could start anew unburdened by centuries of racial violence. The contradictions evident in such discourses are worth noting. First, and perhaps most fundamentally, the idea of California as a frontier, a place to make a fresh start, is a settler colonial discourse premised on indigenous death and erasure. This selective racial history of California and imaginings of racial "elsewheres" are central to the stories told about this place. We celebrate Chinatowns and Mexican food without contending with the extreme racial violence wielded against the groups that gifted us with their diverse cultural traditions. We might mention contemporary racism against Black people in California but quickly sweep the issue under the rug because the problem couldn't possibly be as bad as in the South.

Importantly, the idea of California exceptionalism, of the state as free from racial violence, was also likely exacerbated by the fact that we conducted this research during the height of Donald Trump's first presidential term, which likely implicitly configured in respondents' interviews. For example, Dolores grew up in housing projects in a mostly Mexican American area in East Los Angeles, raised by parents from Mexico. She wore a Nike shirt to the interview with the words "East LA" printed proudly on it. During her interview, Dolores emphasized the racism she had experienced outside California, which she often noticed when traveling: "I've traveled to Mexico, Canada, different parts of the United States. And as I'm getting older, I'm getting scared to go different parts of the United States. I'm gonna be honest. I . . . I just like California . . . um . . . I don't really go out anymore, I see a lot of racism going out. Chicago is where the rest of the Mexican Americans are, so it's nice. But going out . . . I don't like that feeling anymore."

Dolores remembered well this feeling of dis-belonging when growing up under the governorship of Pete Wilson. She described him as a "super racist like Trump." Even so, that kind of racialized assault on certain immigrants was still thought of as an anomaly in California, and one far in the rearview mirror. By contrast, Trump was seen as a stand-in for the racist, unwelcoming place that sat just outside California's cultural border, America's underbelly.

Our survey findings underscored this tendency to think of California as being more hospitable than the rest of the nation. We found that while 57 percent of Californians strongly agreed that racism is alive and well in the United States, that rate dropped to 40 percent when respondents were asked about California specifically.[26] In most cases, when asked about California, respondents who felt that racism was alive and well in the United States shifted their responses from "strongly agree" to "somewhat agree" or "neither agree nor disagree," suggesting that Californians perceive racism to be more of a problem outside California than in it.

We argue that while there are important differences between how different respondents view racism and inequality in California, there was an overall tendency to think about California as a place with softer, somewhat better race relations than the rest of the country. Still, we note some important racial differences. We found, for instance, that the gap between perceptions of racism in California versus the United States on the whole was especially pronounced among Asian respondents. While 60 percent of Asians strongly agreed that racism was alive and well in the United States, the number dropped to 36 percent when asked about California. By contrast, the gap for both Black and Latino respondents was only about 14 percent.[27] These findings map directly onto our interview data, which finds that while Californians seem to think of this place as more racially egalitarian than elsewhere, there are some real differences based on the race of the respondent.

We also found that the extent to which there is a coherent idea of California related to race at all requires a kind of geographic slippage between California and its major cities.[28] One the one hand, there was the California that was synonymous with its large, progressive cities; on the other, there was rural America, which was largely understood as outside of California. This schism happened not only because cities like Los Angeles and San Francisco are more populous than other areas of the state but also because they carry a kind of cultural weight, often acting as stand-ins for California in mainstream conceptions of the place. This slippage also makes certain parts of California even less visible—the places that get less media coverage and that are not typically associated with progressivism, racial or otherwise, at least among those aware that these places even exist.

LOCAL SPATIAL COMPARISON: THE CENTRAL VALLEY AS CULTURALLY BEHIND

Irma grew up in a politically and religiously conservative household in the Central Valley with a White American father and a mother from Peru. She explained that she had never felt any racial bias growing up or living there, not even when speaking Spanish with her family in public, perhaps because she grew up in a small town just outside Merced composed of 60 percent Latinos. Asked if she felt that racial discrimination was an issue in her area, she summed it up this way: "Um, maybe in the Valley it's a little bit different. Maybe it's [less accepted] in Southern California." But when asked if she thought California was different from other parts of the country, Irma declared, "Oh, definitely. I think maybe Texas would, and Virginia would definitely be different from . . .

uh . . . California, I'm sure . . . I'm sure of that." Ruby, another Latina interviewee from the Central Valley shared this view when asked about racial discrimination:

> Oh yeah. Absolutely . . . um . . . I know that there's racist people in our local government. . . . Um, it's getting better there. . . . So, in this district too, there are people running for city . . . city council, and there's a couple of Latinos that are running. Um, but I know there is, I feel . . . I don't trust the cops here. Yeah. It's conse- . . . it's conservative . . . uh . . . in comparison to the rest of California. And when I say conservative, I mean like, there's . . . there's racism in Fresno. I think people are pushed to certain neighborhoods too. I think that they try to keep, like, them, like, in downtown . . . like poor, especially class-, class-, classes . . . um.

Ruby added that Fresno was not as "modern" as other places in California but was still "a little bit more liberal, for sure and, like, not as racist because we are pretty, I think, diverse here in California" than elsewhere in the country. This comment and others like it placed the Central Valley culturally between a progressive California overdefined by Los Angeles and San Francisco, on the one hand, and "the South," overdetermined by its rural areas, on the other. Others described a similar picture. Karen, a White woman who had moved to Fresno because she thought of it as a "melting pot" and a great place to raise her children, said, "I feel like California is probably more liberal than most places and . . . and just [tries] to desegregate probably more heartily than most places. The Central Valley though is always behind, always just a little bit behind the bigger cities like San Francisco and Los Angeles."

Just as the idea of race in California as a state was filtered through comparative logics, the Central Valley was considered to be better than the South but still closer to Southern-style racism than the rest of the state. This idea held up even as respondents tried to make sense of overt racial violence in the Central Valley. For example, Ed, a White man born and raised in Bakersfield, held some progressive views around class disparities but tensed up at any mention of race or immigration. When asked about racial discrimination, he talked about how Bakersfield was a sundown town when he was growing up. He recounted that his parents told him that there was a bridge on Chester beyond which Black people were not allowed after a certain hour. "Don't let the sun go down on your Black ass on this side of the bridge," the sign said. Sundown towns can be a tricky thing to verify, especially in California where racial terror was often de facto rather than ordained by law.[29] What we do know is that California has a long history of racial terror that has driven entire racialized populations out of specific towns and parts of cities, such as in the 1870s and 1880s, when Chinese and Chinese Americans were driven out of dozens of towns and cities throughout California.[30] These terror tactics to maintain a racialized social order that limited the freedoms of non-White people in California may have even served as a model for the sundown towns that would become prominent across the country in the decades following the abolition of slavery.[31]

Alicia, who was born and raised in Bakersfield, knew all about the Chester Bridge sign. We interviewed her in Fresno, where she had moved to attend college and remained, dedicating her life to working on public health challenges facing Black mothers. She recounted having experienced overt racism growing up:

> Swept under the rug but also as well as those that were overt. So, I remember in high school because in high school . . . the first high school I went to—Byrd High—it's in the part of town that's known for being a little anti- . . . um . . . anybody but White people [*laughs*]. . . . So, um, and historically, because they used to have a sign on Chester Avenue that went over the overpass into . . . into the city that said no N-words allowed. . . . So that was within our recent, I guess seventy-five-year history.

Ed saw this all as an unfortunate problem of the past and felt things had since "calmed down." "You know, that was twenty or thirty years ago. . . . I think that Bakersfield's far more progressive along ra- racial lines than it's ever been before." When we asked him to explain further, he seemed regretful and apprehensive. "I don't, you know, I've . . . I don't like . . . I don't like this line of questioning because I'm gonna sound White."[32] Ed was not the only one who seemed to self-censor. Perhaps because of the long tradition of overt racism in the Central Valley, the tenor of our conversations about race with people there differed significantly from the ones in Los Angeles. While most interviewees in Los Angeles spoke freely on the topic, many in the Central Valley spoke in hushed tones when discussing anything remotely related to race or immigration. These whispered interviews revealed how a place's culture shaped the responses we received on race and racism. Another aspect was a culture of avoidance, clearly demonstrated in our interview with Kim, a Black woman in Fresno, who confessed that after experiencing racial discrimination at the Olive Garden restaurant in nearby Clovis, she avoided going to Clovis altogether.

These interviews highlighted the ways that the Central Valley was not only geographically and figuratively between San Francisco/ Los Angeles and the rest of the nation but also culturally between the two. This was the sense that Bai, an Angeleno, got, despite having never been to the Central Valley. We asked him: "So in terms of racial discrimination, do you think LA is different from other parts of California?" He responded:

> Um, I'd say LA is more open. It's more open than say Fresno or Bakersfield or whatever. Oh, so you . . . you think . . . um . . . like the Bay Area and LA are, like, a lot different from the Central Valley. Okay. Um, actually, I've never been to the Central Valley so I wouldn't know. [*laughs*] Yeah . . . I feel like, you know, there's less . . . there's less . . . uh . . . less racial . . . uh . . . it's just mostly Hispanic and like Caucasians around here, from what I heard. Okay. So, you think it's like . . . uh . . . the more diverse a place is, the less discrimination.

Bai's understanding was of a Bakersfield, or Fresno, "or whatever" that was racially behind Los Angeles not only in terms of the culture but also in terms of demographics. Much like the portrayal of the "South" or "Midwest," California's Central Valley was seen as lacking diversity, despite having very similar demographics to Los Angeles.

These findings raise questions about how Californians in the Central Valley describe race relations in the state and in their respective region. What does the vantage point of being geographically inside but discursively outside California allow someone to see about how race functions in the state? For the most part, Central Valley respondents talked about race in their region in a similar way that Angelenos did, emphasizing diversity, immigration, and the state's progressive ethos. However, many were quite aware of the cultural differences between Los Angeles and cities like Fresno and Bakersfield, even though the two regions actually share similar racial demographics.

Respondents emphasized that the Central Valley was still better than the South, even if not quite robustly Californian and despite evidence of overt racial violence in the area. For example, Travis, a White PhD student at the University of California, Merced who grew up in Fresno, told us that he had recently seen a local video of "a bunch of cops shooting a Black kid with a . . . a baton or something . . . of a Black kid that had been shot." Nevertheless, he went on to say the following about racial discrimination in the region:

> I'd say it's probably a little . . . it's not as bad as the South if that's a barometer. Um, which is a shitty barometer. But I just assume everything kind of . . . it's just kind of racism. I mean, you have . . . you could probably find a Confederate flag in Merced if you tried. Like . . . but you'd have to put effort into it. I can think of exactly one like, that I've seen in a population of 80,000. Uh, if you go to the foothills, maybe you'll see two. Okay. Like, if that's gonna be like, the metric you're gonna use for, "How hostile is this environment?" Whereas I'm relatively sure that the state flag of Mississippi has the stars and bars on it.

Just as the idea of race in California as a state was mediated through comparative logics, so too was the idea of cities and towns in the Central Valley.

Our interviews in the Central Valley made clear the limits of belonging in a progressive California while also revealing the way that the Central Valley occupies a kind of cultural liminality when it comes to the racial "wokeness" and progressiveness associated with the state. This part of the state might be better than Texas but was still not living up to the California ideal. Rather than the Central Valley revealing the contradictions of race in California, this positioning of the Central Valley as not quite the California that we know actually helped to reify this idea of California itself.[33] In this way, the discursive maneuver of seeing California as "not like Texas" required ignoring the parts of the state that might resemble Texas. Yet constructing a discursive boundary between California and places like "the South," "Texas," and "Middle America" was just one of the ways that Californians made sense of racial inequalities within its borders.

Blackness and the Limits of an Exceptional Framing

We have shown the ways that Californians sometimes minimize their own knowledge of and experiences with overt racism in favor of more harmonious views of race inequalities in the Golden State. We see this narrative strategy happen across racial groups, but for Asian American and Latino respondents, we found that there was often a dissonance between the stories they told about being directly and negatively impacted by race and their reading of this place as relatively free of racism. Their experiences underscore the safety that comes from being a sizable minority and living racially segregated lives. They also reveal some of the costs of integration in this less-than-perfect place, as we see with Sanjay's experiences where the price of belonging may require that one be prepared to laugh off or minimize racist incidents and jokes. While these experiences of Asian and Latino respondents expose cracks in the veneer of California's racial liberalism, the discourse around "Blackness" in the Golden State and the lived experiences of Black Californians further test the limits of multicultural belonging.

In this section, we first turn to the interviews with Black respondents who, despite sometimes minimizing their experiences with racism, told vivid stories about how racism had impacted their lives. Their narratives were almost always afflicted with the subtext of these things happening in a place where they were not expected to happen. More broadly, we also want to better understand how Black people figure into the discourse about race for respondents more generally. Are Black people imagined as part of California's diverse, liberal state? If they are invoked, does it trouble these more parsimonious ideas of this state as "not like Texas"? We suggest that in asking how Blackness figures into discourses about race and racism among Californians, we learn a lot about belonging—and its limits.

California's Black population is relatively small but accounts for an outsized share of the population experiencing incarceration, homelessness, and poverty in the state.[34] This overrepresentation among the Californians that experience the most precarity in the state is one of the many reasons that we must think critically about where Black people and Blackness figures into our analyses of this place. If nothing else, centering Blackness in this context helps us better understand the possibilities and limitations of racial liberalism.

We know that discourses of multiculturalism can often co-exist alongside practices that reify anti-Blackness.[35] While this contradiction is not specific to California, it may be particularly pronounced here. During interviews, despite the veneration of diversity, respondents rarely mentioned Black people when discussing California's diversity.

Black people and Black culture were absent even from the most superficial level of belonging related to cultural consumption and collective identity. For example, in lauding diversity as a kind of Californian virtue, respondents often referenced Mexican food and Koreatown but never mentioned Black cultural enclaves like Leimert Park, soul food, or even the rich contributions of African Americans to music in California. More striking was the fact that, while Black people were largely absent from discourse about the positive benefits of multiculturalism, they were often at the front of respondents' minds when they did explicitly acknowledge racism, particularly racial violence. Indeed, the few dozen interviewees who spoke briefly but directly about police brutality and racialized over-policing always conjured up images of Black people as the victims of such injustice. Sometimes these comments were explicit, sometimes implied. For example, Alana, an Asian American respondent, said, "you know, I have a luxury of not walking around . . . ha- . . . like walking around and not being afraid of, like, being attacked or compared to, like, other- other . . . um . . . communities, right? Um, I don't have to live in fear when I get pulled over by, like, a police officer."

In comments like this, Black people's (and sometimes Latinos') interactions with the police acted as a sort of shadow or underbelly to California's racial tolerance. This feeling was palpable among respondents throughout the Central Valley and may come as no surprise when we consider that Kern County, where Bakersfield sits, was once dubbed "the Killing County,"[36] because it led the nation in the highest number of police killings in the country.[37]

These perceptions of anti-Black and sometimes anti-Brown state violence layered on top of otherwise easy race relations led some respondents to talk about race in California as a complex racial system. This was the case with Luv, a Hmong respondent who had spent her early life in a primarily Mexican neighborhood. She moved to an all-White neighborhood in elementary school and was very conscious about structural and interpersonal racism in California. She described the feeling of being on the other end of racialized and patronizing offers to "help you Brown people" or play with the "little Brown kid." Despite this and other experiences, she shared that race had not proved to be very salient in her life. She said:

> Yes, I am Asian American. When I'm hanging out with my friends, I don't racialize myself. One time, someone asked me and my partner . . .

was like . . . oh, you guys are in an interracial relationship. And I was . . . what the hell is an inter- . . . oh! And I was like, ew. It . . . ugh . . . no. Like, it . . . it was uncomfortable. And it sat weird with me because I don't look at my friends, and I don't look at my partner and go, oh my god, you're a different race. I'm just like, well, like they have names.

Luv felt that many of her own experiences with race were specifically related to living in California. This way of seeing race came in part because of the particular position that Luv felt that Asians occupied. Despite being Hmong, which she described as "jungle Asians," she felt she could "pass in a way in which, like, my friends who are Black or African American cannot."[38] In another part of the interview, she explained that "Hispanics and African Americans" are on one side and "Caucasians" on the other. "It's almost like this big war." Paradoxically, though, Luv still felt like race was not a problem in Los Angeles because of its progressive culture: "There's, like, such a melting pot of all kinds of different groups." Ultimately, Luv opted to fall back on ideas of Los Angeles as generally progressive despite her awareness of how racism and racial conflict affect others. But anti-Blackness and sometimes anti-Latino sentiments still loomed in the background.

In general, our interviews with non-Black respondents were peppered with brief mentions of spectacular and everyday racism against Black Californians, but this did not seem to dampen the overall view of the place as relatively good in terms of race relations. We saw this when Gina, a Latina from the Central Valley, casually admitted that her company intentionally refused to hire Black people. In another interview, Katie shared that she saw racial inequality as an issue in Los Angeles, even while she held that it was worse in Texas, a place she knew well since she had gone to college at the University of Texas at Austin. As a White woman, she admitted that she was concerned about what she called "secret racism," recounting an instance where she recommended two friends who happened to be Black women to rent an apartment in her building:

> After the guy met with them, he was like, "Oh no, we found someone else." Like, maybe they did find someone else, but it didn't feel like it. It felt like they didn't want two Black girls living in his apartment. . . . So, I feel like it is definitely still a thing. . . . Here, I feel like people don't talk about it as much—they are pretty relaxed with it—but racism is definitely still a thing.

Katie was not alone in her casual, matter of fact, and fleeting mentions of racial discrimination. Many respondents, especially those that did not see themselves as negatively affected by racial discrimination, fit the same pattern. You may recall Christian's witnessing of what might be called White privilege at his job. Ultimately, this embrace of vague multiculturalism and bracketing of racism close to home and work, among other factors, left specific questions about how Black Californians understood these racial contradictions in California.

AN EQUAL OPPORTUNITY ANTI-BLACK STATE

Earl, a Black man who had grown up between Lancaster and Burbank (both in LA County) said that he felt racism on a "daily basis," adding: "I could go on and on, but I experienced a whole lot of strong, overt racism" Even so, when asked if racial discrimination existed, he said: "Not so much in California. I think in most states, the racial discrimination is the same. Probably places in the South where they're more overt. It's probably different, but I think discrimination exists to a great degree in America."

Earl was similar to most respondents in telling complex, sometimes contradictory stories about his own racial experiences and in his assessment of race relations and inequalities in California. Like Earl, many respondents would finish their comments on a positive note about racism not being as bad in California as elsewhere. Lurking just below the surface in so many of our interviews was a way of seeing California in relation to other states, as previously discussed.

This sentiment also came through in our interview with Craig, who we met in the previous chapter. He shared that his experiences of being racially profiled by the police were much more common in Los Angeles than in Pennsylvania where he grew up in a middle-class neighborhood. Still, he felt like the racism he experienced in Los Angeles was not always as overt as it might be elsewhere.

> Um, like I've never been followed by the cops when I was on the East Coast but, like, I didn't have a nice car on the East Coast. So, it's like, you don't . . . you don't really know. But, like, you might come across some . . . you might come across some people anywhere who are gonna treat you a certain way, and you're gonna start realizing, like, "Oh, I know why you're acting like this now." Like . . . it's starting to

> make sense. But, like, yeah. I mean, it has to be different. I can't speak on all of California. But if I'm being honest, like, the amount of discrimination that I face hasn't been that overt. It hasn't been that in my face, and it hasn't been on much of a regular basis. Mostly, it's just . . . yeah. The biggest thing that I noticed is just the cops.

Craig then laughed uncomfortably. Despite direct experiences with racism, he made discursive moves that de-emphasized the more unsavory ways that race entered his life. In so doing, he downplayed his experiences with race and racism, particularly when alluding to racialized encounters with the police. He was not the only one to do so.

Rich grew up in St. Louis and moved to Los Angeles to attend college at the prestigious University of Southern California (USC). The campus infamously sits in the middle of a historically Black neighborhood in South Central Los Angeles, and its borders are some of the most heavily policed of any university campus in the country. As a dark-skinned Black man, Rich had many stories of palpable racism at USC, experiences that were not new to him as someone who had experienced racism growing up in the Midwest. He described being on campus as living through an "apartheid," where he was persistently harassed by the police and was constantly asked to show his student identification. When he refused to show it after becoming fed up with being surveilled to this extent, he was put in jail. He shared that none of his White friends had ever been asked to show their identification cards but, in contrast, he had to show his "ten times, twelve times. It became so offensive to me that I took a position where I wouldn't show it to them. By not doing that, by refusing to show it to them, they arrested me. I found out USC has a jail on campus. I didn't know it."

These experiences with the police made it impossible for Rich to give California a pass. He explained that he gets frustrated when people see racist incidents happen and say, "this is not who we are." He retorted: "This is who it is. It's always been vicious. There's a savagery in this country." He concluded "wherever people are, there is racism." Although later in his interview, he added this caveat:

> But I think it's more . . . um . . . nuanced and more . . . it's [racism] not on display really where you just see people, you know, with animus on their face. People kind of go about their business and . . . um . . . and it's a blue state and that matters to me. You know? You could say all sorts of things about California, but at the end of the day it's a

> consistently blue state, and most of them aren't. So, I would hate to be in a red state just because it would feel like I'm surrounded by people who are maybe even . . . uh . . . willing participants in my demise, you know? So even though there's a lot of people here, I have to feel like at least there's a progressive spirit, you know?

Rather than deny the existence of racism and racial disparities in California, Rich, like many other Black respondents, settled on an idea of this place as not as horrific as other places. In making this spatial comparison, they often recounted traumatic experiences with racism in the state, which they either knew were not as bad as what they had experienced elsewhere or assumed were better. Even so, Rich's use of words like "I have to feel" and "at least" to describe his own attitudes toward race relations in his adopted home perhaps told another story. These phrases, uttered almost like mantras, may say less about what kind of California respondents like Rich are actively experiencing and more about what they need California to be. The fact that Rich, like many others in our sample, is a migrant likely contributes to this desire to see California in a particular light.

Still other Black respondents discussed racism in housing and the workplace, often at the hands of Latinos and Asians in mid-level managerial positions. For example, Keisha talked at length in her interview about how she had won an antidiscrimination lawsuit against a former Latina manager. Similarly, Denzel, a Black man in his fifties, was acutely aware that anti-Black racism was not necessarily something that only implicated White people in California. He actually suggested doing the interview for this study *outside* the coffee shop where we first met him because he had just seen a viral video of two young Black men being arrested for simply holding a meeting at a Starbucks in Philadelphia. Denzel had been in Los Angeles for decades but had moved around as a child between Kentucky, Ohio, and Michigan. When asked what role race played in his life, he said he experienced it every day. "Couple of times . . . like all day, every day. . . . I walk by people out in the street, they locking doors because they think I'm gonna rob them." This daily reality defined every aspect of Denzel's life. For instance, it figured into his grocery shopping routine. "Go to the same store, every time, so they don't chase you around," he told himself. "I got to be worried about being my race, where other people can think about stars and space, and it's a great day," he lamented. His management of race was not in the context of a Black-White color line, but rather in a multiracial environment where anti-Blackness still seemed pervasive.

Similarly, Sarah explained, "I've come up against some super racist Latino people, and also super racist Asian people, but then again, it's not everybody. But I was really surprised at that, but I guess I kind of feel like people are just looking for someone to look down on. I don't know." Sarah had grown up between Cleveland and Chicago and experienced culture shock when she moved to Los Angeles and found herself a minority among "minorities."

Unlike many of the non-Black interviewees who believed more diversity led to more racial tolerance, Malcolm felt that diversity was giving way to *more* racism. Malcolm was born in England but moved to New York when he was a child, and then to Los Angeles at the age of eighteen. In his fifteen years in Los Angeles, he had experienced racism regularly in social situations and public spaces. Yet it was the racial makeup of California that led him to see it as "different because it's a multi-racial state. There's more [racism] over here than anywhere else." Indeed, rather than see California as an equal opportunity state as politicians have claimed, Malcolm and others described what might be called an equal opportunity anti-Black state, one where anti-Blackness is rampant and where they were discriminated against not only by White people but also by Latino and Asian people alike. Jasmine recalled similar experiences. She had grown up in Ohio but recounted many instances of anti-Black racism against her at the hands of Latinos in California, particularly housing discrimination, which led her to conclude that Los Angeles was "worse than Jim Crow." She told us, "The whole building was all them. And so, I come up saying, 'Can I look at the one-bedroom apartment?' 'Oh, yeah, well we' . . . it was clear that this was the unit where the resident manager was getting off on excuses . . . come back another day. Then you knock on the door. You know somebody's in there, and they're not coming to the door. On and on and on. And I just said after a while, 'You know what, these people really' . . . and I've had some of them flat out, call me a n—r."

These experiences made it impossible for Jasmine to think about racism in California as better than elsewhere in the country. They also hardened her, like other Black residents, into a nativist position on immigrants—particularly Mexican immigrants—a phenomenon we discuss in the next chapter.

Overall, many of our interviews with Black respondents were similar to their non-Black counterparts in terms of emphasizing California's racial liberalism. However, the overwhelming majority of those offering sharp critiques of this idea were Black respondents, who ultimately determined that despite popular narratives, California was not exceptional when it came to anti-Black racism. Perhaps non-Black respondents also understood this contradiction. Like their Black counterparts, when they did name racism in the state, the experiences of Black people, and police violence specifically, were typically front of mind for them. Yet this absence of Black people in the positive discourse about California's multiculturalism and their hypervisibility when talking about racial violence raises questions about where Black people figure into California's mythos of a multiracial paradise.

Conclusion

In some ways, California might be considered a unique place for understanding racial inequality and how it manifests itself in both overt and subtle ways. In other ways, it is not. Ultimately, we found that most respondents subscribed to a kind of measured racial exceptionalism—not a wholesale embrace of colorblindness but still a normalization of racism and racial disparities. In this, non-White respondents tended to recount experiences where racism and racial inequality negatively impacted their lives. And while these stories were sometimes painful, the majority of respondents across racial groups still chose to downplay them. Rather than amplify those experiences, they were more likely to think about how much worse it might be elsewhere in ways that gave them comfort.

This required respondents to create two boundaries. The first was around California's cultural and geographic space compared with the rest of the nation, especially the South. Many Asian and some Latino respondents also emphasized their comfort in being a sizable group in California, which made them feel like they belonged in ways they suspected might not be the case elsewhere. Rather than the grass always being greener in terms of race in California, what we found is that many imagined that "over there" in Texas or "Middle America" the grass is always yellow, dry, and patchy. That grass was likely seen as even drier in the context of Trump in the White House. As such, interviewees were distinguishing California not only from the rest of the United States but also specifically from Trump's America. One of the ironies about this stark contrast is that, ultimately, California is not very different from much of the rest of the country, where rural areas voted overwhelmingly for Trump while urban areas did not.

Another irony revealed during interviews was how some respondents who could never see themselves living in, or even traveling to, places like the South engaged in their own local avoidance strategies to minimize potential racist incidents. Like Pam and James, whose stories we shared at the start of this chapter, Black respondents avoided places like Oildale and Taft, while others stayed away from affluent parts of town, including Fresno's Fig Garden and neighboring Clovis. Their counterparts in Los Angeles engaged with similar strategies, staying away from places like Santa Monica so as not to test the limits of racial harmony discourse. In some cases, these strategies would be filed away alongside others that their parents may have taught them: to always keep their hands up when encountering the police and visible when shopping. These mundane practices of self-management deserve further attention as they also likely shape folks' experiences in ways that made it easier to create a particular narrative of race in this place. Put differently, by avoiding specific local places they thought would be hostile to them, as Kim did with Clovis, these respondents also likely shielded themselves from more overt forms of interpersonal racism. While such strategies might be necessary for survival, they do nothing to address the structural racial inequalities that manifest in everything from homelessness to homeownership rates, from access to health care to educational attainment. Clearly, the limits to achieving the American Dream in California, defined not just by economic mobility and security but also by the ability to experience what Evelyn Nakano Glenn called "substantive citizenship" has racial overtones. This is as true in California as it is in the United States in general.

Ultimately, though, we do not want to suggest that California is worse or better than any other regions in the United States. State governments in Arizona, Texas, Alabama, and Florida are clearly adopting policies aimed at making life impossible, or at least inhospitable, for immigrants, especially Latinos, and people of color in general. At the same time, we also know that California, like any other place, has its own racial histories and specific legacies that shape contemporary race relations. Given this, it is not our place to make a normative argument about whether California is an easier place to live for people of color than elsewhere. Still, what became clear in our interviews is that residing in California exposes you to a canonized, high-school-history-book idea of "the South," which is important for understanding how people experience race and racial inequality in this state. Here, the idea of the South has productive power, in a Foucauldian sense, in that it serves to obscure the ways that racism actually shapes the social world in cities and towns throughout California, as well as the lives of those we interviewed.

The second boundary involved a kind of normalizing of anti-Blackness—including anti-Black state violence—to maintain a belief in a kind of multiracial dream, a place where race does not mark the life chances of people and where a racially diverse population thrives not despite diversity but because of it. Yet there were many things that contradicted this portrayal including the uncomfortable moments when some respondents themselves espoused anti-Black racism during their interviews. We argue that Blackness and anti-Blackness lingered in the minds of respondents who otherwise fashioned California as a place where they accepted everyone and where everyone could belong. These exceptions to the idea of a progressive paradise are revealing because they show the limitations of the California Dream while also revealing fundamental contradictions inherent in all boundary work, which inevitably involves defining who belongs and who does not.

In California, that discursive border can also be a physical one, as matters of race can easily slip into questions about immigration. The abstract pictures of diversity that many of the interviewees painted papered over actual negative experiences with racism. Importantly, they also often relied on discourses about California being an especially hospitable place for immigrants. Indeed, in a state where more than a quarter of the population is foreign-born and about half has at least one parent that was born in another country, it is nearly impossible to talk about race without discussing immigration and, arguably, vice versa.

Furthermore, we know that immigration and anti-Blackness are intimately related,[39] just as pitting different racial minoritized groups against each other often serves to reinforce racial hierarchies.[40] Given this, we now delve deeper into the question of who truly belongs in California by analyzing attitudes about immigrants and the inequalities that our racialized immigration system produces.

CHAPTER FOUR

IMMIGRANT INEQUALITY IN THE LAND OF SANCTUARY

Cresencio was only sixteen when he first crossed into the United States at the San Diego–Tijuana border in 1970. Most California teens at that time spent their days consumed with typical teenage activities, such as sports, first kisses, high school dances, learning to drive, and quinceañeras. But not Cresencio. He went to work. Over the next two years, he would live in migrant camps after the harvest and spend countless hours picking apples, peaches, figs, and other crops—from sunup to sundown. He would pack six crates a day, six or seven days a week, following the next contract to the next field. While many worked alone, Cresencio was fortunate to work alongside his father, Juan, who already had over a decade of experience as a farmworker in California. Cresencio received critical advice from his father about staying safe from the heat and pesticides, safely storing food and belongings in overcrowded and drafty barracks, and keeping track of bushels and pay. Wearing a handkerchief over his mouth, wet rags on his head, and a long-sleeve shirt, Cresencio worked—even on above-ninety-degree days.

Cresencio's father had accumulated deep knowledge about life as a farmworker. He had been orphaned at a young age in Mexico and grew up with little formal schooling or wealth. A fieldworker in Michoacán, he was recruited to California by the Bracero Program[1] when he was twenty-two years old. For two and a half decades, Juan divided his time between Mexico and the United States, spending up to nine months of the year working the West Coast harvest. By the time Cresencio joined him, Juan had worked in every region in the state. Together, the pair teamed up to earn extra money. "I was young and could quickly climb

https://doi.org/10.7758/uybx4321.1545

the tallest apple trees, shaking branches so that my dad could catch and sort the fruit. . . . They paid us by the crate, so we made a fast team." Cresencio's mother and six younger siblings were in the process of migrating, and much of their earnings went to support this effort. They slept in makeshift cabins with other workers, cooked over campfires, and washed their clothes daily by hand. At night, a small radio connected them to "Laboratorio Mallo," which brought them the sounds and news of Mexican and Latino California, although this would never completely ease Cresencio's homesickness.

Soon thereafter, Cresencio found work at a factory, manufacturing plastic parts for trailers, and after that he worked in Los Angeles' infamous garment factories, hunched over loud sewing machines making women's blouses, children's shorts, and baby hats, six days a week, ten to twelve hours a day for the next fifteen years. The work was hot, sweaty, and backbreaking, but it was a way to make ends meet without constantly having to migrate to new farms. Cresencio never really learned English—he was too busy working. He eventually married Maria, whose family was also from Michoacán, and obtained legal permanent resident status. In those days, it was much easier to process an application, even for the undocumented. The amnesty provisions in the Immigration Reform and Control Act (IRCA), signed by President Ronald Reagan in 1986, would open opportunities for many more immigrants to legalize their status—a game-changing scenario for Cresencio's family and many of his friends and neighbors.

Cresencio and Maria raised three children in one of the Eastside LA's Latino barrios. Though they were able to buy a home and even start a small business, they never really found jobs that provided stable salaries and retirement options. Life became more difficult as they got older because many factories closed, having moved out of the country due to international free trade agreements, while their medical bills piled up. Many of their challenges were tied to healthcare because Maria endured serious work-related injuries that left her disabled and at the mercy of the public health care system. Still, Cresencio and Maria doted on their children as best they could, and Maria, in particular, emphasized the importance of education. She did not have the opportunity to finish high school, and she dreamed that her three children would.

Juan, a strong, six-foot-two bear of a man, even in his senior years, would continue to follow the harvest before taking a full-time job at an

LA nursery near Cresencio and the rest of his family. Though he was the strongest man his grandchildren had ever met, Juan began to deteriorate in his late fifties. Despite having worked in the United States for his entire life, Juan, like Maria and many other Latino immigrants, never had access to employer-based health care, much less preventative care.[2] He died at the turn of the century from diabetic complications, never realizing his dream of returning home to Mexico to retire. By this time, Cresencio and his younger siblings, along with their children and grandchildren, had settled in California. Northeast Los Angeles, with its heavily policed streets and underperforming schools—as well as its churches, family spaces, and immigrant vitality—was now the Mora family's home.

In many ways, Cresencio's story is one of success, indicative of the many individual stories that have come to make California not only a land *of* immigrants but also one *for* immigrants. It's the story of a place where the foreign-born might just get a real shot at the American Dream. Cresencio certainly felt this way. Even though he has little in terms of retirement savings or wealth, and while he worries about his and Maria's access to health care, his children have achieved some measure of middle-class stability, either through education or homeownership. That is enough for him right now.

To be sure, California has long been considered an immigrant-friendly state. As one of the first states in the nation to offer undocumented immigrants driver's licenses, in-state college tuition, and health care coverage, as well as to declare itself a "sanctuary state," in the eyes of many, California seems to live up to its progressive reputation.[3] The Immigrant Climate Index rates California's policies as the most immigrant-friendly in the nation, far ahead of other blue states such as Oregon, Illinois, and New York.[4] Yet demography might be the clearest indicator of how friendly the state is to immigrants as it is home to more immigrants than any other state in the union.[5] Today, nearly half of Californians were either born in another country or have at least one parent that was.[6] In 2024, the governor named June "Immigrant Heritage Month" in honor of the "generations of immigrants from across the globe that have helped shape California's history and progress."[7] As of this writing, California is still the nation's preeminent sanctuary state, serving as a symbol of resistance to Trumpian immigration politics.

Many residents view immigration through this welcoming lens. But there are commonplace occurrences that butt against this otherwise optimistic rendition. For example, studies reveal that many immigrants, especially the undocumented, face discrimination and inhumane forms of exploitation in the workplace, where they are subject to precarious labor shifts, wage theft, and unhealthy and dangerous labor conditions.[8] Even today, agricultural workers in California often experience extreme forms of poverty and live in substandard housing that lacks basic plumbing and other necessities.[9] Many go without important worker protections and experience work-related illnesses at higher rates than those born in the United States. Conditions for these breadbasket workers are so challenging that researchers back in 1998 estimated that the life expectancy of a farmworker in California was forty-nine, well below the average in many developing nations.[10]

Given that immigrants are less likely than US citizens to have health insurance, the precarities and difficulties of immigrant work create spiraling challenges to the health and well-being challenges of families and individuals like Maria and Cresencio. Consider that a study by the Public Policy Institute of California shows that immigrant workers in the state earn about 26 percent less than native workers, a margin wider than that found in other US states.[11] It is no surprise, then, that the poverty rate for immigrants in California is 50 percent higher than that of the native born, or that the poverty rate for undocumented immigrants is 200 percent higher than that of citizens.[12] Beyond the reality of labor, a lot of research shows that many immigrants live in the state's most under-resourced areas, with underfunded and overcrowded schools and neighborhoods.[13]

Let us pause for a moment.

Despite California's well-known celebration of diversity and immigration, immigrants and their families are significantly more likely than US-born citizens to have precarious and dangerous work, live in poverty, and face various forms of segregation. And the largest wage gap between natives and immigrants in the nation is found in California. Concretely, this means that immigrants like Cresencio were likely never paid equally for their efforts, at least not as much as a US-born citizen would have been doing the same work. Add to that his many years engaged in segregated immigrant factory and field labor, and we can only imagine the hundreds of thousands of dollars of lost comparative lifetime earnings that Cresencio experienced because of his migrant status. If California is the nation's "best shot" for immigrants, with the nation's most immigrant-friendly policies and opportunities, these stats remind us that there is, at best, still much room for improvement.

But what do people in California think about this? In the following pages, we take a deep dive into attitudes about immigration, exploring how our respondents made sense of migration, inequality, and the contradictions inherent to immigrant life. We find that upper-working-class and lower-middle-class respondents, for the most part, easily explained that immigration was an integral part of the California landscape, as important as the state's blue shoreline and golden mountains. And even though many acknowledged that immigrants faced structural obstacles, these understandings took a back seat to the idea that immigrants were actually achieving the American Dream. In so many words, they could see stories like Cresencio's, who came during a time when immigration processes were more accessible and lenient, as proof that immigrants had "made it" even as they acknowledged that immigrants today are likely to be exploited, discriminated against, and live in poverty.

Yet how is this so? How could residents see immigrants as the personification of the American Dream and among the most vulnerable? We will explore this puzzle, showing that the answer has much to do with how residents normalize the inequality that immigrants face. Put simply, respondents were able to broadly frame immigrants as "exceptional" hard workers and as folks who had made it because they could mobilize a particular but narrow understanding of the American Dream, which differed from the typical middle-class stability narrative—including a white picket fence—that they hoped to achieve for themselves. In so doing, respondents used the tools of exceptional framing and spatial comparison to adopt an image of immigrants as dreamers who achieved the American Dream simply by making it to US soil and to minimize the precarity and exploitation they experienced thereafter. Because, after all, respondents reasoned, opportunities were surely more ample in the United States than places like Mexico or the Philippines.

However, we also found that underneath progressive statements about immigration and the value of diversity, many Californians viewed the undocumented with deep ambivalence and even as morally suspect. The concept of bounded blame helps to shed light on these residents' attitudes. Indeed, even when respondents reminded us that they disagreed wholeheartedly with Trump's rhetoric about immigrants, telling us they were Democrats, and even when they talked at length about how "hardworking" and exceptional immigrants were, they still somehow lumped the undocumented into a single category and suggested that people in this group engaged in problematic behavior that created social burdens. In this manner, respondents could exalt immigrant workers for their contributions and mourn the structures that seemed to unjustly hold them down, but then also find ways to blame the undocumented for their predicament.

We argue that respondents come to see the inequality that immigrants endure as normal as they fall back on more positive and individualist understandings of immigrants as American Dream achievers and as they reserve their ambivalence and suspicion specifically for the undocumented. In this way, many—though not all—could also softly and indirectly blame the undocumented for somehow choosing to live in inequality. Many respondents could therefore say that immigrants in general belonged in California but the undocumented, specifically, perhaps did not. We elaborate on these findings by first situating immigration in the Golden State. Then we show how exceptional framing, spatial comparison, and bounded blame allow people, including liberals and some progressives, to see immigrants as exemplary workers and dreamers as well as potential burdens to the state.

California as an Exceptional Place for Exceptional Immigrants

When public commentators talk about California and immigration, they often start with a look at the polls and the finding that most residents are pro-immigrant. Indeed, over the past decade, a majority of residents have answered positively on binary questions concerning immigration. This trend is consistent with our survey results. When we asked respondents whether immigrants made California a worse place to live, less than 20 percent agreed with that statement. Instead, the overwhelming majority considered the state better off because of immigration. We also found that Latino, followed by Asian respondents, were much more likely than Black or White respondents to agree that immigrants were a benefit to the region.

Most survey respondents also thought that California was a particularly good place for immigrants, or at least one where they were treated more fairly than they would be in other places. Specifically, we asked respondents two questions: (1) Are immigrants treated unfairly in California; and (2) are immigrants treated unfairly in the United States? Thirty-seven percent of respondents strongly agreed that immigrants were unfairly treated in the United States, but that rate dropped in half when they were asked the same question about California. These results suggest that respondents thought immigrants living in California had a fairer chance at life—such as jobs, housing, and educational opportunities—than immigrants living elsewhere, like the US South.[14]

The interview excerpts that follow show just how the broad majority of respondents thought of immigrants as "good" for the state. We found that many articulated this positive understanding about immigrants by speaking about cultural consumption and labor.

IMMIGRANTS AND CULTURAL DIVERSITY

Marina is a retired Latina teacher living in Los Angeles. Born and raised in California, she told us about the benefits of having so many friends who were also the children of immigrants. Reflecting on the diversity and the significant presence of Latino immigrants, she shared:

> Somebody told me once, in California there's two types of people, Mexicans and wannabe Mexicans [*laughs*]. Because we love Mexican food. Um, I, you know, if you look around, we have Mexican food restaurants, and we have Italian restaurants, and we have Japanese restaurants, and, you know, we have . . . um . . . movies and books and . . . and we just have . . . it's not plain white bread. We've got brown bread, we've got rye, we've got so many different flavors that we can choose from instead of, this is it? This is, you know, all it's going to be. And we don't expand our minds and our feelings and our soul if we're just stuck with one thing. So, I think immigrants bring a lot to the table.

Like Marina, most respondents spoke about the diversity that immigrants brought mainly in terms of the culinary consumer benefits it provided. While a small minority of respondents told us about the positive benefit that various immigrant houses of worship brought to their communities, most largely thought of immigrant cultural contributions to their region in terms of markets and restaurants. And for many, the large number of immigrants and the wide availability of diverse food were primary examples of how special an immigrant-friendly California was. As Katie, a White respondent from Los Angeles described, "Like if you grew up in rural Alabama and you have never seen other places, other people, other experiences, you're probably a little more narrow-minded from someone who's grown up in like LA. LA is diverse, it has so many areas, different pockets that you can go. You can eat Korean food if you want, you come to Glendale, you can try Armenian markets and, like, try new things, so I think it brings, like, interesting bits, so it's not, like, boring, like, everything."

Vanessa, a Latina from Los Angeles, noted the nexus between immigration, diversity, and food when asked about the contributions of immigrants to the region:

> I think . . . um . . . I think LA, not even more than any other place, but I mean, 'cause there's a lot of immigrants all over the country, but LA is predominantly a Mexican city, you know? So, like, if you speak to any other ethnicity, and they haven't eaten any of the Mexican food or heard any of the Mexican music or grown accustomed to our ways, the way we celebrate things, our holidays . . . um . . . then they've been living under a rock because there's no way that you can drive down the street and not see a Mexican restaurant, you know, a Mexican store . . . uh . . . a Latino store. You even go to Koreatown. You go . . . we have Koreatown. We have Filipinotown. We have Little Saigon. We have Little Tokyo. Like we literally have all kinds of immigrant, like . . . uh . . . what's it called? Little cities within our city, you know?

Many respondents believed that California was enriched by immigrants and their traditions, especially their food. This diversity was seen as essential, a critically important aspect of what defined their region. For example, Christian, a Filipino from Los Angeles, talked about the centrality of immigrants to the culture of California: "Yeah, so yeah, you know, somehow you see different cultures mixing together a- and it's somehow . . . uh . . . lucky. I'll say that I'm lucky I'm here in Los Angeles or in Southern California wherein there's a lot of cultures interact[ing] with each other," adding that California was different because "other places somehow . . . um . . . there are also places in America where they may be White supremacist, I don't know what states they are located in, but somehow this, they also start doing some of that stuff against other cultures." When we asked why he thought there weren't as many White supremacists in California as elsewhere, he linked the racial tolerance of the state and especially Los Angeles to its immigrant population: "Well, because LA is more predominantly immigrant. And . . . and [White people] become the minority for LA."

Indeed, the respondents broadly understood immigration as an integral part of what made California a welcoming area. In doing so, they framed California as somehow exceptional and much better than other places by comparison. Many respondents therefore took offense at anti-immigrant discourse that depicted immigrants as cultural invaders. For example, during his interview, Ken, a White respondent from Los Angeles, reflected on how immigrants were part of a broader process that made not only California but also the nation better, stating: "The biggest thing is these people are coming here to give us something. They're not coming here to take anything, they're coming here with their culture, they're coming here with their work ethic, they're coming to be a part of the community. They're not coming with the intention of stealing and taking over, they're coming in to be a part of something that we have been cheering and showing off for hundreds of years, even bragging about how great we are. How foolish of us if we thought no one would want to come here." He saw immigrants as part of a broader diversification process that empowered the state and the nation.

In this sense, respondents understood California as a place that thrives on diversity, not despite it. The consumption of immigrant culture helps shape a broader narrative of California as a cultural sanctuary, a cosmopolitan place of many languages, culinary options, and diverse histories. From this standpoint, the many cultures that different waves of immigrants have brought with them have enriched California culturally and have become a fundamental and defining feature of the state. Many respondents spoke of consuming the diverse foods associated with immigrants as a kind of marker of belonging and a cultural expectation in the Golden State.

IMMIGRANTS AS HARD WORKERS

Beyond food and culture, labor, especially the idea of "hard work" was central to how respondents talked about immigrants. For example, Marina shared:

> You know, most immigrants are coming here because they want jobs to take care of their family. And they're going to take the crap jobs that nobody else wants. I mean if you look . . . do you want to go pick strawberries in . . . in the heat? No. You know, most people don't want to do that. Most people don't want to wash dishes. You know, if . . . if I asked my students, you know, "What do you want to, what kind of jobs are you going to get?" "Oh, my father's going to give me a job, you know, I . . . I'm not going to have to do that." Most immigrants are coming and they'll take anything.

Marina did not see immigrants as criminals or as a source of job competition to be feared in the way she contended that Republicans and right-wing media had painted them. She pushed back against a particular kind of anti-immigrant rhetoric touted by Donald Trump, who infamously called Mexican immigrants "criminals" and "rapists" when he announced his first presidential campaign.[15] Amid pushback even from his own party, he doubled down on this xenophobic rhetoric, insisting that undocumented immigrants were "taking our jobs . . . taking our money, they're killing us."[16]

As one might expect, the majority of the respondents saw themselves as far distanced from the overtly racist rhetoric about immigrants displayed by the right, especially Trump. In the Golden State, where immigrants have a strong presence in nearly every sector of the economy, the idea that immigrants were hard workers who did the jobs "no one else wants" was especially prevalent. Sheila, for example, an Asian American respondent from Los Angeles, thought about how conservatives talked about immigration and stated: "So, I don't think, you know, it's like with the immigrants, would they . . . are they really taking your jobs? I don't think so. In a lot of ways, because I, unfortunately, I don't think the ones that are here already are going to do that work. . . . You're not going to find them washing cars for whatever minimum wage is or below, you know, for ten hours, twelve hours a day."

Ideas about immigration and agricultural labor were prevalent among respondents in both the Central Valley and Los Angeles. Andrés, another Latino from Los Angeles, noted the following about immigrants:

> These people are coming to find jobs, they're not here stealing, they're not here going on welfare. If anyone goes on welfare, it's going to be an American. If you look at the state of Kentucky, it's got the highest rate of welfare people in the union, I believe, is the stat that I read. But no, it's bullshit that these people are taking away from our country, they're adding to our country. Economically and in a work force. Do you see any Blacks working the fields? Do you see any students working the fields? Farming? No. It's backbreaking work that only other people could do because they want to do that.

There are a few important things to note here. First, Andrés was from Los Angeles, not the Central Valley, yet still one of his main images of immigrant labor was in the fields. While Los Angeles respondents could certainly talk about immigrants as dishwashers, janitors, or as construction or factory workers, it was most often the idea of agricultural labor, far from Los Angeles, that often dominated the imagery of immigrants as workers. This idea of the farmworker as the quintessential immigrant may be connected to the importance of the farmworker movement in the state. Indeed, if you are in any major city in California, you are probably not far away from a César Chavez Boulevard, a Dolores Huerta school, or a mural of farmworkers. So, while contemporary farmworkers often toil out of most Californians' view, in fields tucked far away from major cities, it is well known that the immigrant farmworker is an essential part of the state's economy.

Second, Andrés, like other respondents, compares immigrants to native US citizens, African Americans in particular, suggesting that immigrants are more industrious. This discursive move, which on its face celebrates immigrant workers, also serves to reinforce negative stereotypes and pits immigrant workers against non-immigrant Black workers. While it is true that agricultural laborers in the United States are mostly immigrants, especially Latinos, it is also true that the implicit comparison between "hardworking" Latino immigrant laborers and an implied "unwilling" African American laborer has historically served as a sort of racist dog whistle in broader, conservative anti-Black discourse in the United States and even in Mexican media.[17] Furthermore, the celebration of the immigrant as particularly hardworking ignores the economic and legal context in which such labor is happening. Rather than see immigrant labor as structurally determined and often precarious, it naturalizes certain kinds of work as "immigrant work."[18] Ultimately, these comparisons, which were implicit and explicit in our interviews, simultaneously obfuscate and exalt the exploitation of immigrants in ways that also reinforce racial hierarchies.[19]

Still, the idea that immigrants were making important contributions to California through their labor was also widely held among White and Black respondents with few family connections to immigrants. For example, Megan, an African American in Los Angeles, told us the following about the issue: "It's like my friend Monica, told me. She says, 'You know most of us [immigrants], we work . . . we're the ones working the fields.' She said, 'You go out to the fields, there are no White people out there . . . and cause to be honest with you there's no Black people out there. We're out there, we're the one who's working the canneries, we're the one.' She says, 'We are the ones that are pretty much working twenty-four hours a day making sure that production is happening.'" Megan told us that she really wished Trump and other politicians had this type of "sensibility" and understanding when thinking about immigrants.

Jack, a White male respondent from Los Angeles, reflected on the recent anti-immigrant legislation in Texas and other parts of the US South and how such policies could create adverse economic effects because they limited immigrant labor. He explained that those states were "telling the immigrants we are gonna come get you and then there were crops rotting in the field!" He continued, noting that California was an exception because it understood the value of farmworker labor: "In California it's [the] immigrants . . . that's who's gonna pick the vegetables, you know. That's true or otherwise we wouldn't be eating as long as we do." There is, of course, a bit of irony in the fact that agricultural work is hard, exploitative, and debilitating labor, suggesting that California is more welcoming than other states in part because it can have a thriving immigrant-based agricultural economy that overlooks, or perhaps even accepts, this exploitative inequality.

Many interviewees talked about the broader trends in California's agricultural sector, demonstrating that Latino migrant laborers do the vast majority of farmwork. While the service sector in the state is diverse, jobs like janitorial, dishwashing, and housecleaning are also mostly held by Latino migrants.[20] At the same time, it is important to note that exploitation, especially of undocumented immigrants, runs rampant in these labor sectors and leaves migrant workers among the most vulnerable in the region.[21]

Overall, respondents perceived immigrants as hard workers who contributed greatly to the nation and to California. The fact that Southern states had passed anti-immigrant legislation and might be more anti-immigrant places also factored into their opinions about California as a land for immigrants. Though, what stood out for them more broadly was the sense that immigrants had helped transform California through their labor and cultural distinctiveness, making the state a better place to live. In some ways, immigration helped the precarious middle feel more cosmopolitan, providing diverse foods and consumer options, along with service labor, at an affordable price.

Exceptional Immigrants and the American Dream

The broader narrative on immigrant hard work echoes the bootstrapping concepts long tied to notions of American individualism. Alexis de Tocqueville, Thomas Edison, Horatio Alger, J. T. Adams, and other commentators on American life long posited that American individualism was characterized by lone grit and a person's ability to pick themselves up by their bootstraps and experience social mobility through hard work. Such ideas tend to overlook how the government, intergenerational wealth, White privilege, and inequality have long been at the center of social mobility and stagnation in the nation. By glossing over this, American public discourse has moralized "hard work," equating it not simply with success but also with worthy and commendable behavior.[22] By tying this sentiment to immigrants, many might overlook the structures that often exploit and keep immigrants engaged in menial labor, with comparatively fewer opportunities for personal advancement.

We know that respondents think that immigrants contribute to California through their hard work, but how do residents think that immigrants are faring? We wondered if respondents indeed equated immigrants' hard work with their social mobility, or if they believed the difficult labor conditions and inequality disproportionately affected immigrants.

Culling through our interviews, we found that respondents seemed to minimize the structural difficulties faced by immigrants and foreground the idea that immigrants, through their ability to labor on US soil, were achieving the American Dream in California. This view was especially prevalent among respondents who were the children or grandchildren of immigrants who shared stories about how their immigrant parents and ancestors had "worked hard" in the United States. This sentiment shone through especially when we asked respondents about how they defined the American Dream.

For example, Ang, an Asian American man in Los Angeles, told us that to him the American Dream meant "a white picket fence and a stable job." While he felt that he personally could not achieve the dream in Los Angeles, especially with its high cost of living, he did think that many immigrants, including his own parents, had done so. When asked to elaborate, he stated, "I mean, my parents, I see that . . . okay, they came like . . . this was like a lot of other people. They came to this country. They . . . they kind of made a living, and they . . . they supported their family. And, you know, they kind of, like . . . they went through the whole process. And that's kind of like . . . uh . . . achieving the American Dream to a certain level."

Bai, another Asian American in Los Angeles, thought about his parents from Vietnam when he told us that immigrants tend to achieve the American Dream. When asked why, he stated, "My parents achieved their dream by coming here. 'Cause they lost a lot during the war. So, I feel like they accomplished what they wanted." He continued telling us that while his family had not been well off while he was growing up, his parents—especially his mother—had eventually been able to stabilize herself in a career and even helped him pay for college.

Perhaps the clearest evidence of the connection between immigration and the American Dream is how respondents were able to talk about both in the abstract, as a sort of truism in American society. Hence Leah, a White respondent from Los Angeles, explained to us how she defined the American Dream: "Um, I mean, I feel like it's a thing about . . . I feel like it started as an immigrant dream. . . . Like come to America and live free." Here, freedom is broad and abstract and does not need to be specifically connected to economic stability. Rather, it is simply proof that international migration had occurred. Similarly, Sen speaks of immigrants and the American Dream in the abstract as inherent to the United States. When asked what the American Dream meant to him, he explained:

> Um, well, when I think of that I just think of . . . my mind goes to immigrants in this country and . . . uh . . . building a life for [themselves] that [is] in contrast to where they came from . . . so to me that . . . throughout the history of, America's history, different immigrant populations have come in waves and all within the lure of the American Dream, which is because, like, the idea of . . . uh . . . you know . . . uh . . . achieving a life that is . . . uh . . . you know, more stable, more, you know, just better than what they could have achieved in their home country.

Importantly, this broad sentiment of the American Dream was also shared by those without close immigrant ancestry. In his interview, Tony, a White man who grew up in northwest Fresno, reflected on how many immigrants are more enthusiastic about the American Dream than people born in the United States are. He noted that "these immigrants that come inside, have seen it in so many other ways, that they get here, and they see that they can have it, they just have to go and get it. Um, it's awesome." Also reflecting on the American Dream, another respondent, an African American in Fresno, thought abstractly that the American Dream was about freedom as well as people who "come to this country" and were able to "build things and a better life" for themselves and their family.

A person does not have to be politically liberal or have sympathetic attitudes toward immigrants to note the link between the American Dream and immigration. Even conservative respondents with scant ties to immigrants in their family or friendship networks made the connection. For example, Jacob, a White conservative man from Bakersfield with strong anti-immigration views, had this to say: "I think the American Dream . . . is that you could come to America, or you can be born in America."

On the left and the right, immigrants and non-immigrants, including those skeptical of their own ability to achieve middle-class standing, often defined the American Dream as tied to immigration. This understanding was so prominent among respondents that when we asked Grace, an Asian American Republican respondent in Los Angeles, about whether she had "heard of the American Dream," she answered immediately "the American Dream for the immigrants?"

Indeed, although respondents understand immigrants to be exceptionally hard workers, they also know that they perform backbreaking labor in jobs that "no one else wants to do." How, then, do they reconcile immigrants living the American Dream with immigrants living in a state of inequality? As in the previous chapters, we argue that this ability rests on the practices that help them to minimize structural explanations of inequality. Specifically, we found that respondents leaned into exceptional framing and used abstraction to tolerate such inequality and in some cases even develop an optimistic account of immigrant achievement. We elaborate on these ideas in what follows.

REDEFINING THE AMERICAN DREAM FOR IMMIGRANTS

Andrea was born in Fresno to undocumented Mexican parents. Her father worked decades on dairy farms, and her mother was a stay-at-home parent. Although she noted that the part of town she grew up in was "very diverse," there was always an important distinction between Mexicans and White people where she lived. The latter were "definitely not the majority" but had consolidated their "power in terms of economics." She remembers living among people who displayed "prejudice" against Mexicans, but she did not really understand or name it as such until she was a young adult. To her, the racial hierarchy in the Central Valley felt pervasive, often positioning Latinos, and especially Latino farmworker families, near the bottom.

Her family "bounced around a lot" as her father searched for a more permanent agricultural job. In the process, they found themselves homeless for a while and dependent on community food banks and extended family support to get by. Those were rough times. She remembers living with her parents and two siblings in a single room and in a small shed and even sleeping in the family car for a time as the family struggled through poverty. Food pantries and charity drives were sometimes the only way that her family got by; a family meal at Burger King "was a luxury" back in those days, she recalls. And although she is a native Californian, she can only remember a handful of times that her parents took a day off from work to enjoy the beach. By most measures, her family's story is one of intense economic struggle, reflective of the working poverty that many Latinos endure, often while working full-time or almost full-time but not making enough to meet the cost of living in their area.

Today, her parents are semiretired agricultural and service workers. She helps them out economically because they are "still struggling to be secure." Still, when asked about how she defined the American Dream, Andrea turned to her parents' story, weaving common understandings of the concept that emphasize migration, hard work, and the freedom to relocate. She noted: "I definitely feel like, that searching for a better life encompasses what the American Dream is." She paused and then continued: "My parents came to this country for a better life." In many ways, Andrea felt that her parents' arrival in the United States in and of itself provides some proof of the American Dream. It was in leaving Mexico and its relatively poorer economic mobility prospects there that her family was able to come to the United States and toil here, north of the United States–Mexico border. To Andrea, her parents left a potential life of extreme poverty in Mexico to labor and find a shot at making it in the United States.

Importantly, Andrea was not blindly accepting of the American Dream. Seeing her inability to purchase a home and the rising cost of meeting her expenses in Fresno, she was skeptical that her generation could achieve middle-class status. She told us that she felt the American Dream was a "lie" and was just used to distract folks, especially "communities of color," from the inequality that abounded. Her cynicism stemmed from her own experience. She had gone to college, incurred debt, and still could not find steady employment that paid enough to keep up with the cost of living in Fresno. At that time, she was balancing a few side hustles in hopes of one day landing a government job with Fresno County.

Yet despite telling us that she felt the dream was a ruse, she also could see her parents, even with their economic struggles, as having achieved the American Dream because they had come "in search for a better life." She could hold both understandings of the American Dream at the same time: the immigrant-based one that rests on the idea of mobility and labor in the United States and another that defined middle-class standing for her—a "white picket fence"—which felt out of reach. Immigrants like Andrea's parents had one specific dream premised on work, while she had another based on material comforts and economic stability.

The immigrant–American Dream link attributes "work" and "opportunity" to immigrants while overlooking other definitions tied to middle-class stability. This is the immigrant American Dream that California is so emblematic of. Yet to view immigrants as dream achievers involves sidestepping the economic aspirations and stability that society seems to apply more generally to the American Dream, at least for those born in the United States. Immigrants can achieve the dream without necessarily standing on firm middle-class ground or achieving the broader economic security gains that are tightly connected to ideas of "making it," such as homeownership and stable employment. Immigrants, then, can be emblematic of the American Dream without necessarily attaining anything close to a "white picket fence." Likewise, California can be a land of immigrant dreams without needing to be a land of immigrant middle-class stability. By repeating and buying into the immigrant-American Dream link, respondents minimized the structural and systemic nature of immigrant inequality.

BETTER THAN "THIRD WORLD" COUNTRIES

There are also other ways that abstraction allows people to see immigrants as dream achievers. Rene, an Asian American respondent from Los Angeles, spoke to this when asked what she thought of the American Dream: "Um, be . . . achieve anything they want in life. Uh, you know, because when you look at like other countries, like third-world countries, they don't really have the same opportunities, you know? Or they don't at all [*laughs*]. . . . Uh, because . . . uh . . . because of the, where they live, just because of . . . it's unfortunate because . . . uh . . . people, a lot of people don't, a lot of people don't get to choose, well some people don't get to choose where they . . . they're brought up, where they live, where they're born, you know?"

Her response reflects the way that abstract global, spatial comparison figures into the immigrant–American Dream link. That is, the idea that immigrants could be personifications of the American Dream rests on the understanding that the United States is a much better place to be than the "Third World," which includes many of the Latin American and Asian countries from which many immigrants in California came. This perspective was evident in respondents' comments about immigrants coming to "build a better life" or when they mentioned that their parents or loved ones came from a "poor" or even "poorer country."

In such an understanding, moving to the United States is synonymous with opportunity. Yet, importantly, the move does not have to be one from complete and utter poverty to the United States; it can simply be the perception that a move to the US brings about improved conditions. For example, when Jane, an Asian American woman from Los Angeles, was asked about the American Dream, she noted:

> Um, I think having the freedom to do . . . um . . . a lot of things . . . uh . . . I think also having a lot of options. Um, I know I speak to my cousins in Thailand and they're my age. And after college they graduated as well, but they had a very hard time finding jobs. . . . She had a very hard time and she's very more savvy than I am. I think . . . I think she's honestly a lot better, but in Thailand there's just not much opportunity. I think in the United States, the American Dream is definitely that idea, that a lot of opportunities here. Yeah.

Once again, the idea of movement from a lack of opportunity to the United States with its more apparent opportunities was key. This idea was also prominent among those in our sample who came to the United States when they were children, even if they could not remember their time in their home countries or never spent any of their working adult lives there. For example, Gina, a Latina respondent born in Mexico, migrated to Madera at two years old. Her father worked in agriculture and her mother was a seamstress. She recalls growing up poor, wearing handmade clothes, and not having much money for toys or vacations. She began working small jobs at the age of ten and now works as a full-time bookkeeper. When asked what the American Dream meant to her, she noted: "I mean, we came here to start a better life. I did." Indeed, even though she came when she was two and has never lived anywhere else, she has a deep sense that her migration to the United States was connected to better opportunities. Later she would continue this line of thought when reflecting on why she was grateful that her family moved to California: "Um, [here] you can go from dirt poor to dirt rich, you know. You can win the lottery [*laughs*], or you can just, you can achieve a lot of stuff where you can't do that in other countries."

For Gina, the idea of opportunity was synonymous with the United States, including California. Even though she only lived in Mexico for a short while, she had a deep sense that moving to the United States afforded her opportunities for social mobility that she otherwise would not have had. More broadly, she revealed an abstract understanding of the process as not simply about her story or her migration but as a more conventional immigration-to-America story.

Once again, even among respondents without a significant connection to immigration, many thought of the immigrant-American Dream link using spatial comparison. For instance, Aisha, an African American woman born and raised in Los Angeles, noted in her interview: "I think everybody's looking in some way for that American Dream: peace, freedom, better education, better access to all the things that we have in this country that are positive things that don't exist in more impoverished countries. That's why people come here. So, I get it because—put yourself there. If I were in a bad situation, no clean water, under a dictatorship, or whatever, I'd be trying to flee too."

Here, Aisha reminds us, movement to the United States is not simply about social mobility or moving from an impoverished country. It is also about fleeing authoritarianism. Some of these same sentiments were echoed by many Asian respondents, including those of Vietnamese and Chinese descent who noted that their parents fled a war or communism.

The important thing about such remarks—even when coming from someone who has never lived in another country or only has vague memories of their time outside of the US—is the way that the comparison works in the abstract to reinforce the golden tint through which many view immigrant life in California, and the United States more generally.

We are not suggesting that there are no economic differences between the United States and countries in the Global South or between California and Latin America or Southeast Asia more specifically. There are certainly many differences and likely more opportunity for class mobility in California than in many of the countries from which respondents and their families came. Yet we are stressing that this sort of spatial comparison, and the idea that life in California is better than life in other places for immigrants, was often taken as a truism without nuance or much reflection on how exploitation and inequality touches immigrant lives.

Moreover, the use of spatial comparison was not necessarily connected to concrete material realities. Our respondents stated plainly that immigrants move here for opportunities and a better life while not always emphasizing that immigrants reach the middle class or obtain a "white picket fence." Instead, the dream was focused on migration from a comparatively poor place to the United States for opportunities and to achieve a "better life," however abstractly imagined.

Respondents' understanding that the presence of immigrants was related to the American Dream was closely tied to a global comparison that saw the United States as an ostensibly better place to live. While some respondents connected this view to political opinions, most respondents thought that the comparison was more natural, something taken for granted. Paul, a White man from Los Angeles, summed it up this way: "The American Dream is really something for everyone to look at in third-world countries. You know, freedom to pursue what you wanna do. Freedom from the norm, not having to be already heavily taxed. You know, American Dream. I think it's really, again, it's really everybody's dream. Again, we just have maybe a better opportunity here than most places in the world."

On the whole, respondents seemed to understand that the main contribution of immigrants is their exceptional labor. Their presence alone is sufficient evidence to many that the American Dream is alive and well in California. But it is one thing to think about immigration writ large; it is another to better understand just who—or which immigrants—respondents believed actually belonged in the Golden State. As we dive a bit deeper, we find that respondents relied on important racial—and especially legal—boundaries to define who they felt belonged in the state. These boundaries provide insight into the ways respondents thought about immigrant belonging.

(ASIAN) IMMIGRANTS AS ENTREPRENEURS AND JOB CREATORS

By and large, when thinking about the contributions of immigrants to California and how they made the state a better place to live, respondents emphasized immigrants' ability to roll up their sleeves and work hard. Additionally, some respondents thought more broadly about the economic contributions of immigrants to the state through their entrepreneurial abilities. Indeed, in California, immigrants are heavily entrepreneurial. Recent reports note that they are significantly more likely than those born in the United States to launch their own businesses and that, in any given year, about 42 percent of new companies in the Golden State are founded by immigrants.[23]

Accordingly, respondents tended to reflect on how immigrants' savviness, long working hours, and ability to employ others benefitted the state. For example, Pepe, a Latino in Fresno, noted, "Uh, immigrants? I think . . . uh . . . they're . . . especially here in California, I believe that they create small businesses, and small businesses, they have to be run by employees or something. . . . So, I think they create jobs for different people and then I think they benefit." For him, immigrants' efforts create opportunities for others and the state writ large. Christina, an Asian American respondent noted that immigrants in California faced many challenges but still persevered and "created small businesses, created a lot of jobs, and somehow, those jobs, they're already configured into the economy."

Some respondents were particularly clear about the bad rap that immigrants got, especially because they were used as scapegoats in conservative media. Monica, for example, told us: "I think immigration is good. I think we can always learn from other . . . uh . . . people from other countries, and . . . um . . . I think a lot of them come here and they start businesses, and I think that's really good. So, I'm not one of the people that think . . . that immigrants are bad, and I'm not one of those people that blame immigrants if I'm not doing well myself."

In all these ways, many respondents thought of immigrants as entrepreneurs and as an important part of the California immigration story. Many believed that this understanding was rarely appreciated in conservative and Republican circles.

At times, the idea of the immigrant entrepreneur went beyond small businesses, as respondents reflected on how particular migrants were transforming elite economies. For example, Jerry, an Asian American respondent from Los Angeles, pointed out that immigrants had transformed Silicon Valley and the tech market in California. He stated, "Like how many Indian and Asian immigrants have created billion-dollar companies . . . you know? Um, that have created so many, so many jobs, you know, pays for one thousand, ten thousand immigrants that, you know . . . that are . . . that haven't, you know, created as many jobs." For him, the impact of immigrants on California came through entrepreneurial efforts, large and small.

Importantly, when respondents talked about immigrants as entrepreneurs and job creators, they typically had Asian, rather than Latin American, immigrants in mind. Latin American immigrants were mainly understood as "hard workers" who labored in service and agriculture. This sort of racialization of immigrants and their contributions came rather naturally, often from Asian and Latino respondents themselves. Latinos reflected on their parents' efforts as laborers, and while some Asian respondents did the same, they were also more likely to acknowledge co-ethnic small businesses and restaurants in their neighborhoods. Qiang, an Asian respondent in Los Angeles noted: "Well, immigrants, you know, they're doing a lot of the work. . . . There are Asian restaurants . . . uh . . . Asian people own their own business, a lot of them are immigrants. A lot of them were . . . um . . . mostly came from . . . um . . . some Asian country and they came to America and try to achieve their American Dream by owning their own business and working at their own restaurants and small business. You know, they try to achieve their own dreams by being a sole proprietorship type of company and doing their own work there."

Latinos are actually a highly entrepreneurial group in California as well, establishing close to a million small businesses in the state, more so than any other community of color.[24] Yet the equating of Latinos with hard work and Asians with job creation overlooks this fact. This conflation only emphasizes, loudly, that Latinos are workers—laborers rather than creators.

This racialized aspect of Latinos' labor contributions to the state also reflects a broader aspect of the immigrant imaginings among the respondents. It was often, but not exclusively, Asian respondents that thought of Asian immigrants and their entrepreneurial capacities when thinking about the broader question of immigrants in California. For example, when asked about immigration, most Asian respondents spoke of Asian migrants and Asian business owners. Yet most Black, White, and Latino respondents imagined Latinos—often undocumented workers—as prototypical immigrants. In this manner, Black and White respondents were less likely to talk about Asians, much less Asian small business owners, when thinking about immigration writ large; and Latinos were likely to reflect on the experiences of their parents, families, or friends. While some Latinos mentioned

Latino immigrant small business owners, they were outnumbered by those who imagined Latino immigrants purely as low-wage workers. Respondents did not seem to be aware of the fact that Asians represent the fastest growing immigrant community in the Golden State and that Latin American migration has actually decreased. These findings echo much of the research that shows that individuals usually picture Latinos, especially Mexicans, when asked to think about immigration writ large and the undocumented in particular.[25]

Illegality and the Limits of Belonging

The majority of respondents held positive feelings toward immigration. If they were asked to declare a binary pro- or anti-immigration position, nearly all would likely claim to be pro-immigration. Moreover, many took pains to distance themselves from those they perceived to be on the far right of immigration, especially those that seemed to deem all immigrants as criminals or to lament the "Browning" of the nation. Yet we also found that, among many in the precarious middle class, the extent of enthusiasm expressed toward immigration had its limits. Importantly, respondents' ambivalence centered on the issue of documentation and the question of what impact the undocumented in particular had on their region and the state. Some of these sentiments mirror broader trends found in US public opinion polls, which consistently find that support for immigration decreases when respondents are asked about "illegal" immigrants.[26] The Public Policy Institute of California documents similar trends at the state level. Californians express overall support for immigration; however, the level of support wanes considerably when respondents are specifically asked about providing services to the undocumented.[27]

The interviews echoed much of this ambivalence about the undocumented, even among those that consider themselves, in principle, to be pro-immigration, and even among those that distance themselves from more conservative political viewpoints. We argue that these individuals see the undocumented as a sort of litmus test to their more progressive stances on immigration and the golden-colored lens through which they see immigration in California more generally. When discussing the undocumented specifically, broader ideas about the benefits of diversity and the value of immigrants and their labor to the economy seemed to take a back seat to the more pressing worries around the economic and, for some, even moral cost of "illegals" to the state and nation.

Specifically, we found that many respondents found ways to classify and homogenize the undocumented as a group separate from legal immigrants and citizens, whose activities were suspect and, ultimately, potentially burdensome. We unpack these forms of reasoning, showing how these particular respondents engaged in bounded blame, effectively forming a symbolic boundary around the undocumented so they could keep imagining California as a land of and for immigrants.

"ILLEGALS" BECOME THE PROBLEM

Karen was born in Los Angeles but was raised by her single mother, a conservative Christian, in middle-class neighborhoods in Fresno and the surrounding towns. She graduated from a private Christian college but shared that she has drifted away from her conservative background. On reflection, she disclosed: "As I've gotten older, I've become a little bit more . . . um . . . liberal in my thinking." She explained that this has caused friction with her parents. She described her mother, a registered Republican, as someone who felt like immigration is making the United States "lose its identity"—an assertion Karen highly doubted.

Karen worked part-time helping to run a small business, but she said that it was a "struggle," and at the time of the interview, she felt like she and her husband were living "month to month." Drawing on her more progressive principles, she felt that the government should help people who are suffering, though she noted that it is complicated because there are so many of them. She also told us that she thinks immigration is good for society because the resulting diversity yields many benefits. Yet when probed further on her beliefs about immigration, Karen struggled to reconcile her progressive principles of welcoming others and providing a social safety net with the issue of documentation status. She noted: "Um, I know . . . I guess it's kind of a, like . . . a . . . I mean, I don't know, immigrants, the more people that are here, the more people that can work and help the economy but then, you know, if they . . . if they're look-, you know, looking [at undocumented immigrants], then they're having to be helped from the government as well. So, it's kind of a catch-22: you're damned if you do, damned if you don't have things."

While Karen noted that immigrants contribute to the economy, she focused on how some with undocumented status might have to be helped more than others. In Karen's case, she thought the value of immigrants could offset the cost of helping immigrants. Later in the interview, she connected, albeit tentatively, the potential poverty of the undocumented experience with crime: "Um, I mean, like, we don't want poverty, you know, these are obviously things that we, like, crime . . . you don't want those things. So, as we think about that as tied to immigration or tied to illegal immigration then, you know, then that's bad, that's a problem, then illegal immigration is really, really bad [*laughs*]. So, um, but if you think about them as separate issues, then they're separate issues. So, I don't know, I guess it depends on how you think about it."

Karen used speculation to suggest a link between undocumented status and socially undesirable conditions like poverty and crime. Speculation allowed her to suggest this link while not fully owning it. She did not definitively say that she thought undocumented immigration led to crime and poverty. Instead, she said that she might consider these concerns when thinking of the issue because others might consider them. When she thought about the issues "separately," that is, when she thought only about whether she supports immigration overall, she expressed a positive view. But when she thought of the undocumented specifically, she grew more hesitant and ambivalent.

This example underscores the need to better understand the power of speculation. In suggesting, but not owning, stereotypes about immigrants, Karen is able to think of herself as having a progressive set of values, except when it comes to undocumented immigration. In this way, she is able to create a categorical boundary around the undocumented, who exist in an ambivalent political space, but maintain her overall views about immigration as a net good for society.

Like Karen, Ang generally thought that his views differed sharply from those held by conservatives, especially Republicans. Born and raised in California to Asian parents, he told us that he enjoys living in a state where diversity seems valued, although he noted that there has been significant tension, and the state is not perfect on issues of racial inequality. A self-described "moderate Democrat" who felt that the nation would be "a lot better when Trump leaves office," he worried that the right had maligned the image of immigrants to the broader public. He disagreed with the idea that the undocumented were criminals because he noted that even citizens, and people born in the United States, were "causing trouble. You know, they're doing crime or whatever." For Ang, there was nothing particularly criminal about the undocumented. But later in the interview he added, "And obviously, one thing I wanna say is . . . obviously if someone is undocumented and, like, if they really have to survive, you know, they might do bad things, so [*laughs*]. They have no choice."

A few things are important to note about this initial part of the interview. First, Ang was generally positive about diversity and felt that, in general, immigrants were unfairly portrayed by Republicans. Yet he was also able to quickly tie immigrants to crime, not necessarily because he felt that immigrants had criminal intent, but because he thought there were "good" and "bad" people in any group, including the native-born, documented immigrants, and the undocumented. Ang also suggests that some undocumented "might do bad things" because their structural position leaves them with difficult choices "if they have to survive." During the rest of the interview, Ang expressed a clear understanding of the systemic difficulties in the immigration system. He described the path to citizenship as "broken." He continued: "Um, but I don't know, I mean, sometimes in the country, you know, of course, there's, like, a lot of people that are undocumented and maybe they can't get, you know, citizenship and they have to, like, do things to survive. So maybe they steal. . . . But then the thing is, a lot of people, you know, they steal, and they steal it all the time. And that I don't think it's good. I'm sure it's not all immigrants. But sometimes, like, I feel like, you know, the majority of people here are immigrants anyways."

Here Ang displays the essence of bounded blame. He essentially takes what is a structural problem—"people can't get citizenship"—and suggests that it leads to impossible choices and criminal behavior among a bounded group, the undocumented. What he understands as a broad and systemic dysfunction—the lack of a path to citizenship—is then linked to individual criminal behavioral responses within this group. Ang's view differs from broader arguments, like those posed by Donald Trump and even some of the anti-immigrant respondents in this study, that suggest that immigrants bring criminal intent with them as they cross into the United States. Instead, this is a more nuanced and qualifying type of argument that depicts immigrants as responding to a broken or difficult situation that leaves them little choice but to commit crimes.

Ang's hesitancy does not suggest he sees immigrants as "bad" people but rather as ordinary people trapped in bad situations. He acknowledged that immigrants can be "hard workers" but then noted that the structure does not reward this population. Later in the interview, Ang returned to the topic to ensure that he was understood as not blaming immigrants themselves. He continued:

> I don't bla- . . . I mean, to me, I don't blame people for trying to, like, come into America. 'Cause a lot of people are coming from countries where they just can't even live or whatever. It's like . . . it's so poor, or no opportunity or violence and all that. So, they obviously wanna get away. . . . The problem is, like . . . uh . . . they wanna, you know, they come here. Yes. The problem is it causes a lot of tension. Because people, they don't want . . . they're just so afraid that, you know, other people will come and they'll take away, like you say, their livelihood. Or maybe they'll bring violence with them or something like that. Which, it could happen.

Once again, Ang pointed to a difficult situation and created space to suggest that problematic situations can lead to crime and other problematic behavioral responses. Importantly, he lays out this logic in a hesitating manner—he spoke about possible criminal behavior with many qualifying "ums" and pauses. Yet, at other times when speaking about immigration's beneficial impact on diversity and the plethora of ethnic food, he was much more assertive and supportive, signaling that his ambivalent stance concerning criminal behavior is more low-key and perhaps a position he rarely communicates. Still, he ponders these issues.

Similarly, Fernando uses the same logic, suggesting that undocumented immigrants' difficult situation leads to poverty and therefore crime. A Latino born and raised in Fresno, Fernando told us about his difficult childhood and being raised by a single mother. In the interview, Fernando expressed his feeling that corporations were winning in today's economy, often at the expense of the middle class. "Cause they're the ones that get . . . I mean, I feel like they're the ones that get the big tax breaks." Thinking about the areas he lived in, he noted how political allegiances coincide with class politics. He said he was a Democrat because, "I mean, I feel like I'm for . . . for the people, but

Republicans, I don't- I don't know, I think that they're kind of like . . . uh . . . I don't know, more people . . . I don't wanna say rich. But I feel more . . . I mean, upper-middle or . . . or wealthy people kind of lean more to Republican." Moreover, he explained that he generally appreciates the diversity of California and sees himself as someone that "gets along" with others and respects others' cultures. He then noted, "But, I mean, I'm proud of . . . of, you know, being . . . to be Latino . . . I mean, 'cause we're like . . . have some good values and . . . and Latinos are known to be, like, hard workers and stuff."

Fernando lamented that there was no clear path to citizenship now and stated that because of current immigration politics, undocumented immigrants are not "able to accomplish what they would accomplish before, like, bringing their family over and . . . and becoming American citizens. I mean, everything has gotten harder, so I feel it's harder for them to get a job without, you know . . . uh . . . proper documentation or whatnot."

Like Ang, Fernando believed that the difficult context of immigration policy creates problems that stand in the way of immigrants' well-being. Yet he stopped short of explicitly connecting this sentiment to the broader understanding of corporations and inequality. Fernando can see exploitation and difficulties for the undocumented, and he can also blame corporations for creating inequality, but the broader set of links between these two forms of social ills remain unconnected.

Fernando believed that the undocumented do not exist in a meritocratic system that rewards them for to their efforts: "Because then what do they become? Because then how else you supporting yourself over here? You're either working under the table . . . which now you're not paying taxes. Or you turn to uh . . . doing illegal things."

Here, Fernando makes a logical leap to suggest a link between undocumented status and criminal behavior. Similar to Ang, he seems to equate the hardships that immigrants face to criminality. He clearly sees a difficult structural situation and then imagines criminal intent and actions. By not directly claiming that immigrants are immoral and criminal, both Ang and Fernando could imply that immigrants were criminals while still distancing themselves from Trumpian and conservative rhetoric on the issue. The undocumented, then, are not a problem in and of themselves. Indeed, many such respondents held a systemic understanding of the experience of the undocumented.

They could point to exploitative labor conditions for those without protection, and how the undocumented had very little access to well-paying jobs. But they would also make a logical leap to suggest the potential for criminal behavior, even though studies have long shown that immigrants, including the undocumented, are less likely to commit crimes than those born in the United States and that the presence of immigrants reduces crime in neighborhoods.[28]

Even though Karen, Ang, and Fernando, among other respondents, were clear that their politics differed substantially from conservative anti-immigrant groups, including Trump supporters, their interviews did leave open the possibility of connecting immigration to crime, a long-repeated trope spread by conservative media and politicians and by many people across the nation. In their minds, undocumented immigrants seemed to have a latent propensity for crime that could be primed by the difficult circumstances that they endure. Respondents saw future behavior and future criminal intent as a problem linked to the undocumented.

Importantly, the type of logic that sees categories of individuals as living in a problem situation and then engaging in problematic behavior is not exclusive to the undocumented. Scholars have long argued that progressives and the Democratic party more broadly connect poverty, especially the poverty associated with Black people, to criminality in similar ways.[29] What may be occurring here is a similar logic, often an anti-Black one, transposed onto the condition of undocumented immigrants. This may be why scholars have explored the empirical ways that anti-Black racism is closely correlated with anti-immigrant sentiment.[30] The respondents seem to provide at least some qualitative clues to how this relationship might be at play. Yet we also found that this was not the only way that respondents revealed their ambivalence about the undocumented. Many also relied on broader arguments about the law to constrain their support for immigration.

THE LAW IS THE LAW, NO "CUTTING IN LINE"

Some respondents had negative views of undocumented immigrants mainly because they saw them as disregarding the rule of law. Here, bounded blame worked to lump all undocumented people into a single group, regardless of their reasons for migrating or their personal stories.

This homogenization made it easier for them to view the people in this group as a group, and as one that was culpable, and even morally criminal. By binding undocumented people together and projecting moral suspicion on them based on their legal status, some judged these immigrants as responsible for their unequal condition.

This form of bounded blame had two different orientations. First, there were individuals that thought that simply not having documentation was wrong because "the law was the law." The idea that being undocumented was "illegal" framed their perception of the issue and overshadowed broader sympathies. We found that a range of respondents in our sample, but especially African Americans, expressed this type of ambivalence.

Howard, an African American respondent in LA whom we met in the previous chapter, for example, made clear in his interview that he had "nothing against" immigrants, noting how much he valued the diversity in Los Angeles. Born in Texas, he attended a historically Black college but has lived in Los Angeles for two decades and has a wife and two young daughters. Although he considered himself a political "independent," he said he usually votes Democrat. His more progressive sensibilities came from his experience of not being able to find a job in California that would pay enough to keep his family afloat and stay on top of mounting medical bills. He said he thought the government should "have more of a responsibility to help those who need help," and he tells us that he wishes that state and federal agencies would create more jobs and assist the homeless. He strongly opposes guns and thinks that society has a long way to go before it reaches racial equality. He appreciates that California is a lot less overtly racist than his home state of Texas but laments the various racial "microaggressions" he has endured while living in the Golden State, including some at the hands of Latinos and other people of color.

When discussing immigration, Howard expressed some progressive opinions and made sure to tell us that he sympathizes with the plight of the undocumented. For example, when asked about how immigrants contribute to the California economy, he made sure we understood that he disagreed with people who portray immigrants as an economic burden, noting: "The immigrants that I've known, and even immigrants that I've not known but just seen, interacted with on a surface level, they may be doing jobs, they're hardworking. . . . Again, they're hardworking, and they are contributing to the economy, because they're paying in their taxes, they're spending their money locally."

In this, Howard didn't see immigration as a problem per se. He even complained that politicians, especially Trump, attempt to scapegoat immigrants for political gain. He noted, "This is a made-up problem, to garner votes for people on one side or the other." He believed that undocumented immigration suddenly became a problem in conservative circles because it became non-European, explaining, "Immigration has been going on since this country was founded, before this country was a country, people were immigrants. But they were immigrating from different places. It was never an issue." When asked about how immigrants shape the culture of Los Angeles, he took a national perspective and explained that immigrants tend to hold onto or "stay true" to their culture: "But in reality, I think that's the definition of what the US is supposed to be. It's supposed to be a number of different cultures, so it's complicated. But if you're asking me my personal opinion, I think they contribute to being culturally rich and diverse, and you can't get enough of that."

Still, later in the interview when thinking about the broader politics of the current moment, Howard brings up the undocumented specifically, noting, "I wouldn't say that I have a problem with someone who is undocumented or illegal. I think that the problem comes in where you hear a family talk about . . . well, they're separated families. [They say], 'My father immigrated here illegally, and settled in and had a family, so the children were born US citizens, but ICE comes along and gets possession of the father and deports him.' And they've effectively separated family. That's not a good thing."

At this point, Howard seems much like many of the pro-immigrant respondents who lamented family separations and called for immigration reform. However, he continues:

> But you knew that game before. And I can't . . . I can be upset with the methods, but I can't be upset that the laws are followed. I think it's a law in the hands of the wrong people that can be used in a very discriminatory manner, but it's still the law of the land. So, I think for a lot of people it's a sketchy subject, a touchy subject. But the way I see it is in black-and-white, you've got to follow the law. And if you happen to get caught, there's going to be consequences, and you've got to be ready for that.

In this case, Howard had a clear sense that immigrants, including undocumented ones, contribute to the economy through their "hard work" and that they enrich the state. However, undocumented immigrants, by nature of being "illegal," created a clear boundary for him. While he could express sympathy for these immigrants personally, he felt that they should be subject to consequences for not following the rule of law. To him, immigrants were hardworking and often good people who happen to be "living a really hard life," but at the end of the day, they were "illegal" and had to face those consequences.

Howard's response to the issue of immigration was rife with contradictions. On the one hand, he made clear that he had immigrant friends and empathized with the plight of undocumented persons. He was troubled by family separations. Yet he also acknowledged that his empathy had a limit and did not supersede his commitment to the rule of law. Laws had consequences. At no time did he consider that immigration laws needed to be reformed or might be unfair. His reasoning was that while he could be sympathetic to the conditions of the undocumented, they still needed to face legal consequences.

Another expression of bounded blame emerged when respondents expressed the idea that the undocumented, simply by being unauthorized, were already morally suspect or even criminal. For example, Aisha was working freelance in marketing, and told us that she sometimes votes for independent candidates if they seem more progressive than the Democratic alternatives. When asked to describe her political worldview, she stated that she is "more liberal." She continued, "I guess I would be distinguished as a little more socialist in thinking, like free health care, free education for all, free post-secondary education." When asked about racial diversity in California, Aisha noted, "People of color in this country have had a rough time . . . economically, socially. All people of color get labeled, get mistreated, get profiled more so than others."

She lamented how the police treat "people of color" and noted that minorities have often been mislabeled and mistreated in society. Still, she explained, she did not think White people were bad because she lives her life "trying to see God in all people." Later, when reflecting on California's social problems, Aisha further expressed her progressive tendencies by telling us how bothered she was by income inequality in the Golden State: "For one of the richest states, at least supposedly, to have the biggest rate of poverty is actually an embarrassment, I feel, like, because it doesn't make any sense for a state with celebrities and all these corporations, things that we have here to . . . have so many people sleeping in tents . . . for me that's a problem."

When asked about immigration, she conveyed a great deal of empathy, stating, "People who are immigrant families are worried about being separated from their families, and it's heartbreaking. It's heartbreaking to hear about. We hear about kids being held in small rooms and mistreated. That's not something that I would do." Still, her warmth toward immigrants waned a bit when asked how immigrants shape the economy. To this, she explained that she was worried that the undocumented "work hard" but get paid under the table and thus do not really contribute to public coffers. "It's a little bit different because there is no tax," she said, suggesting that this type of immigrant labor does not contribute as much as formal labor.

Toward the end of the interview, when asked what "American" means to her, Aisha brought up the undocumented to emphasize the idea that they are not fully American and suggested their intentions were morally suspect:

> That's a trick question. Okay, why am I an American, I say? Well, I'm born and raised here, but then I have to say somebody who wasn't born here, wasn't raised here, can that person not be an American? I mean, of course, someone who was not born or raised here, of course they can. It's just like, what does it mean to be . . . I don't know how to say it . . . to be a French citizen? If I go through whatever process to legally get that denotation, I deserve to have it. Now, if I sneak into the country and I'm undocumented, I can be working and all that stuff, I can have friends and family here, but if I'm flying under the radar, how can I be a proud citizen of that country if I'm flying under the radar? That's kind of how I look at it.
>
> So if you're born here, raised here, cool, but if you were not. [If you] in youth immigrated to America, and let's say, you . . . you pay your dues, you've gone through whatever it is to become a citizen or you're . . . you're working on them, you know, to me, should you be considered American? Yes. If you . . . you paid your dues. If you don't pay dues, again, I look at it like if the tables were turned, if I go to some other country and I'm just hiding out or whatever the case, and I don't go through what they say, "Here are our rules," then I don't deserve

to be called a Spanish citizen, or a French citizen, or whatever. I think that should be standard across the globe. That's just my thing.

Aisha noted that the "rules" of the country should be followed in order to become truly American. She suggests that those that "sneak in" cannot be fully American or likely "don't deserve" to be because they did not follow the rules and "pay their dues." In this way, she restricts ideas of Americanness and belonging to only those that are legal, who have "paid their dues" by obtaining legal status or were born in the United States. She saw a bright line between the good, potentially American documented immigrants and the bad un-American undocumented immigrants. The boundaries of legal status played an important part in how Aisha blamed immigrants. So despite her more progressive politics, she believed that legal status was a sort of litmus test for immigrant belonging.

Ultimately, these respondents conveyed a lot of sympathy for immigrants and even valued their contributions. They could see immigrants, including the undocumented, as "hard workers" and "good" people, but their support seemed to stop there. Documentation created a bright red line and delimited the boundaries of further support. It was as if their progressive politics had a limit—the law—regardless of its justness.

Some respondents thought about "fairness" and the law when thinking about the undocumented. They suggested that undocumented immigrants that came into the country by "breaking the law" had not waited their proper turn in line. For example, Qiang, a registered Democrat, told us that immigration was a net good for society because immigrants contribute to the local economy. But he drew a clear boundary when it came to the undocumented, noting: "You try to . . . um . . . break into a country and you're not allowed to, or not legally . . . uh . . . documented to come here because some people . . . uh . . . died to come to this country . . . uh . . . where some people try to sneak into this country, and it's not fair. And if somebody had to die to come to this country as opposed to . . . uh . . . somebody just trying to sneak into this country by building tunnels or whatever. And . . . um . . . you know, it's just not a fair opportunity for everybody." This sense of unfairness was echoed by many other respondents who suggested that undocumented immigrants somehow "skipped the line" or "cut in line" and got to the United States without the proper documentation.

Let's briefly consider the issue of "paying one's dues" or "waiting in line." Those who arrived before 1972, like Cresencio and his family, had a relatively easy path to authorized status. Family-sponsored wait times were not as long as they are now,[31] and some fortunate braceros, like Cresencio's father, were sponsored by their employers. Those immigrants without access to an employer- or family-based status adjustment but who arrived before 1982 could take advantage of the amnesty provisions in the IRCA, signed in 1986 by President Reagan. They just needed to show proof of continuous presence, pay a fine, and display "good moral character."[32] This policy was a game changer for many Latino immigrants, including those in Cresencio's extended network.

But in the 1990s, the visas became much harder to obtain as demand increased, and the cap on annual family reunification and employer visas from heavily sending states, such as Mexico, barely inched upward. At the same time, congress passed a set of policies that made those who came without inspection subject to re-entry bans of up to ten years,"[33] even if they were married to a citizen or had given birth to one. The bureaucratic protocols in place after the 1990s made "the line" longer, stricter, and riskier.

Today, those seeking to apply for a family visa in Mexico will likely wait decades before they see movement in their applications. The Cato Institute notes that, in cases where applicants are not spouses, children, or parents of US citizens, sponsors "will die before their immigrant relatives can migrate."[34] And any person who crosses into the United States without a visa or inspection is subject to fines, deportation, and the prospect of a decade or more apart from loved ones in the United States, even if they seek to adjust their status. Asylum cases are routinely denied at the border, and those that are processed have no clear path to adjustment, often leaving migrants in a liminal legal status.[35] Altogether, this creates a system where one can spend decades living, working, and studying in the United States without papers and without a viable option for status adjustment.

Still, many imbue the idea of "the line" and "waiting one's turn" with moral judgment. For Qiang and others, undocumented status is proof of immorality rather than a symptom of broader issue connected to the byzantine and neocolonial structure of citizenship and immigration policy. Many people make these logical leaps despite having empathy for immigrants' conditions because they elevate noncompliance to a defining feature of an immigrant's character—even though immigration is actually a geopolitical process rife with contradictions and inequalities. It cannot be reasonably compared to waiting in line at a school or in a store, and yet many still do rely on this association.[36]

THE MIDDLE CLASS EVENTUALLY PAYS

Some in our sample tried to reconcile their more progressive sensibilities on immigration with their understanding that the middle class would somehow eventually have to pay for the cost of the undocumented. Even respondents who told us that immigrants contributed to the economy through their hard work had a sense that immigrants and their children would in the future end up costing the middle class in direct and indirect ways. These respondents saw the issue as a hidden cost and eventual social harm that would specifically affect an already squeezed middle class. In other words, they blamed the undocumented, however abstractly, for potentially burdening the middle-class in particular.

For instance, Sun, an Asian American in his late twenties, was born and raised in Fresno in a "farming family" that was mainly working-class. He remembered living with his eight siblings and parents in a two-bedroom apartment for many years and working out in the fields, usually after school, weekends, and in the summer. He started college at a nearby state school but dropped out when he realized he could not make enough money to support his new family. At the time of the interview, he was taking an online course to finish his degree and working a full-time job as a mechanic.

During his interview, Sun noted that politicians, especially Trump, talk about immigration as a "major problem." He especially resented the criminalization of immigrants in conservative media. To him, immigrants were like his parents and the incredibly hard-working undocumented farmworkers that he worked alongside for many years in the fields. He believed that US-born voters and politicians should "try to put themselves in others' shoes . . . if you were trying to escape something horrible . . . what would you do?" He continued, "Morally, well, these people, they are suffering in their country, they want a better life. Who is it that we should not allow people to seek a better future?" And he laments that immigration laws have become far too rigid. He also disagreed with the framing that immigrants steal American jobs. He told us, "No immigrant is just going to come in and take what we do. It's . . . that's just some kinda stupid myth going on [that] people are saying." Sun held many of the views that immigration advocates empathize with and, in this way, diverged from those that understand citizenship and documentation procedures within the "law is the law" frame.

Yet later in his interview, Sun hesitated, especially when considering the increasing cost of living in the Central Valley. He told us that he had recently heard that the governor was looking into creating a way to fund health care for all residents in the state. He was upset by this, noting, "They're going to fund $20 million into providing health care for [undocumented] immigrants. I saw that, and I was pissed. I'm not paying for It. I can barely afford for me and my family. . . . And so, I'm like, I'm cool with that, but help us too, you know?" He then proceeded to detail how difficult it was to get by with the increasing cost of living in the Golden State. Now, to be clear, the state of California did move to expand health care coverage options for low-income undocumented immigrants in 2024, but it is unclear that working Californians, particularly those born in the United States into the middle class, would have to pay for it.[37]

In short, Sun expressed a great deal of sympathy for immigrants, including undocumented ones. He saw them as exceptionally hard workers and important for diversity in the Central Valley. Yet he also saw a tradeoff between what the state could spend on immigrants versus what they could spend on those in the working and middle classes. He seemed to think that providing the undocumented with the services they required, such as better access to health care, would come at a potential future cost and potentially cause harm to the squeezed middle. Sun could see immigrants as hard workers who helped the economy writ large but still see the cost of their needs and services falling on him.

Lori, an African American respondent, saw the economic burden of immigration a bit differently, but agreed that the overall cost could eventually hurt the middle class. She considered herself a Democrat, which was tied to her identity. She explained, "I guess growing up, that's what African Americans were voting. I really didn't have a say. . . . 'You're a Democrat.'" Lori had a technical certificate in radiology and had spent many years working in the field, though she recently moved on to work in a more administrative capacity at a nursing home. She sometimes works part-time providing elder care to help make ends meet. When asked what economic class she considered herself, she stated, "I'd say working class, because we no longer have a middle class. That's pretty much gone." Indeed, she complained that rich people in particular have been given tax cuts, which she saw as unfair and leading to growing inequality. She faulted Republicans, noting, "They want that two-class system. The lower and upper. No in-between with the tax cuts. And everything for the middle class is really being eliminated."

When asked how she felt about the economy, she continued to lament that manufacturing opportunities for the middle class seem to be closing. It is this specific view of the economy and the government that seemed to color her understanding of immigrants' impact in California. She continued, "I feel that . . . I'm not against immigrants, but I'm against people that are here illegally. And I feel that society . . . because they misuse them, because they don't have papers, they make the salaries bad for everybody." Lori's antipathy was based on the fact that the undocumented seemed to drive down the wages of others. She noted that the system is exploitative and treats immigrants unfairly but then further argues that this mistreatment shrinks the salaries of native-born workers.

And while there is research that considers the extent to which immigrants displace work for low-skilled US-born laborers,[38] Lori felt that immigrants were a threat to the middle class as well, noting:

> I have a friend that owned her own home health care business, and her client passed away. She worked with seniors. And now she's looking for a job, and every person in home health care, the agencies, wants to pay her like $11, $12. And she was like, "I didn't even get paid that in the nineties." And it seems that it's not comparable. . . . If you're trying to pay people $12 an hour . . . that's nothing. That's not $100 a day. So, it's difficult, and I feel that because they don't have papers, and they work under the table, then it pushes the salary down for everyone.

Lori viewed the undocumented as having a larger social cost for even the middle- and upper-working-class. Later in interview she would reaffirm to us her appreciation of immigration writ large but then also convey her reservations about the undocumented. She told us, "There's a lot of great things that immigrants bring. It's like a melting pot. . . . So, immigrants bring in a lot of culture, they broaden your horizon. They make you think out of the box. And I feel that they shape the state of California, but again you have to do it the right way, and you have to do it the legal way." Indeed, Lori would also later tell us that if "you come here illegally, you are breaking the law."

The preponderance of evidence on undocumented immigration and salaries suggests that immigrants serve as a complement to native job opportunities and do not necessarily "take jobs" from those born in the United States. There is also a great deal of evidence that the entrance of immigrants into a region helps to grow the local economy, creating more opportunities for others.[39] Still, the research on immigrants' impact on low-skilled labor is mixed, and scholars have suggested that immigrants might displace lower-educated African Americans from employment opportunities. What is clear, however, is that the idea of immigrants taking jobs or depressing salaries is a message heard beyond conservative media.[40] Lori offers an example of a Democrat who holds these views as well.

While Lori was concerned with how immigrants impact salaries, Rose registered concerns about the impact of the undocumented on local government coffers. An Asian American Democrat and self-described "liberal," she told us of the various ways that immigrants bring diversity to Los Angeles. Yet when asked about the undocumented specifically, her tone shifted as she expressed more ambivalence about the issue:

> I don't know, you know, I think that sometimes people are so desperate, you know, that they just have to do what they have to do. But by the same token, I do understand the view of people, they're saying they're undocumented, they're illegal, you know, my niece-in-law, bless her, you know, and she's up in Napa, where a lot of undocumented are, you know, are up there because, you know, they work, and she is White. And she complains bitterly about how they do, you know, take up a lot of resources, you know, that the government has so, you know . . . and . . . but you know, that's . . . that's her views because she's in it, you know, she's smack in the middle of it, and her kids are, you know, [at] school with all these kids who don't speak English, you know, and, you know, it's, you know . . . it's just, again, the differences as they are taking up a lot of resources or whether it really is . . . yeah, I think that . . . yeah, they do . . . they do, but it's because we offer it, and it's . . . it's there for them to take, you know, right? I mean, it is to help them, you know?

Rose seemed clearly supportive of immigrants and saw them as important to California. Yet when she spoke of the undocumented, she was much more ambivalent. Stating several times "I don't know" and peppering her answers with some hesitancy at the end, she uses a vicarious discursive tactic to suggest opposition to the undocumented. She does not directly say that she thinks immigrants use up resources. Instead, she told us the story of her niece to suggest stereotypes about economic burden. This is similar to Lori's telling us about her friend's inability to get paid a fair wage. These respondents offered seemingly biased assessments of immigrants without fully owning their views and without seeming outright biased.[41]

To some respondents, the idea of immigrants costing society by using resources coincided with a broader understanding of economic scarcity and tradeoffs, now or in the future. Dina, an Asian American respondent in Los Angeles who described herself as liberal, told us that she empathizes with the undocumented and understands how they might come "illegally" without proper documentation, especially if they are fleeing a dangerous situation. She noted that she doesn't think that "they're taking away from anyone, like here, like any American citizens . . . uh . . . taking any . . . any benefits away from anyone . . . I mean, we should help them, and as far as, like, them taking people's jobs, they're really doing jobs that Americans don't want to do anyway." She felt much empathy for them and noted that they are only really here to work and be safe. Yet quickly, in the same sentence she wondered aloud. "They just need to be . . . they just want to be safe. They just want a safe place to sleep. So, but at the same time, yes, I mean, it's like, where are . . . where are we gonna house these people? And how do we care for them? We already have our . . . enough homeless people as it is. I really have no idea." Dina did not display the anger that Sun did when he wondered why he had to pay for undocumented health coverage. However, her interview still suggests ambivalence and a seeming trade off that pits the cost of the undocumented as a harm because they take resources from other needy constituents, such as the state's unhoused population.

In some ways, Dina created an imaginary tradeoff and future harm that she saw as emerging as more undocumented immigrants arrive. Similarly, Oscar, a Latino from Los Angeles and another self-described liberal, saw the tradeoff as not simply involving resources that the undocumented need now but as broader "crowding up" of city spaces.

He said he did not think that immigration was a problem at all but then stated: "Illegal immigration, I would say, I can understand how that can be a problem. Because there's only so much space, only so much resources for so many people. If people are coming and restricted, without being documented, that's crowding up the country. That's more people in schools, more people in jails. That's crowding up everything, so I can understand how that could be a problem. But I'm not going to say it's just a bad thing, immigration. I think there are good things too, especially if people come legally and they have a skill and they can work here."

Later in the interview, Oscar told us that he knows of undocumented immigrants who came to the United States and work hard but get a bad rap just because they lack papers. He sympathized with them but still considered them to be potential burdens and to bring with them costs to society.

Overall, the ambivalent respondents broadly recognized the many benefits of immigration in California and strongly appreciated how exceptionally "hardworking" the undocumented were. Yet their support seemed to have a limit. While the amount of sympathy they held for the undocumented varied, many respondents left the door open to contemplating stereotypes and stoking broader fears about the moral and economic costs of this population. Their pro-immigration stance was bounded, with documentation status serving as an important limit to their broader liberal or progressive political tendencies.

Conclusion

In 1994, while Pete Wilson was running for reelection as governor of California, his campaign ran a highly publicized advertisement. Using grainy black-and-white highway footage and foreboding music, the ad began, "They keep coming. Two million illegal immigrants in California. The federal government won't do anything to stop them at the border but requires us to spend billions to take care of them." In a second ad, Wilson's campaign used the same grainy footage to note that "illegals" come the "wrong way" and break the law. Riding the wave of anti-immigrant sentiment in the state, Wilson easily won reelection.

To some, 1994 seems like eons ago. Yet Wilson's legacy lives on in many ways. In downtown San Diego, a bronze statue of him welcomes shoppers to an urban retail area. Even though activists, including

Dolores Huerta, have called for its removal, many support it and it remains to this day.[42] Wilson has become a welcome commentator in many congressional district events, using the issue of immigration to boost support for Republican candidates in the Central Valley and along the southern coast.[43] Just as state legislators declared California a sanctuary state, others used Wilson's politics to oppose this move and warn of an immigrant takeover.[44] In 2024, a state assembly candidate ran a series of television ads in Southern California titled "Governor Pete Wilson was right."[45]

Today, a significant minority of California politicians proudly support the aggressive Trumpian immigration actions characteristic of his second term. For example, some sheriffs and mayors have encouraged local efforts that violate California state sanctuary policies, especially those limiting local law enforcement from cooperating with federal immigration agencies.[46] As they do so, these elected officials often paint California's undocumented as criminals and undesirables, reminding us all that the Golden State is not entirely blue. More recently, conservative organizations have become more visible and unapologetic throughout the state, especially in the Central Valley and the inland regions of Southern California, with reports of Confederate flags flying over schools.[47] In this context, such a flag might be read both as a signal of White supremacy premised on anti-Blackness and the romanticization of slavery and as a display of anti-immigrant resentment.

Let us recall Cresencio, who came to the United States in the 1970s to join his bracero father. Today a grandfather of five, he suffers from injuries related to a lifetime of factory and manual labor. He and his wife have difficulty meeting the rising cost of living in the state. Still, he feels lucky and indebted. To many of the respondents, his story might represent the embodiment of the American Dream, proof that California is a place for hardworking immigrants. Some might even use his story as a way to hit back at Trumpian immigration politics, which are often seen as extensions of Wilson's stances.

Yet others might see Cresencio's story, and others like his, as greyer. To be sure, Cresencio was lucky. He migrated at a time when legalization processes were more lenient. Unauthorized migrants coming more recently face the likelihood of remaining undocumented for decades, with little legal reprieve. Their stories, and to an extent Cresencio's, tell of exploitation and uncertainty but also of hope and faith. To understand just how respondents made sense of this nuance, we must examine how they deal with contradictions and how they try to reconcile them.

In this chapter, we have focused on how participants grapple with issues around immigration. We found many respondents venerated the hard work of immigrants, including the undocumented, viewing them as the embodiment of the American Dream and proof that California is a land *for* immigrants. We also found many individuals narrowed the idea of the American Dream when referencing immigrants, defining it simply as an ability to labor on US soil, the chance to come and work rather than getting a "white picket fence" or an opportunity to gain economic stability. In this way, they could see immigrants as dream achievers who, despite having to endure occasional exploitative work conditions or being stuck in the bottom rungs of the labor market, were still better off than they would have been if they had stayed in their home country. After all, the Golden State offered more opportunities and was freer than Michoacán or Manila. In this way, we argue, people often downplay the inequality experienced by immigrants or see it as tolerable.

Respondents' sentiments make sense in terms of exceptional framing and spatial comparison. By seeing immigrants as exceptional workers and embodiments of the American Dream, respondents often overlooked the fact that many immigrants, documented or not, still had not achieved economic stability in an unequal California. Reasoning that immigrants were better off here than in their own home country allowed them to dismiss contrasts with the US born, even when they revealed how immigrants faced vast inequalities, cruel labor conditions, and limited mobility. The practices we describe allowed respondents to look beyond inequality, to park it on the side, and see immigrants as "still making it" in the land of sanctuary.

Our findings also reveal how legal status can serve as a marker of moral worth, even among those who see themselves as generally pro-immigrant. Many respondents, including some self-identified progressives, linked undocumented status with potential criminality. The vast majority arrived at these conclusions without reverting to the language of "cultural threat" or the dehumanizing anti-immigrant language peddled by the right.[48] Instead, they hesitated, hedging their words and suggesting that the difficulties of undocumented life could lead some immigrants to engage in criminal behavior just to survive.

When respondents linked the undocumented with crime, bounded blame came into full display. By making this connection, many could wonder aloud about whether undocumented immigrants' behavior was contributing to their difficulties, however imagined, and they could question why the undocumented didn't "just get in line." Discourse about undocumented immigration offers a window into the limits of immigration support and shows how ambivalence can serve as a stand-in for bias in a progressive state.

Before moving on to the next chapter, a note on how respondents imagined the race of immigrants. By and large, when asked to conjure up a picture of a working-class immigrant or an undocumented immigrant, respondents imagined a Latino, especially a Mexican person. In contrast, when they pictured immigrant entrepreneurs and economic contributors, Asians often came to mind. While this racialized imagery matches some of laboring classes' demographics, it also distorts ideas about Latinos and Latinidad.[49] It obscures the fact that Latinos are also professionals, artists, and part of a vibrant middle-class whose contributions shape the state far beyond field and factory work. This type of racialization positions low-wage laborers as distinct and unable to offer creative and dynamic social, economic, and political contributions to California. In this way, Latinidad becomes flattened, understood as synonymous with certain kinds of racialized labor and nothing else.

Moreover, the fact that Latinos were significantly more prevalent than Asians in discussions of immigration shows how the latter group can easily fade into the background. While Asians, like Latinos, are often understood to be perpetual foreigners, our findings show that they were rarely brought to mind among non-Asians. Beyond discussions of entrepreneurship, Black, White, and Latino interviewees simply overlooked this group, and instead spoke at length about Latino labor migration. These findings reflect broader research that shows how the experiences of Asian immigrants fall to the wayside during discussions about immigration.

Taken together, the findings presented in this chapter reveal the limits of belonging in a diverse state. They show how immigrants are seen in contradictory ways, both as achievers of the dream and as potentially suspect. Immigrants make California great, diverse, and productive but perhaps also socially burdened. By holding on to these contradictions, respondents could see themselves as mainly pro-immigrant and as living in a mainly pro-immigrant land that opens doors for all. And with this understanding, it became easier for respondents to normalize the inequality that immigrants faced—to see beyond it.

In the next chapter, we continue to examine how people make sense of inequality by exploring how respondents engaged in discussions about the future. This approach, we argue, also provides insight into how they understand their own sense of belonging in a state that always feels two steps ahead of the rest.

CHAPTER FIVE

BELONGING IN THE FUTURE

Living with large and often growing inequality is not just a feature of Los Angeles or California, it is a centerpiece of life in the United States. This is as true in big cities as it is in towns throughout the country, raising questions not simply about how folks understand inequality but also how long they believe it must be endured. If you see growing inequalities as part of an economic or political cycle, then, arguably, it will pass and give way to better conditions later. However, if you see inequality as built into the system, into our social structures, into our state policies and power arrangements, then you might see it as a defining feature of our society, with no escape, no reprieve. We thus need to focus not simply on how people think about the present, with its widening divides, but also how they envision the future, including the fate of their communities and regions.

In this chapter, we zero in on how people talk about and imagine the future. In chapter 2, we looked at how people think about their individual future trajectories by examining how they perceived economic inequality and their personal chances at upward social mobility. Here, we focus on how folks imagine the collective future of their communities and the state more broadly. This analytical focus, we argue, offers a window into foundational questions about how people in the precarious middle class make sense of how inequality evolves and develops over time. It also reveals a great deal about how people think about belonging. By narrating stories about what is to come, respondents also painted pictures of who they thought California's future was supposed to be for.

https://doi.org/10.7758/uybx4321.4604

We argue that the future is a place where the intersectional nature of inequalities around race, class, and immigration become pronounced, as people shift from thinking about individual experiences to collective trends. Some respondents, we found, imagined a future of economic growth that included less inequality and more diversity. For this group, the future seemed to be one that lifted all boats across communities, with more high-rises, more job creation, more diversity, and many more tech booms. These respondents engaged in exceptional framing about the future. They imagined that California's future would bring the returns that the California present had not, mainly through technology and economic windfalls. They saw any social pessimism connected to inequality in California as temporary, bound by the here and now and sure to dissipate or at least feel less acute in the future.

We found that region mattered. Respondents in the Central Valley were much more likely than LA residents to see a gold-tinted picture of the future, mainly because they saw the Central Valley as somehow "on the verge" of positive developments. Many believed California's agricultural towns and Central Valley cities were poised to create the state's next big economic and social boom because they had developed at a slower pace, behind Los Angeles and the Bay Area, where growth was seen to have come too hard, too fast, and too unevenly. This sense of imminence paired with comparably fewer visible manifestations of extreme inequality, such as homelessness, made discourses about the future among people in the Central Valley less foreboding, even among Black and Latino respondents.

However, we also found that a smaller group of respondents saw the future as rife with contradictions, with inequalities of such a magnitude that it would fundamentally reshape who could remain and be visible—and who could belong—in California. The state's increasingly unlivable major cities, rapid displacement, and the homelessness crisis—all with pronounced racial dimensions—colored respondents' visions of the future. It seemed that, to these respondents, who were mainly but not exclusively Black and Latino, there was something about talking about the future and inequality in an intersectional way that made them less likely to naturalize and minimize social divides. Some of these respondents even wondered if there would be any Black communities left in the Golden State when it was all said and done. Still others wondered if Latinos, with their demographic majority, would ever be considered agentic drivers of the state's future rather than omnipresent but invisibilized workers.

In the following pages, we describe why discussions about the future matter, noting how the future has long been an important window to understanding how folks make sense of the present. We then examine respondents who had comparatively positive renditions of California's future, seeing the inequalities of today as something that could resolve themselves in time, especially as technology lifted all communities. We show how respondents relied heavily on exceptional framing and spatial comparison, along with a fair amount of abstraction, to create a narrative of what was to come. We then analyze the tensions embedded in these renditions of California's future, showing that many Black respondents and some Latino respondents were wary about an Asian and White future that erased Black presence and invisibilized or even demonized the omnipresence of Latinos.

Inequality and the Stakes of the Future

Sociologists have spent a great deal of attention analyzing the present and the past. Much less research has focused on the future. This is not to say that social theorists have ignored the future entirely. W. E. B. Du Bois, for instance, critiqued the utopian linking of social progress to time and instead cautioned that we might actually be moving toward what he sometimes referred to as the "ugly future."[1] He contended that the future is more of a dialectic between the hope of a better world and the disappointment of past failures. French philosopher Simone Weil came to the same conclusion, claiming that "the future is made of the same stuff as the present" to underscore how current social dynamics, if not addressed, would inevitably continue into the future.[2] Closer to home, in *City of Quartz*, Mike Davis examines the future of Los Angeles from the vantage point of the abandoned socialist community of Los Llanos. He suggests that it is from there that we can glean more about the future of inequality in the city. He asserts that "the best place to view Los Angeles of the next millennium is from the ruins of its alternative future."[3]

Sociologists have increasingly taken up the idea that a lot can be gleaned from discourses about the future, whether people are talking about their outlook on their own lives or more broadly about what the world could or should look like. And, within the subfield of science and technology studies, scholars are beginning to think critically about the sociological importance of the future in a number of ways.[4] This "sociology of the future" or "sociology of expectations" is interested in the future as a terrain of struggle in and of itself but also as an arena that shapes the present. Cynthia Selin offers the term "anticipatory knowledge" to make sense of knowledge forms and practices that are oriented toward the future but shape human behavior in the present."[5] At the risk of sounding like social science operates in the realm of science fiction, scholars examining these issues hold that the future can also "become the present" because beliefs about the future shape how people behave in the present in ways that do actually shape the future. This is why images of the future and discourses of the future are quite important to researchers, especially those who take seriously the agency of social actors to mold the world around them.[6]

Examining people's thoughts about the future can offer a distinct perspective on how they understand the world and their place in it. Looking at the perceptions of race and demographics in the future, Michael Rodríguez-Muñiz coined the term "forecasting," which he defines as telling a "story about the future, what it means and how one should feel about it."[7] We find that the future is a terrain of interpretation and disputes over symbolic power, or as Rodríguez-Muñiz notes, "forecasting is a practice of world making." Similarly, as sociologist Richard Tutton notes, "discursive constructions of the future are not simply imaginative in the traditional sense but are thoroughly social practices. These practices are in turn implicated in forming certain materialities and with letting loose both intended and unintended consequences."[8] Thinking about who gets to belong in the future is just one of the areas where we see what is at stake when people imagine the future.

This epistemological shift toward the future may shed light on the fundamental questions about inequality and belonging in California addressed in this book, partly because California is a place that has been constructed as always, already in the future. Indeed, in political discourse and in the popular imaginary, California is often depicted as the nation's "tomorrowland." Headlines like NPR's "California Is the Future of American Politics" or sayings like "as goes California, so goes the nation" help sustain the idea of California as already in the future socially, demographically, politically, and economically. Los Angeles politicians Kevin de Leon and Anthony Rendon summed it up well this way: "California was not a part of this nation when its history began, but we are clearly now the keeper of its future."[9] Asking questions about the future in a place like California begs the question: If California is the future, what kind of future is it?

More broadly, we suggest that perceptions about the future of a place can also offer a window into more foundational questions about inequality and belonging in the present. For example, what does it mean when people imagine a future with increasing inequality and when they see this future as unfixable, as inevitable? How might we understand belonging when people cannot imagine people like themselves thriving or even existing in the future? Ultimately, we are interested in the worlds revealed as interviewees make sense of the future of inequality in their neighborhoods, their cities, and the state.

Exceptional Framing and Tech-Driven Futures

Most of the people we interviewed imagined an economically booming future for their cities and the state, which is not surprising given the ubiquitous discourse about California's economic prowess, especially its leadership in building the economy of the future. While elsewhere in the country, many have concerns about whether places will bounce back from times of severe economic downturn, the dominant narrative we heard about California was that it was somehow shock resistant. In other words, interviewees believed that while the state might take hits, it was, after all, already seen as in the future and, thus, did not have to reckon with the issues that other states might have to deal with, including reorienting their economic development plan in the context of postindustrialization or going green. In this way, respondents saw California as an economic model to be followed, with its future-oriented economy featuring self-driving cars, gig economies, and housing bubbles that only rarely burst.

This narrative was pervasive among respondents, even as they were also aware of growing economic inequalities and wondered about who would benefit from development. Ang, a respondent from Fresno, was asked: "Looking ten to twenty years into the future, how do you imagine your community to be?" He explained: "Um, in twenty years, I see it's gonna be more developed. Probably, people with, like . . . uh . . . probably a lot more people with, like, better income. Like, a lot more money. Um, maybe people, like a lot of people from, like, the . . . I guess, like, the new generation. Where they have these, like, good-paying jobs or something like that in tech or whatever. And probably, like, fancy cars, more development."

This booming future was often linked to perceptions of the role of Big Tech in the state, which is not surprising given its prominence in and outside of California. Indeed, it is difficult to overstate the importance of tech in the narration of California's future for several reasons. First, tech itself is an industry that is always oriented to the future, marketing itself as bringing the future that we may not even be able to imagine to us in the present. Second, tech makes up a huge share of California's economy. Although defining the boundaries of the tech industry is challenging, estimates suggest it accounts for roughly 17 percent of California's overall GDP—about twice the share of its GDP at the national level and second only to the state of Washington.[10] So materially, it is certainly the case that overinvestment in tech is driving the state's economic boom in the same way that some would argue it is driving inequality. Finally, to the extent that tech is an industry that we might place geographically at all, its home, its birthplace, its primary physical geography, is Silicon Valley, even though scholars have argued that people often reduce the tech industry to this one place in a manner that obscures the real ways the tech industry is shifting local economies and social dynamics around the country.[11] In any case, tech then is one of many reasons why California, a state that has already thought of itself as foreshadowing the future for the country, becomes solidified as such.

Laura, who grew up in East Los Angeles in primarily Latino working-class neighborhoods, was one of many participants that pointed to technology when asked about the future of California, explaining, "I only see it going upwards . . . especially since like, you know, we have all the big tech companies here, we're innovating." Another respondent, Joy, echoed this sentiment when describing the future of her neighborhood in West Los Angeles:

> Oh God, it will be one of the most booming, tech driven, I don't know how much more can expand because of where it's . . . but oh man, I think diverse, but like a modern Silicon Beach type of situation, probably more younger . . . a lot more younger people will be in the neighborhood, owing homes, all of that, but definitely one of the most

> progressive areas in LA, hands down . . . YouTube headquarters is there. Google headquarters is there. Yahoo is there. All of these, I'm missing one, some of these big tech companies are all around here, so it's just natural.

Between 2020 and 2022, a number of large tech companies set up headquarters in Los Angeles. They joined some five hundred other tech companies already peppered throughout the Westside of the city in various neighborhoods now referred to as Silicon Beach. Some cities and towns around the area even began to use this technology reference in their marketing and promotion websites. On the website playavista.com, for example, boosters write "From titans like Google, Verizon and YouTube Space LA to creative powerhouses like 72andSunny and the University of Southern California's Institute of Creative Technologies, Playa Vista has become the Westside address of choice."[12]

Regardless of whether respondents lived this close to the tech companies, they often imagined California's economic growth as inextricably linked to the inevitable growth of the tech sector. Some respondents had a clear sense that technology could bring jobs and other forms of growth, while others were vaguer. Yet in the narratives of most respondents, the excitement about technology was palpable and linked to opportunity. As Jorge, who was born in Honduras but came to the United States when he was four years old, told us:

> I think . . . I think our economy's gonna be way better. I think the . . . the jobs are gonna be ten times better. Um, schools are gonna be ten times better. Everything's gonna be more educated, more better . . . because . . . uh . . . part of it has to do a lot with . . . um . . . technology. And technology . . . uh . . . has really taken over our lives. Like, you know what I mean? Now you . . . you could, like, do three . . . 3-D printing and stuff like that. You could build stuff, like, you know, with technology. You could own stuff; you could own businesses with just having technology. And you . . . you could even help . . . uh . . . across the country because you could send money, like, through technology. Like, basically everything. Like, you know what I mean? Get your money from your bank, you could do everything through technology.

Jorge, like Joy and others, saw California and especially the LA region as on an upward trajectory. Even when these respondents expressed uncertainty about the present, which had fewer opportunities for the middle class, they believed that the future was likely to offer opportunities that they assumed would lead to prosperity.

Let us reflect on this. For these respondents, the future was exceptional compared with the present. While present trends might look bad, with rich people getting richer and poor people getting poorer, the future would be different. Here, the individual optimism respondents used to describe their personal trajectories were projected onto an abstract future. Clearly, abstraction played an important role in these more gold-tinted renditions of the future, as many respondents could never clearly identify just how or through what causal mechanism technology would create an exceptional future. This abstract future, though, was able to save respondents from an anxious and uncertain present, with its high cost of living, including skyrocketing housing costs. Abstraction and exceptional framing of the future both worked to make the inequalities of today feel less stressful, less foreboding to respondents.

We found that even among respondents who were unsure about how they would fare personally in this new economy, many echoed this optimism. For instance, Howard—who supported his wife through serious health challenges while making ends meet as an Uber driver—at first appeared to be critical of major technology companies. However, as he envisioned the future of Los Angeles, he speculated that it would be "a harder place to live in the future financially." He continued:

> I just see prices continuing to rise and wages not rising to meet that. I think that people will probably be less connected socially. The interaction we're having now might not be as commonplace just because of how technology, and how people would rather not touch one another anymore. Maybe that's more for me, cool. But I think there will be good things as far as ease of life, it'll be easier to live here for those who can afford it. I think they're going to have some fantastic things going on with probably driverless cars and things of that nature. I don't see it as a dark future or anything like that.

Like others, Howard expressed reservations about the future and how affordable it might be for people like him in the upper-working class but quickly pivoted when he thought about the role of technology. The future might be uncertain, but it might also be one where technology provides "fantastic things," allowing for a more positive and parsimonious take on California's trajectory. In choosing to downplay the difficulties of life in the Golden State, Howard and others engaged in a sort of exceptional framing about an abstract "fantastic" future, which allowed them to maintain their idea of California as a place for innovation and opportunity.

On the surface, the future looks golden to many Californians, a narrative that aligned with the tropes they were likely told and told themselves. Although these narratives of technology-driven development and rising prosperity are especially pronounced in California, they are not unique to it. As sociologist and Black Studies scholar Ruha Benjamin warns: "The dominant story told by techno-utopianists to lull us to sleep is that the world's major crises can be solved with even more investment in their energy-intensive digital dreams, which usually also means less public participation and collective dreaming."[13] Indeed, in this vision of the future, tech would benefit everyone, even those who are systematically left out of such narratives and those who have fallen on tough times.

Of course, many of the respondents were not blind to the implications of the trends around them. Inequality was also at the front of their minds as they told us of their fears about being priced out of Los Angeles, increasing homelessness, and traffic congestion. Others were less worried about how present inequality might impact the future, and some thought the changes happening at the time might be signs of a good future to come. They explained that the increase in gentrification over time made the future look bleak and that there might be fewer opportunities for the middle class to make it. They also spoke of the economic changes that have come with technology and development in more "naturalized" and inevitable—but positive—terms. For example, Jason, who worked in the tech sector within the film industry, opined at length about how unaffordable Los Angeles was for lower-middle class residents like himself. He was unsure how long he could continue to live in Los Angeles given the cost. Yet when thinking about the future, he was somehow able to minimize the negative impact of continued gentrification and see the upside. He told us:

> Um, on that same block, this apartment . . . uh . . . this company came through and started building small houses . . . they're like three stories high, but each unit is, like, more than a million. So, I just feel like a lot

> of the properties are gonna come up more in the million. It's gonna be really diverse. Uh, we're gonna have . . . uh . . . young people living here, like, people who work in tech, people who work in, like, law firms . . . those kind of jobs . . . stuff like that. I think we'll see more younger families coming out here. Um, film people . . . I bet as well. I mean, I know . . . I know at least four other people that I work with in this neighborhood that live here. Um, so I just feel it's gonna be like that. Less people are gonna be like . . . uh . . . um . . . families who . . . who lived here in the nineties with kids 'cause all those people, the kids have grown up, a lot of them moved out, and the families don't want to deal with, like, the people, you know, the parents are still [living] there.

Jason believed that the myriad and entangled economic and demographic changes would give rise to a new neighborhood that looked much different from the old. It is interesting how rather than seeing these changes as having a negative impact that pushes families out, he reflected on the future as a sort of natural development, one where younger people who worked in tech would naturally move into homes and organically change the character of the place. Change was neither good nor bad. It was natural and inevitable as technological developments unfold.

Some respondents thought of the displacement of the less wealthy as the displacement of the less prepared, a kind of latent survival-of-the-fittest logic that deemed those that did not fit neatly into California's future as a mere casualty of an inevitable path toward greater development. For example, Ang, an Asian American from Fresno, forecasted the future of the region this way: "And then, like, the . . . I guess, the poor people, they're gonna have to, like, move elsewhere. East or whatever. Um, maybe . . . I think . . . I think the economy, like in this area, I think it's going to be . . . it's just going to be better. Because there's gonna be more people with more money coming in."

This idea of California's communities being on an upward trajectory, even if that involved the natural displacement of some communities, was present in interviews across race and region. Andrés, for example, had a similar way of imagining inequality in the future. A third-generation Mexican American, he had grown up in Texas but lived in an Eastside Latino working class suburb just outside Los Angeles proper. Like Ang,

Andrés saw the future as somehow resolving some of the current problems related to inequality. Using a kind of bounded blame logic, he told us: "When you look at Van Nuys, there's a lot of great communities and there's a lot of crappy communities within this one community. But that's the story of Southern California. Look at my area, there's nice homes and there's crappy homes that people just don't want to take care of. But I think in the future, it only has to be positive."

To Andrés, inequality is simply the story of Southern California, the way things work, in part because of the failings of those at the bottom who refuse to take care of their homes. Yet he believed technology would improve matters, even if that did not mean the elimination of inequality completely. He explained: "Here in Van Nuys, they're going to build some kind of a monorail down Van Nuys Boulevard. If you go to Van Nuys Boulevard right now, it's pretty much empty offices, empty buildings, feels more like a third-world country, where all you have is goods shops that are selling stuff outside. It's not a Beverly Hills . . . but I think that's going to improve a better group of businesspeople, they're going to open up better businesses and in turn it's going to hire more people."

Andrés thought that while inequality might still be with us in the future, it would be less present and visible, less of an issue when you consider all the improvements that technology would bring. By connecting offices, commerce, and communities, technology would somehow make Los Angeles' "third world country" tendencies feel like a thing of the past. While he did not explicitly mention immigrants, Andrés's reference to third world countries raises questions about how he imagines the role of immigrants—especially those from the Global South—in this technologically advanced future.

This uncomfortable tension between the idea of development as an ultimate good alongside the idea that some will be left behind, lingered in the air during most of our interviews, especially in Los Angeles. Even so, many respondents still envisioned California becoming increasingly wealthy and increasingly "better." Those who could not make it, the families with failing businesses, they claimed, would simply have to pack up and move because that is part of the natural path toward progress. In this way, many respondents believed that the future of California entailed a sort of social Darwinism that would ultimately lead to a brighter future—one where the likelihood of ongoing inequality was papered over.

Spatial Comparison and the Central Valley of Tomorrow

Perhaps the most optimistic future scenarios came from Central Valley respondents. More often than not, they painted a picture of the Central Valley's trajectory as booming and livable, where development would come at the right time. It was a vision of the future that was somehow protected from repeating the mistakes made in the state's larger cities, with their homeless epidemics and overcrowded freeways. This vision of the future, we argue, stems from the region's position as an in-between place.

Perched roughly equidistant and inland from the Bay Area and the Los Angeles metropolitan area, the Central Valley sits between, or perhaps outside, ideas of what California is supposed to be economically and culturally. We have discussed in previous chapters how the region has been an agricultural hub for at least a century. Indeed, early colonization efforts often touted the area as a farming utopia and a place ripe for development.[14] It is worth repeating that the region supplies nearly 40 percent of all fruits and vegetables grown in the United States.[15] Yet despite its important role in providing the food necessary for the social reproduction of the state and country, the Central Valley is often left out of the dominant narratives about California. The area is not one of the well-known cities of San Francisco, San Diego, or Los Angeles, nor is it on the tourists' beaten path. It is instead a kind of in-between place, literally and figuratively. This context helps explain why so many respondents talked about the region as a place where good things are still to come.

Repeatedly, respondents used spatial comparison to create a positive vision of the Central Valley's future. For instance, Marisa saw a future Fresno with a lot of opportunity, diversity, and affordability, especially compared with the Bay Area. "I feel like there's gonna be a lot more mix of people, because I think a lot of people move here and kinda, eventually, I feel like people always move here, all the time, from different parts of California." She imagined a very different future for the Central Valley than what major headlines were professing about the Golden

State. Where some saw a demographic exodus, Marisa saw a population boom. Alana, who we met earlier, had a similar outlook:

> I think that . . . I think that it's gonna grow in a positive way for a lot of, like, housing development, and that comes with more people. Um, but hopefully, more businesses as well to keep the economy going. Um, by getting more of that middle class, I think that's gonna contribute to keeping, like, the city alive. Um, and it . . . and I think, like, with, like, the generations lining up, like, there's gonna be more, like, hardworking working-class people. Um, that are gonna do much better off than our parents. So, I'm hopeful that there's gonna be more investment and development in the area. Uh, and just seeing more of a growth overall.

Alana's comments were not grounded in specific data about population movements or anything else. She just had a gut feeling that the future would be bright for the region. At the time of our interviews, the broader discussion about a California exodus had not yet reached its pinnacle. Still, many interviewees talked about a middle-class squeeze and moving to other states. Data from 2023 would later show that most of the state's population loss came from Los Angeles and the Bay Area. By contrast, between 2015 and 2023, the Central Valley actually saw a modest population gain—certainly not a boom but also not a decline like the higher-cost cities in California experienced.[16]

Yet whether grounded in a feeling or hard data, many people in the Central Valley shared a sense that they were on the verge of something big. Critical to this sense was the belief that the region could attract new kinds of people and new industries. And precisely because of the Central Valley's economic and geographic position, often behind its big-city counterparts, respondents saw economic development in the area as a collective good rather than rife with contradictions. Mary, a respondent introduced earlier, shared this view of the region's future. She told us that Fresno was starting to "take off." She explained, "I just see the companies coming here and I see, actually see, the starting to take off. I see, I see Fresno, actually . . . um . . . because it's [been] a little ghetto here." Even when they noticed inequalities growing in the Central Valley, many respondents believed that development would result in a net good. Even if development was connected to congestion, inequality, traffic, smog, and other ills in the big cities, many respondents in the Central Valley saw it was a net positive for the region.

Compared with Los Angeles and San Francisco, cities like Fresno were seen as more affordable, more livable, and with more room to grow. Aracely underscored this during our interview with her when she talked about a friend who lived in the Bay Area: "I have a friend [*laughs*], for example, who lives in the Bay Area, and he's an architect, and he has a really . . . he makes really good money . . . um . . . educated, you know, and everything. But he . . . I asked him on the last trip, I went, when I was in the Bay Area, and I said, 'Hey, so are you planning to buy, you know, property?' But he can't . . . he lives with the expense of life in the Bay Area."

Aracely was in her early thirties and had just been laid off from her job as a case manager in the medical field. While she was not earning enough to own a home, she told us that she lived comfortably with her mother. Still, she believed that it would eventually be easier to buy in the Central Valley than in other, higher cost-of-living areas. To her, Fresno represented the chance to one day fulfill her American Dream of homeownership, even if the goal seemed out of reach at the moment.

Other respondents used spatial comparison to highlight the lack of congestion in the Central Valley and to predict that traffic would not be negatively affected by new growth. Irma, for example, who lived in Merced, stated the following when asked how she liked the region: "I love it because it's so small. Like, you can, like, go to, like . . . everything's so close. It's not like you have to get on the four different freeways to get to your job. So that's something that everybody needs to appreciate. Like my boyfriend, who comes from LA. He's like, 'How do you not appreciate this? You're, like, ten minutes away from your job.' You know? So that's a good thing . . . and I think a lot of people from the Bay Area come here because it's a lot cheaper to live here."

It is true that it is cheaper to live in the Central Valley than most parts of the Bay Area and many parts of LA County, but it is also the case that home prices, along with other costs, have increased dramatically in places like Fresno. In 2016, a typical single-family home in Fresno sold for about $198,000, more than doubling over the next ten years to $420,000. In this sense, the Bay Area and Los Angeles are not the only areas where "everything is going up," even if rising prices are not felt as severely in other parts of the state. Yet optimism about the future of the Central Valley allowed many of the interviewees in this region to downplay these trends, even when they felt them personally, by talking about the higher comparative cost of living in Los Angeles and San Francisco. Spatial comparison served as a foil that helped people in the Central Valley downplay the economic trends negatively affecting them and shaping inequality in the region.[17]

And even when respondents saw some cracks in the veneer, they found comfort in the fact that, at least economically, Fresno was not as aggressively expensive as elsewhere in the state. For example, in her interview Marissa initially told us about Fresno: "Um, I just, I feel like everything is just getting more expensive and I just feel like it's never going to end [*laughs*]. And it's tough, it's tough. It's like, you work hard to buy a house, like that's the goal, we're going to buy a house, but then it's like, the housing market, and the housing value, and it's something you can't predict ever. So, it's kind of just, kind of like, you hope for the best and the house is just terrible."

Later, Marissa downplayed these sentiments and spoke optimistically about her community, explaining: "I think this area . . . um . . . will always have a lot more opportunity, as opposed to where it's more expensive [like] going towards, like, the Bay Area. I feel like there's gonna be a lot more mix of people, because I think a lot of people move here and kinda, eventually . . . I feel like people always move here, all the time, from different parts of California."

For Marissa, the earlier worries about affordability become obscured by the fact that there was always a more expensive place to the North and South, places where middle class stability would seem even more out of reach. In other words, while Marissa did feel anxious about homeownership at the time, she also saw Fresno and the broader Central Valley as places that would eventually boom and even become more livable in the future.

This optimism about the economic future of the region was intertwined with a healthy dose of "if you build it, they will come" ethos. In such narratives, the Central Valley would be in a position to court folks away from the overcrowded and unaffordable Bay Area and Los Angeles. For example, Shontay told us: "That's already happening in some areas in Fresno, they're like, y-y-you're right here, you drive down a little bit, you're like, whoa! It's like you're not even in the same city. And I feel like, with our high-speed railroad, hopefully within twenty years it will be developed, and that will bring a lot more people here.

I mean, there are already people like, from the Bay Area who come here and buy property because they know that's coming."

Indeed, perhaps the greatest amount of excitement came when folks in the Central Valley talked about the impending high-speed rail that would connect the region to Los Angeles and San Francisco. Although voters passed a ballot measure in 2008 authorizing funding for the construction of some segments of the rail, the project has been stalled and plagued with political and corporate infighting.[18] Still, those in the Central Valley that we interviewed were especially enthusiastic. Kim, for example, told us "Like, it, it's got the bridge going, everything. You know. They finna put a high-speed rail. Yeah, they finna put a high-speed rail from LA to the Bay. So, I say, Fresno gonna be booming. I mean, yeah."

In the aggregate, those in the Central Valley tended to see the future as an opportunity for their region to finally thrive, to catch up with the gains made by the bigger cities, only with less congestion and, somehow, with less economic difficulties that already beset the bigger cities. The region was "on the verge" and its booming future was just a matter of time. And while respondents here often also noticed important inequalities and questioned the shrinking of middle-class opportunities, their reliance on spatial comparison allowed them to see a much more optimistic future for them especially compared with Los Angeles and the San Francisco Bay Area.

Toward a Multiracial Future

We found that more economic development, in our respondents' visions, also meant more people. But what kind of people? Who did folks envision in the future? And what did they imagine in terms of the future of the state's famed immigration and racial diversity?

We found that at first glance, most respondents seemed to imagine California's racial future as a multiracial and diverse one. An important part of this rainbow future frame had to do with a perceived increase in multiracial people in the state. This was true of respondents across regions. For example, Tiffany, a Black Los Angeles resident, predicted the following: "Especially in California, there's a lot of . . . I mean, it goes on in other places too, but specifically California, there's a lot of . . . uh . . . uh . . . commingling and there's a lot of . . . um . . . interracial marriages. And so, because of that, you have a lot of . . . um . . . you know, biracial or [*laughs*], you know, just mixed kids. So therefore, it's not even the color of skin. 'Cause everybody will just look Brown."

And Ivan, a Latino in Los Angeles, told us his vision of the city as much more "mixed" as well. He stated, I think it'll . . . it'll be harder to tell who's who, you know? I think it'll be harder to see, like, you know, what language do you speak, you know? Um, that's good and bad. I mean, because it'll be so racially mixed or . . . not so racially mixed, but I think it'll be more racially mixed. I think there'll be more people living together . . . um . . . speaking English."

Here Tiffany and Ivan provide us with related, but slightly different, predictions. Tiffany thought development would bring more people who would mix and create a larger multiracial Angeleno population. Ivan believed development would lead to an increase in the mixed-race population and also create opportunities for diverse immigrant communities to come together and possibly bond over learning English, for example. Still, in each of these narratives, the potential pitfalls of growth and diversity, from interracial conflict to multidimensional racial hierarchies, were downplayed, while a type of multiracial, multicultural vision was emphasized.

Some respondents were specific in their predictions about how the state's racially ambiguous and mixed-race future would unfold. Andrea, a Latina respondent from Fresno, told us that growth would be fueled by Asian and Latin American migration:

> Yeah. Um, gosh, I don't know. I feel like if in the next ten to twenty years, if a lot of our border issues don't get, like, fixed, I will definitely feel like there will be an influx of . . . um . . . immigrants from Latin America being, like, Central America, and even way more from, you know, like, South America, depending on what happens globally. Um, I definitely feel like, geographically, like, we will have more Latin American immigrants in terms of, like, migration trends. Um, we have big communities . . . more Indian communities . . . um . . . so, like, Asian . . . [from] Asia . . . but I think there's definitely so many different ethnicities. . . . Um, so I don't know. I don't, I mean, maybe it gets Browner.

To Andrea and others, California's future demographic changes were clearly tied to present-day migrant flows. Andrea saw a "Brown" future in California's tomorrow, potentially implying that it would also be less White—and less Black.

A Future for Whom?

While some respondents imagined a future of economic growth and diversity—with few inherent contradictions—others had a more skeptical take. Some pointed out that economic growth could exacerbate inequality and raised questions about the future of racial disparities. For example, when asked to think about the future, Grant, a White man who grew up in a working-class family in West Los Angeles, shared:

> I think, you know, the divides gonna become greater and greater between . . . um . . . you know, the . . . er . . . I think it'll be primarily tech and health care professionals who are doing like exceedingly well. They're . . . they're gonna be doing a lot better than they even currently are, and I think the homeless population will also rise and like the lower le- . . . the middle class will, you know, either go one or two ways. I think we're gonna get rid of the . . . the middle class will get smaller and smaller . . . um . . . so there would be, you know, a bigger, stronger, you know, higher class and a stronger, l- larger lower class.

Grant envisioned present-day economic inequalities as worsening in the future. Like Grant, Marina, the retired Latina teacher we met in chapter 4, imagined a dystopic economic future for her South Los Angeles neighborhood: "Well, I think un- unless you're a millionaire, you're not going to be able to afford a house here. . . . Um, I think it's, I think it's going to go, who's got the money? So, depending, you know, if you're White, Black, or purple, if you've got the money to be able to afford the houses, if you're not, you won't."

Some respondents conjured up vivid imagery of inequality and how it would impact the physical geography of their neighborhoods. For example, Joe, a Latino from Los Angeles, shared his concerns about the future being one with persistently high levels of inequality: "I honestly imagine it like a slum in Guatemala, which is when neighborhoods look very dangerous and poor, bars on the windows, neighborhoods with walls around them, and armed guards. That's what I think, what LA and the big cities in the US are gonna look like in twenty years.

[Everyone] will be protecting themselves like this, the whole economic divide is not going to end very well."

Vanessa, a Latina respondent in Los Angeles expressed similar concerns:

> I feel like if the cost of living doesn't like . . . if I feel like if the cost of living and the wage situation and the homeless situation doesn't get addressed, like, quickly, it's going to spiral completely out of control. And I feel like it's going to end up looking like it does in every other third world country where it's, like, well, you have the complete slums on one street and, like . . . uh . . . really, really nice house on the other street, and there's no one in-between. And I feel like if that doesn't get addressed, then there's literally going to be no one in-between.

Indeed, although most respondents described the future in ways that helped them soothe their present-day anxieties about a middle-class squeeze, some did not. For these respondents, the contradictions in the state dampened more sunny pictures of the future of their cities and of California more generally. To them, comparisons to places like "Guatemala" or "Latin America" foretold the dangers of what could happen if present-day trends continued.

There are two things to point out before we continue. The first is that tales of the future have direct implications on belonging. In telling us about a gold-tinted future, those with more optimistic scenarios saw the present downtrodden as also somehow being lifted up or as naturally disappearing or moving out of the state. But respondents like Grant, Joe, and Vanessa predicted that the only ones that would really belong in the future were the wealthy—those that could find ways to be on the winning side of an increasingly unequal California.

The second thing to note is the role that comparison plays. When Joe compared a future California to the "slums" of Guatemala to describe a dire future, he is pointing to an abstracted and racialized picture of Latin America as a negative comparison. We do not know whether Joe meant to suggest that the large presence of Latinos coupled with racialized inequality could create this menacing, foreboding future, or if he simply invoked Guatemala to represent slums and hyper-inequality. Regardless, as philosophers from Jose Martí to Gloria Anzaldúa and Eduardo Galeano have noted, Latin America, with its perceived racialized inferiority, has long been characterized as a sort of dangerous alternative mirror, one that the United States, with its Protestant values and European heritage, dare not mimic.[19] In some ways, Joe may have been invoking these racialized tropes about Latin America as he imagined a dangerously unequal future in the Golden State.

TOWARD A WHITER AND MORE ASIAN FUTURE

Some respondents directly linked their sense of how unlivable the future of California would be to current racial disparities. In these future scenarios, a class and racial hierarchy reigned in the state, with White and Asian communities benefiting the most from California's growth and inequality. When asked what kinds of people will be living in the city in twenty years, Kim, a respondent in Fresno, predicted the following: "It's gonna be very diverse. Yeah, you know. It's gonna be a lot of, I don't know how to describe it. It's gonna be, like more, seem like a lot of Asian Americans that's gonna come. You know, because they get that, you know, they go to school, you know . . . they get that, you know, the education. And they move and, like, you know. I say, it's going to be very . . . because we booming, I mean."

Similarly, Sheila, an older woman of mixed Korean and Chinese heritage said of Los Angeles: "This area's always been a slow movement, a slow change. I think it'll get more expensive like anything else. Um, I think it's becoming . . . it'll become more and more Asian." Both Kim and Sheila have a sense that California will attract more Asian migrants and, interestingly, Kim directly connects this population expansion to a growth in educated Californians who will help make the state "boom."

Others saw a Whiter future, or at least a less Black one. For instance, Terry, a White man who had grown up with parents living paycheck-to-paycheck, first in Flint, Michigan, and then in cities across the Southwestern United States, felt that his experiences had made him hyperaware of the inequality around him in Los Angeles, where he had settled many years ago. Thinking about the future, he projected that Los Angeles would be "changing to a very White . . . very White, very bougie White . . . tech, disposable income" city. He saw less room for people of color in general and for Black and Brown communities in particular.

Similarly, Arturo, a Mexican American man who grew up poor in a town along the California–Mexico border, was skeptical of the idea that the state would continue to prosper economically and still maintain its diversity. He said this about Los Angeles:

> Yeah, well, if things keep going the way they are, I think it's gonna be even more White. I don't know the racial ethnic be- breakdown of the community, but I imagine seeing a lot more luxury apartments and condos and even more, like, high-end restaurants in the community. Um, so that's kinda what I imagine ten years from now if things . . . don't, something doesn't happen that can help change things or . . . uh . . . turn things around.

For these respondents, the future was not merely for the rich. It was reserved for White and possibly Asian people specifically. Unlike narratives that emphasized continual diversity in California, these respondents saw a direct connection between economic development and racial displacement. They attested that the changes happening all around them were, sometimes slowly, ridding their neighborhoods and the state of certain communities of color. For example, Aaron, a Latino in Los Angeles, explained: "Okay. I believe in ten to fifteen years, it's going to be predominantly Asian. I believe financially, they're going to be better off than we are."

As some of our respondents in Los Angeles and the Central Valley imagined increasingly unequal, dystopian futures, they sometimes invoked spatial comparison to the Bay Area. Our interview with Linda provides such an example. Linda grew up in Minnesota and, even as a young person, dreamed of moving to a more diverse place that was "less boring." She was generally progressive on all issues and was one of the many White interviewees in our sample who had a structural racism analysis and a critique of economic disparities. She lived in Silver Lake, an area in Los Angeles that had become more "hipster" and gentrified over the past decade. When asked what she imagined her neighborhood would look like in ten to twenty years, Linda responded, "Like Silver Lake. Yeah, I think it'll be a lot wealthier, more expensive to live. I think it'll be Whiter, um. Yeah, I think it'll be like . . . and further down the road, we'll all be San Francisco, probably."

Now, to say we are all going to be Silver Lake or San Francisco conjures up slightly different images of the future, but both images immediately invoke gentrification. Neither place is particularly "Brown." Silver Lake, a neighborhood in Los Angeles, has experienced rapid neighborhood change in recent decades, which has decreased the Latino population substantially, and San Francisco is one of the cities with the lowest proportion of Latinos in California. While Latinos make up at least one-third of the population in most of California's major cities, and often more, in 2021, Latinos represented only 14 percent of San Francisco's population.[20] Furthermore, San Francisco's Black population, which stood at 13.4 percent in 1970, has been on a steady decline ever since. Between 1990 and 2021 alone, the population decreased by nearly half, from 10.9 to 5.7 percent.[21] At the same time, the Asian and Asian American population in the city has been on a steady increase, now comprising about one-third of San Francisco's population—second only to White people, who comprise 42 percent of the population.

We note these demographics because, while many respondents had racialized pictures of the future in their minds, they did not always explicitly explain them. We suggest that Linda, in invoking Silver Lake, and especially San Francisco, was painting a particular economic and racial picture of the future, one that involved Black erasure and Latino decline or invisibility.

A FUTURE WITHOUT BLACK PEOPLE

Many saw the future of California as decidedly "Whiter" and "more Asian, which often meant that they also saw the future as "less Black" and to some extent "less Latino." Black respondents were more likely to directly link their present-day anxieties about displacement to their predictions of the future. As Jesse, a Black respondent in Los Angeles, explained, "I see a future where they're running people out. Cause a lot of the older African American people, their kids are all gang bangers, they're all on to other shit. And some of [the other African Americans] left the neighborhood when they became educated. So now the older people are dying, and you have all these White people coming in gradually, and I've seen them. And not only that, [the Los Angeles Police Department] has a presence in my neighborhood, so they're not going to fuck up and act stupid in there. You know what I mean?"

Jesse was echoing many of the frustrations that Black activists across California have long sought to bring to light—the fact that, whether through gentrification, racialized policing, or other means, Black Californians are feeling increasingly displaced within their state. And this is more than just a feeling. A 2024 report from the UCLA Black Policy Project found that the state's Black population shrank from 2.2 to 2.1 million between 2000 and 2020, leaving the population at less than 6 percent.[22] At this rate of loss, some activists contend that historic places of Black middle-class life, including Oakland and South Los Angeles, will no longer exist.

This reality even led some Black respondents to imagine their own futures elsewhere. For example, Kim discussed her concern that the Black population was getting smaller and smaller in Fresno. She predicted that the trend of African Americans moving out of state would continue and told us that this made her consider leaving as well. She explained: "I plan on moving and buying a house in Atlanta, Georgia. So even [as a Black person] you see your future maybe somewhere else. Yeah . . . how do I say it? I like the, I like the motivation . . . motivation in Atlanta. There's a lot, a lot of Black-owned businesses. A lot of Black doctors . . . African American doctors. I mean, that's gonna let me know, I'm a say more motivational because like say, out here you don't see, like you don't see that, you know. You know what I'm saying?"

To Kim, the issue was not simply a decreasing Black population in Fresno. It also involved a deeper sense of mourning of a lack of "motivation," a feeling she thought she might find in a place with a substantial Black middle class. Kim, like others, saw Atlanta as a sort of dream of what could be—a place where "Black" and "doctor" were not mutually exclusive, and where she did not have to feel like an extreme minority. In her framing, she was naming both the abject social status of Black people in Fresno and their decreasing numbers.

Respondents like Kim are not without cause in fearing that California is heading in a direction where there will be increasingly fewer Black people and where those who remain cannot thrive. While Black people constitute only 6 percent of the state's population, they make up anywhere from 25 to 40 percent of its homeless population,[23] 25 percent of its incarcerated population,[24] and 18 percent of people living in poverty.[25] In a state that was already racially and economically divided, such trends are ominous, especially when projected into the future. They conjure up images of eventual Black displacement, erasure, and even death.

This specific image of a future California is palpable in Black communities across the state. In 2022, for instance, the Oakland Museum of

California ran an exhibition on Afrofuturism.[26] The open-air entrance of the museum featured a wall measuring 20 x 15 feet painted with the words: "There are Black people in the future." The piece, by interdisciplinary artist Alisha B. Wormsley, could be seen as a simple and joyful declaration of Black life and living. But many people also interpreted it as a manifesto of sorts that was especially powerful in the context of a city once home to the first chapter of the Black Panther Party and a sizable Black middle class that is now a place notorious for its anti-Black violence and displacement. "There are Black people in the future" can be seen as a piercing, loud testimony that Black people, against all odds, will survive. This statement was particularly palpable in the context of the exhibit, which took place during the COVID-19 pandemic when early data showed that Black people were overrepresented among the dead. Beyond that moment, the question of whether Black people will be in the future is an inherently provocative one in the California context, where Blackness is often rendered invisible and the future of the state is imagined as many things, but rarely ever Black.

AN OMNIPRESENT BUT INVISIBLE LATINO FUTURE

While discourses about the future of the Black community in California are premised on the idea of demographic erasure, discussions about the place of Latinos in California's future are much more complex because they represent the majority population in the state—a trend predicted to continue over the coming decades.[27] And while similar discussions about displacement, racism, and even police brutality were also thought to apply to the Latino community, it was difficult for respondents to imagine the complete erasure of this community that constitutes almost 40 percent of the state's population.

Even so, present-day experiences with racialized gentrification have left some Latino respondents wondering about what the future might look like at the neighborhood level. Many respondents were particularly worried about the effects of gentrification. For example, Georgina, a Latina pharmacy technician in her late twenties who lived with her father, noted that her neighborhood in Los Angeles hardly has any Latino families anymore. Growing up, she recalled, "everyone was Hispanic" around her. And while the neighborhood was not "rich," it was certainly better off than other poor and working-class neighborhoods farther east.

Yet, at the time of the interview, she noted that it was mainly White, non-Latino couples without children who populate her block. When asked if she saw the same, Latino demographic possibly living there, she responded, "Very less . . . very little I mean. It's getting to be a lot more like Caucasian background [than] more than what I used to see when I first lived here." Later she added, "If it keeps going, it's going to be really hard for our kids to be able to grow up in a neighborhood like this."

To Georgina and other Latino respondents, the question was twofold. On the one hand, it made her think about gentrification and whether future generations would be able to live in the communities that their parents had chosen for them. When she referred to "our kids," she alluded to the possibility that Latino children more generally might not have a place there in ten or twenty years.

But the question of whether Latinos would still be present did not automatically mean complete erasure. Instead, Georgina questioned what roles and what neighborhoods this extremely large population might have available to them, which makes sense in a state where Latinos are the demographic majority. It is hard to imagine the Latino population completely absent in California, unlike the Black population, which is less than one-sixth its size. Though, even in this context, gentrification and widening inequality still raised concerns about just where Latinos would be—physically and socially—in the future of the Golden State.

Latino activists in California have long argued that, while Latinos drive the state's workforce population, especially in the agriculture and service sectors, they still face dramatically unequal opportunities and often live in places that lack desirable resources, like good schools and quality public infrastructure. In 2023, the Brookings Institution analyzed wealth data in the six states that currently house the largest percentage of Latinos in the country. They found that California had the widest Latino-White wealth gap compared with every other state analyzed apart from New York. For perspective, in Illinois, White households had about two times as much wealth as Latino households, while in California they had nine times as much.[28]

These concerns about Latino displacement and opportunity, we found, also dovetailed with concerns about Latino representation. If the reigning image of Latinos brought to mind manual labor, then they were not necessarily imagined as the professionals, cultural innovators, and state leaders—or more broadly, the makers—of California's future. Indeed, Latino activists have long decried the invisibility of their communities even in the context of being a majority in California. Much data back up this argumentation. While Latinos are nearly 40 percent of the state's population, they make up less than 6 percent of licensed attorneys, about 6 percent of physicians, and less than 18 percent of engineering degree graduates.[29] Representation in government is also spotty because while Latinos have increased their presence on school boards and in the California State Assembly, a 2022 report by the Latino Public Policy Institute found that, compared with other ethno-racial groups, Latinos in California had the largest representation gap in terms of state-level political appointments.[30] Media activists and congressional inquiries have long shown that Hollywood has historically snubbed Latinos despite its frequent filming and producing in the state with the largest Latino population in the country. Activists have recently mounted social media campaigns to shed light on their concerns and demonstrate that "Netflix has a Latino problem."[31]

This inequality and underrepresentation have led some Latino respondents to believe that conditions would stay the same or get worse in the future. For example, Dolores, a research consultant in Los Angeles, told us the various ways that Latinos were seen as second-class citizens in the city. She said that the Latino students at her private college in the 1990s were always assumed to be staff rather than students, how waiters at "fancy brunch places" seemed surprised to see Latino patrons, and how White clients were always surprised that she has two graduate degrees. "Like in [these] situations, I [also] like to say 'oh and my older sister is a professor. My younger sister is an attorney.'" And in many ways, Dolores believes that the future will be the same. When asked how things will be in Los Angeles in the next ten to twenty years, she simply said, "the same . . . just because of institutionalized racism."

For Dolores, like Georgina, issues of gentrification, inequality, and racism brought up questions of future displacement and belonging for Latinos. The question was less about whether there would be "no Latinos" but rather where Latinos would be and whether they would be seen as neighbors in middle-class neighborhoods, patrons of fancy restaurants, and professors, attorneys, and researchers. Dolores also mentioned the role of Latino politicians in Los Angeles, noting their increased representation there. Still, given that Los Angeles is close to 50 percent Latino, the community is still underrepresented in elected positions in the city, just as they are across the state.[32]

In all, these respondents pushed back against a general understanding of a Californian future that is more diverse racially and where technology would bring benefits for all. Instead, they saw present trends projected into the future. So while they understood that Latinos could not be so easily erased, they did wonder if Latinos could ever be the agentic makers, dreamers, and creators rather than the state's invisibilized, laboring backdrop.

A LATINO THREAT

In contrast, a minority but still significant number of respondents across the political spectrum viewed Latinos as "too present" and almost threatening. For them, Latinos represented a sort of looming demographic threat whose unchecked growth would sour the state's image. No other group was singled out as a cultural, demographic, and even moral threat the way that Latinos were. The respondents making such claims were few in number but stand out because they narrated ideas of a dystopian Latino takeover. Rather than see diversity in the present or future as a positive, they saw it as a cultural threat to the state.[33]

For example, Clay, a White man who grew up in a wealthy household on Manhattan's Upper East Side but has since settled in Los Angeles, was among the few respondents who thought that the city's economy was getting worse. He directly linked these perceived changes to immigrants. When asked what he thought the future in Los Angeles would look like, he said:

> What it's gonna look like in ten to twenty years, you should know, it's like downtown LA. You know, downtown . . . where a lot of places look like a third-world country down there. And believe me, I know what third-world countries look like, like they should be. But, you know, it, it's really . . . 'cause right now, the state is, it's kind of early to really state. You know, I think that my community, that people 'cause it's the government, for the people, of the people, by the people, should actually get together and just say, "Look, we're not against immigration, it's illegal immigration. We don't want to open borders to a bunch of criminals."

While Clay did not explicitly invoke Latinos when he imagined the future, his comments were profoundly racialized, reflecting what Leo Chavez claims is a sort of Latino racialization rooted in a fear of a Latino takeover of the state. Criminals are equated with "illegal" immigration, which is correlated with the idea of "third-world country." These ideas are not neutral—they communicate an ominous future threat rooted in present anti-Latino fears.[34]

Later in the interview, Clay mentioned race specifically. He told us that he worried that the state's demographic change, becoming more Latino, and political shift to the left, was driving out White folks like him. He continued, "I mean, am I gonna get in trouble for being White down the line? I don't know. Um, I'm probably the biggest threat to my security. If I find myself in a position where I decided to run my mouth or something . . . um . . . do I become the subject or the object of someone's scorn?"

Clay believed the future was menacing because he imagined the implications of what political and population shifts meant for White Republicans like himself. His sentiments are similar to those that scholars have found among White conservatives in the rural South and elsewhere in the United States today. Indeed, Arlie Hochschild reminds us that many feel like "strangers" in what they understand as "their own land."[35] We found echoes of such sentiments in the diverse metropole of Los Angeles, which has direct implications for where we think racial bias is rampant in the United States.

Ed, a White Republican in Bakersfield, told us that he feared that he no longer fit into California's future. As a White male in an increasingly Latino Central Valley, he worried that Mexican immigrants were coming and not doing enough to assimilate. He shared, "What I am saying is, if Mexico is so bad, if we're going to say it this way, why are you coming over here trying to make America Mexico?" Ed also mentioned that he worried about California becoming more Democratic and that he often considered moving to a place that was more conservative—"a redder state."

In many ways, respondents like Clay and Ed reflect much of the discourse found in right-wing conservative circles. They are deeply concerned that Latinos are "taking over," that immigrants cannot assimilate, and that the Democrats are helping to create conditions that will drive out White conservatives. To a certain extent, such thoughts stem from economic fears and longing for recognition, but we argue they are also based on deeply ingrained racial biases about who belongs and what the future racial hierarchy should look like. The loss of a White majority has likely sparked racial fears in people like Ed and Clay, and these fears have become intertwined with discussions of criminality and economic anxiety, occupying a central place in their imaginings about the future.

We also found vestiges of the "Latino takeover" narrative among other residents, including Democrats of color. For example, Keisha, a Black Democrat from Fresno, expressed concerns about California's "Mexican" future. She had seen the African American population of the city dwindle in her neighborhood for years and associated this demographic shift with a rise in the Latino population. She noted, "I think, eventually, the Mexicans are gonna take it all over. I really . . . I can see that happening. They are really . . . it's already so many. We close to LA, you know, so LA is already gonna get overcrowded. And they gotta go somewhere, and it's gonna be here. Yeah."

Keisha was asked, when imagining the future, did she see anyone who looked like her, or specifically, if she thought African Americans would live there. She responded: "I think the people who . . . the older people who have already been here. So, yeah, or we might start moving out too. It might be somewhere that gets a little bit cheaper. And we might all head that way because it gets so out of control that we might just all have to just up and leave . . . I can see it all being taken over, yeah."

Unlike Clay, Keisha did not equate Latinos or immigrants with criminality, but she did express concern about the growth in their numbers. And while her comments are inflected with forms of bias, they should also be contextualized. Writing about Black and Brown relationships in California, Edward Telles and colleagues argue that both groups hold distinct stereotypes about each other, many of which get reproduced through numerous means, including racially biased media depicting people in both Black and Latino communities as criminals and policies that effectively segregate groups into under-resourced neighborhoods and schools.[36] We can thus position Black and Brown conflict, which operates bi-directionally, as partially a vestige of settler-colonial systems that have long sought to divide people of color.[37] While there are many examples of cooperation, coalition building, and people defying neat categories, this does not happen automatically. Instead, these processes must be nurtured and built through community education efforts and structural change.

By contextualizing anti-Latino sentiment among some African American respondents, we do not mean to explain it away. Black respondents were indeed among the small contingent of respondents who referred to Latinos as "taking over" or as a looming threat. Some conservatives' fears were based on their sense that too many Mexican immigrants were arriving, somehow changing the character of the state in a way that made White people and culture feel at risk. But for Keisha and respondents like her, fears of a takeover were also rooted in what such demographic changes meant for those that experience anti-Black discrimination, loss, and increased precarity in an increasingly Latino state.

Conclusion

Throughout this book we have shown how people can downplay and normalize inequality even when they are directly subjected to its negative effects. We argue that this normalization aids the often-silent reproduction of inequality. Examining how people talk about the future, we note, makes many of these trends explicit. Indeed, thinking about the future allowed respondents to engage in a kind of world-making where they could channel their optimism and anxieties about living in a state booming with prosperity and inequality. We found that most respondents, across racial groups, had an optimistic view of the future and thought it might save many people from their present-day difficulties. Just like exceptional framing helped respondents believe that their individual trajectories would be better than the norm, optimism helped them feel like the future would be better than the present and the inequalities around them reduced.

Technology and the perceived benefits it would bring to the economy seemed to be at the center of a great deal of exceptional future-framing among respondents. Many were excited by the imagined spectacle, replete with self-driving cars, robots, and unprecedented innovation, which transformed into hopefulness, a sentiment that was less pronounced when they thought about the present. In their imagined future, one that seemed closer to reality when we were finishing writing this book than it did at the onset of this project, the economy would also be booming and somehow lift all—or most—boats. In this, the difficulties of today would somehow fade away. Some respondents believed strongly that, in the decades to come, this imagined high-tech future would also involve significant racial mixing and multiculturalism. Respondents did have different ideas about what this "Browning" would mean, for example, an increase in the number of multiracial people or more multiracial neighborhoods, but they were in agreement that the trend would keep the Golden State unique. California's diversity would increase as its technology-driven future boomed, keeping the state ahead of economic and demographic trends elsewhere.

We also suggest that geography shaped respondents' perspectives on the future of California cities and the state in general. Some of the clearest articulations of a booming and diverse Californian future came from Central Valley respondents who believed that economic and infrastructure developments to come would transform the region. We argue that this optimism is based on this region's structural position in California, materially and discursively. Unlike many of their LA counterparts who underscored the potential negative consequences of such economic booms, respondents in the Central Valley tended to frame the future as about a region realizing its full potential. The Central Valley, and Fresno specifically, was on the verge of something big, if only the future would arrive. This Central Valley optimism underscores how the region is often omitted from broader narratives about the Golden State.

Yet for a smaller group of respondents, the future looked less golden. People in this group had a tendency to see the interconnectedness of racial and class inequality. These respondents believed the present sent out signal flares of a future of growing inequality, less livability, and catastrophe. Black and Latino interviewees, in particular, while they seemed hopeful about their individual futures, lingered on the often-racialized inequalities they saw around them when painting a picture of the future of their neighborhoods and cities. They rarely imagined other Black and Brown folk settling into high-rises or being at the front of future hiring lines. Instead, they imagined that Whiter and wealthier, non-California-born people would ultimately benefit from the state's bright future. They conveyed this through stories of their relatives moving out of state and informal ethnographies of the gentrification of their neighborhoods. They feared the displacement of entire communities in the future and a worsening of the already extreme structural inequalities baked into California.

Perhaps because of these tensions, the economic boom that they saw happening around them, which fueled their imaginings of the future, was only partly welcomed. Instead, these folks approached questions about the future of the state with more ambivalence, more trepidation, and more worry. These anxieties concerned the collective future of their own families and Black and Latino communities more broadly. In other words, for some, the troubles of the future are already here, most visibly and viscerally felt by those from racially and economically marginalized communities. As scholars interested in the construction of space have suggested, the landscape and built environment around us is produced through not only struggle but also messages about who belongs and who does not in a given social space.[38]

Additionally, we found that in discourses about California's future, Latinos seem invisible despite their omnipresence—always in the background, perhaps as gardeners or servers but never as media or political leaders in the state where they represent the majority population.[39] Black residents underscored how years of racialized displacement were coming to a head; at the same time, these residents noticed the absence of Black people in what seems to be planned for their neighborhoods and cities in this diverse state.[40] And though many respondents expressed a belief that the Golden State's future seems to be booming and diverse, others envisioned a much more somber scenario that raises questions about inequality and racial hierarchies. Du Bois warned us that the future will not save us from the present. If we heed that warning, what we will see is that rather than a bright future, the future of Black and Latino communities in California may be much more cloudy, and much more fraught with present-day racialized inequalities that color the possibilities of tomorrow.

CONCLUSION

Traffic backs up around 3:00 PM. If you are on Interstate 80 in Berkeley on any given afternoon, you might notice a cluster of folks on the pedestrian bridge that spans that highway, just south of University Avenue. Holding bullhorns, signs, and banners, they seek to call attention to pressing social issues—climate change, immigrant rights, anti-Black state violence, and the rising tide of authoritarianism—while breaking the monotony of the daily commute. Here, you see people of all ages protesting, from children to the elderly, waving, sitting, and sometimes dancing, or leading the small crowd in lively chants. The protests can be so loud and colorful that they are hard to ignore, even for drivers in a hurry. To some, these efforts might seem like a waste of time, but the activists likely believe that this moment, this exact moment in economic and political history, is as urgent as ever. Nothing seems more critical to them than disrupting the quotidian and drawing people's attention to the unequal systems and structures that shape and define who we are. In so doing, they seek to shake up and shake off our consent to the status quo, to make us reflect on the many ways that we are all implicated in the reproduction of inequality, near and far.

In this book, we have tried to do the same by taking a step back and shining analytic light on the sense-making that happens in the everyday in an unequal California and an unequal nation. Specifically, we have focused on the aspiring middle-class, those upper-working- and lower-middle-class folks who do not feel quite economically stable and who might drive past those same activists on pedestrian bridges, wondering what all the fuss is about. The protests may or may not resonate

https://doi.org/10.7758/uybx4321.7857

with them but, like everyone else, they have to contend with the growing material and symbolic inequalities that so stubbornly shape their routines, their sense of who belongs, and their dreams for the future.

Through in-depth interviews and survey data, we have shown how even those that do not experience the most devastating effects of inequalities are not completely blind to them. Even those who are not regularly tuned into these issues worry. Inequality came up unprompted frequently in interviews, including how the middle class is experiencing new forms of precarity and how economic opportunities seem much less attainable than in previous generations. The people we spoke to were aware of the structural nature of such inequalities, pointing out how government policies favor the rich and how wealth begets wealth, as examples. Some could even describe the historical legacies of colonialism and slavery and the effects of our flawed immigration system on inequality today. In so doing, they revealed a keen awareness of how race, immigration, and class affect people's lives and life chances.

At the same time, we found that respondents tended to minimize structural explanations of inequality, claiming that they thought the problem was "not so bad," or that it was something to be acknowledged but not actively contested. We saw this at the abstract and broader level, when folks told us that the middle class was getting squeezed, or that immigrants got the short end of the stick, only to quickly pivot to suggestions that those who got ahead simply "wanted it more" or found a way to overcome their circumstances. We also observed this tendency at the personal and immediate level when respondents downplayed their own experiences of inequality, their own negative encounters with racism, and their own feelings of dis-belonging, in favor of a more optimistic view that emphasized individual determination and a sense that they could personally overcome hardships with hard work, patience, and a bit of luck. By emphasizing individual striving and minimizing structural challenges, they could come to see inequality as normal.

But how, exactly, did they do this? How were they able to downplay structural barriers, especially when they understood how systemic inequalities operated in their day-to-day lives? We found that respondents engaged in three practices—exceptional framing, bounded blame, and spatial comparison—to minimize structural interpretations of inequality and, in so doing, to breath a little easier.

Exceptional framing, for example, permitted people to emphasize a highly agentic narrative of their own trajectory, and to thus position themselves as in more control of their future than statistics and trends would suggest. As a result, they could maintain a sort of social pessimism, which emphasized the abstract structural processes undergirding inequality, as well as an individual optimism that emphasized one's ability to beat the odds. This dual understanding could exist because folks distinguished between these ideas at different levels. Structural explanations, for instance, helped them make sense of broader trends among the "middle class" or "immigrants" writ large. Yet they avoided applying such understandings when making sense of things at the personal level. Instead, respondents tended to shift to individualistic ideas about hard work and viewing themselves and their futures as exceptional.

Spatial comparison also helped respondents make sense of inequality by creating a lens through which the inequality of one's environment could be compared with another place, however abstract. Such comparisons often served to soften or minimize the inequalities around them. For example, respondents acknowledged the presence of racism and racial divides in California but still suggested that the situation might be tolerable, or even acceptable, because things were surely worse in "the South," "Texas," or other regions of the United States. In this way, respondents were able to consider the racial disparities around them as "not too bad," even as they sometimes recognized the ugly and structural ways that racism was reproduced in the Golden State. This kind of spatial comparison often rests on abstraction. That is, respondents did not need definitive proof that things were worse elsewhere—sometimes they just felt it. Similarly, even when respondents acknowledged that immigrants were exploited and subject to unequal conditions in California, they still mused that things might be worse for them if they had remained in "Vietnam," "Mexico," or some other "developing country." Many respondents shared this view even if they had never been to these places or knew little about them. Spatial comparison allowed them to minimize inequality in California, to naturalize it, because the situation was surely worse elsewhere.

Finally, bounded blame, the third strategy we identify, helped respondents frame the downtrodden in both individualist and structural ways. Respondents could imagine poor people, especially those who were homeless or undocumented, as living under an unfortunate set of structures that made life difficult for them. Yet at the same time, they also saw these groups as engaging in behaviors that served to reproduce their circumstances. For example, they could acknowledge that immigration laws were unfair but still wonder why "illegals" didn't just find the desire, means, or information to "get in line." Similarly, they could bemoan how difficult it was for an unhoused person to get ahead but then wonder how their drug use, mental illness, or financial practices had led to their predicament. This tendency to individualize the structural conditions of the downtrodden essentially allowed respondents to minimize the systemic inequalities that these groups faced while also elevating narratives focused on individual responsibility.

Taken together, our findings are evidence of how individuals come to normalize, accept, and even reproduce the inequalities around them. We argue that this process does not require individuals to be apathetic about inequality or to wholeheartedly embrace it. In fact, we found little evidence of apathy and few indications that people subscribe to overtly religious, political, or cultural ideologies that blatantly support unequal conditions.

Instead, many respondents told us, sometimes in great depth, that inequality was unjust, painful, and a scourge on American ideals. On the left and the right, respondents understood the system to be rigged for those at the top, even if they disagreed on if, or how, the government should respond. In general, respondents were conscious of and bothered by the way inequalities were structured in the United States, particularly in California.

We also found that sense-making is often a nuanced process, not easily pegged as evidence of resistance or acceptance of the status quo. For instance, we found that respondents drew on a range of complex cultural references, including stereotypes, personal experiences, politics, and the media, often indicating both structuralist and individualist understandings of inequality. In opening the cultural and cognitive black box to reveal how this material was fashioned into frames, comparisons, and boundaries, we revealed the implicit ways that inequality is silently reproduced, tolerated, and even uncomfortably accepted.

From Making Sense to Consent

Ultimately, our findings have implications for how we might understand the role of sense-making in our analyses of contemporary forms of hegemony. While we agree with much of the work that has delineated how consent is manufactured from above, we posit that there is still much to be learned by examining how individuals arrive at their worldviews and how they ultimately come to see power relations, including those relations that create and sustain inequality, as ever-present, normal, and accepted aspects of our society. Specifically, our work points to three important directions for developing a sense-making approach to power.

THE POWER OF INDIVIDUALISM, MYTH, AND AGENCY

The first direction concerns the enduring power of individualism. We show that many people can hold both structural and individualist understandings of inequality and that the two are not mutually exclusive or even two ends of a spectrum.[1] They can in fact, co-exist comfortably as sets of understandings that are elevated at different points in time.[2] Even individuals with more elaborate structural understandings of inequality than most can have individualist interpretations of some issues. Additionally, while some respondents relied mainly on individualist interpretations, this was not the case with structural explanations. This observation coincides with some survey findings that suggest that individuals holding purely structuralist orientations to inequality are incredibly rare.[3]

However, we suggest that it is not simply that individuals can hold two types of explanations about how society functions but rather that they can learn to consistently minimize structuralist accounts in favor of individualist ones. They learn this by employing the strategies that we develop throughout this book. We argue that the normalization of inequality is a process, not simply an adopted stance, which emerges as people attribute meaning to the world around them.

We argue that one reason individualist accounts of inequality become powerful enough to overshadow structuralist ones is that they draw on widespread and deeply institutionalized stories about what America is and what it means to be an American. Indeed, ideas about individualism and meritocracy undergird much of the American Dream ideology and the relationship between social mobility and opportunity. Popular myths about immigration reinforce these ideas, especially when they exalt the ways that immigrant labor helped build the nation or suggest that immigrants can achieve the American Dream through hard work. These overlapping myths reinforce individualist interpretations, making them easy and tangible ways of describing the world.

At the same time, we contend that individualist interpretations are powerful because they offer an agentic, protagonist-driven, approach to describing inequality. Inequality and its effects are understood to be the result of the efforts of principal actors who engage heroically (or tragically) in world-building.[4] By falling back on individualist explanations, individuals like the people at the center of this book can see clear cause-and-effect patterns in the world that stem from personal behavior. Structural explanations, on the other hand, lack the kind of agency and simplicity that individualist explanations offer them. They instead emphasize history, institutions, and abstract social patterns that seem less tangible than the more direct idea that one's behavior leads to specific outcomes.[5] Some may therefore find it easier to downplay factors such as legal status, racial background, government policies, and even luck to explain inequality. In many ways, individualist explanations provide cleaner, simpler, and more agentic descriptions of the social world.

It follows then that contemporary theorizing about hegemonic forms of power could benefit from deeper engagement with processes of sense-making. By exploring the types of explanations people have about inequality, *how* and *why* individualist explanations come to trump structural and systemic ones, and where such narratives come from, we can identify the important role that discursive strategies play in forging consent more generally.

TEMPORALITY AND CONSENT

A second direction that our work points to concerns time and temporal framings. Centering sense-making reveals that social conditions, including inequality, are understood not simply in the present but also, critically, in relationship to the past and future. These temporal comparisons bring the present into sharp view, revealing implicit understandings of the possibilities and limits of social change.

Importantly, we find that temporality operates on at least two distinct levels, the social and the individual. Individuals use time to better understand the structural processes that operate at the societal level. This was evident in our study when respondents spoke about the future of their communities, cities, and state. For some, the future represented a sort of collective hope and promise to resolve the problems of today. In this, many respondents told us that inequality, and its ensuing social ills, could resolve themselves naturally in the future with the rise of new technologies and the inevitable pace of social progress. By framing the future this way, the interviewees could imagine inequality as evanescent, something that would dissolve, and was therefore tolerable, at least for a while. On this social, abstract level, the future is a place of relief. One only has to bide time and presumably not get so worked up about inequality while waiting for better conditions to emerge.

Yet to others, temporal reframing does not necessarily carry with it optimism. Instead, it can inspire fear and dread, especially when the future is viewed less as a balm for the present and more as an exacerbation and projection of present-day problems. We observed this phenomenon when Black and Latino respondents argued that gentrification and displacement would only get worse in the future, eventually erasing their communities or rendering them invisible. In this rendition, inequality feels less temporary and more inevitable, like a fixed feature of our society.

We also found that framings of the past operate in the abstract at the social level in similar ways, inspiring both hope and fear. This was evident in respondents' assertions that today's middle-class salaries could no longer secure homeownership in California "like they used to" and that their communities were better off "back in the day," before demographic changes or before the economy turned. In these instances, the past stirred up anxiety and unease about the present.

Thinking about the past, however, can also offer hope about one's present circumstances. This was evident when respondents characterized the past as part of a linear historical trajectory that moved toward inevitable social progress. This view helped soften present-day inequalities, in part because it highlights that social change is inevitable. The past that was often conjured up was not as loud as that past that inspired anxiety, but still important. A person who believes the present, with all its warts and difficulties, is better than the past might also be able to see current social conditions as normal and believe they will eventually improve.

Temporality also matters at the individual level as well as people make sense of their own personal experiences. Some can imagine their personal futures as bright, even if the present is beset with difficulties.

This attitude helps them understand their current social problems as more tolerable, not because they will go away on their own, but because they can resist and chart an independent trajectory for themselves, free from structural determinism. Believing in individual agency and self-efficacy when considering their own personal trajectory, such respondents could envision themselves as an active change agents who can stave off the effects of inequality on their lives and possibly the lives of others.

Ultimately, then, temporality has implications for understanding how hegemony operates. On the one hand, thinking about the past or the future might lull people into believing that current difficulties might eventually resolve themselves, if only we stop worrying about them. On the other, it might serve as a clarion call to resist and engage in acts of social change. In this book, we argue that future and past narratives mean different things to different people at the social and individual level. Tracking these differences through a sense-making approach provides a clearer picture of how hope, fear, and other emotions help to sustain hegemonic worldviews and the status quo itself.

PLACE AND THE POWER OF COMPARISON

The final direction that our work leads to concerns place, which, we argue, does a lot to manufacture consent for the status quo. In this book, we have shown the many ways that California—historically presumed to be the pinnacle of the American Dream—served as an important ideological backdrop for respondents to draw conclusions about the nature of inequality. Minimizing inequality often means conforming to a specific idea of the Golden State as a place where social problems might not be too difficult to solve or too permanent to overcome. The idea of California standing in for a kind of optimism is reflected not only in popular culture—from songs to movies—but also in numerous marketing campaigns, first by colonization agents and later by the film industry, politicians, and tourism campaigns. These have origins in settler colonial fantasies and the literal marketing of the state as a land of dreams and continue to shape the narratives people create when trying to make sense of inequality in their lives, in their communities, and in California broadly.

Place also matters at the local level, whether that be the region you live in, the city or town you call home, or even your neighborhood or block.[6] While we do not systematically discuss these different levels of place in this book, we posit that they are critical to informing Californians' sense of how inequality operates. For example, many Central Valley respondents provided an optimistic account of the future, where the inequalities of today somehow fade away. This narrative, we suggest, is rooted in the imaginary of the Central Valley as a kind of in-between region, not just geographically but also in terms of the promise and perils of what California may have to offer. Because of this, many saw their region as ripe with possibility or "on the verge," destined to avoid the difficulties that have beset places like Los Angeles and San Francisco. In this way, for some respondents, the Central Valley embodied the quintessential dream of California—a place of abundant possibility, where the dream is always on the horizon and never in the rear view, where inequality may be here today but is destined to dissipate.[7]

Spatial comparison gives us the clearest view of the effects of place on achieving hegemony. When individuals minimize inequality because it does not fit into their understanding of place, they are often holding a singular and often idealized image of an area. And even when they encounter direct evidence that counters this ideal, spatial comparison swoops in to keep it intact. A person, for instance, might view their community as beset with difficulties but find this tolerable as long as they think it is comparatively better than other communities, even abstractly. This might also look like brushing off racist incidents as "not too bad" because they do not conform to their understanding of Los Angeles, or California more broadly, as a cultural melting pot. Spatial comparison helps to dull the discomfort of inequality such as when you see racial tensions as tolerable because they are not as bad as those found in the US South.

By highlighting how place matters for sense-making around inequality, the point is not to tell a California story but instead to underscore how geography figures into narratives about inequality and how that in turn shapes how we live with, make sense of, and sometimes justify inequality. This book does not merely offer a California-specific takeaway. Instead, we suggest that readers think more deeply about how people might make sense of inequality around race, class, and immigration across places, from big cities like New York or Atlanta to other areas with differing levels of racial diversity and inequality. How might people across the United States use spatial comparison to make sense of inequality in the places they live? Or might they engage in different narrative practices entirely? How might they draw on local histories and mythos of where they live to help them grapple with problems that can be hard to stomach but which are likely here to stay? These are some of the many questions that we hope will naturally follow from this study and serve to deepen our understanding of power and consent.

THE LIMITS OF DIVERSITY

Our analysis here underscores that while increased racial diversity may lead to more racial integration and tolerance, it also can lead to segregated diversity, complicity with racial inequality, and the minimization of racism. Additionally, the situation in California suggests that economic growth, even when checked by a relatively progressive political machine and a direct democracy governance structure, still leads to an extreme concentration of wealth at the top, precarity on the bottom, and a feeling that the middle is being squeezed out. And yet many remain hopeful about their own prospects for social mobility and their ability to pull themselves up by their bootstraps and out of such intense levels of inequality.

What we learn from the vantage point of California is that creating a seemingly welcoming context for immigrants and for racially diverse migrants cannot solve the many problems that a growing, racialized economic divide imposes on communities. We suggest that in contexts like these, greater racial diversity often simply means greater racial inequality. Perhaps we might go as far as to say that the growing racial divide is made more tolerable and digestible if it happens in such a "welcoming place." Among many of our respondents, we found a comfort in the narratives about this place, some relief that despite it all, they still found a version of home here.

All of this has implications for belonging. When a person feels accepted, part of something larger than themselves, they can more easily minimize the inequality around them and learn to live with it. Indeed, we find that belonging in the Golden State often means understanding the structural patterns of inequality that run deep but never being so worried about them to stop believing in the possibility of the place. This is perhaps why so many social commentators have found fault lines and earthquakes apt metaphors for social relations in California.[8] People in the Golden State are aware of the deep fissures that lie just underneath their feet and the risks they entail, while the mark of a true Californian is actually to not worry about earthquakes. When newcomers experience their first shaking of the earth beneath them, it can feel like a big deal. But the mark of a "true Californian" is to say, "I didn't even feel it," or "Oh, it was just a 3.2." The normalization of inequality works in a similar way. It carries inherent risks to the social order, but retrofitting our lives to fix it seems insurmountable.

We might think of the more critical respondents in this book as a kind of early-warning system for earthquakes. These respondents were more skeptical and concerned about the future, not just for them but for their communities and cities as well. Instead of imagining a beautiful future with more wealth and diversity, these respondents sent out signal flares about what inequality in the present may ultimately hold for the collective future. This group was overwhelmingly Black and Latino respondents who despite their nearly middle-class status, did not see people like themselves easily thriving in a future California.

Taking their warnings seriously may be more urgent now than ever. In this era of ever-reemerging Trumpism, California has been on the defensive—defending its values, its policies, even its demographics. The state has certainly been at war with Trump himself but also with the Trump agenda, which has included a frontal assault on education. "Go to Berkeley" exclaimed Governor Ron DeSantis in a speech announcing the banning of diversity, equity, and inclusion funding and ethnic studies in Florida.[9] Conservative supporters reiterated that if one wanted to be corrupted by critical race theory and gender studies, then California seemed to be the best place to do it—a "last bastion" for liberalism. From this principled perch, one can walk around the cities of Berkeley, San Francisco, or Los Angeles today and see lawn signs that read: "We believe love is love, science is real, Black lives matter, water is life, no human being is illegal, feminism is for everyone, and kindness is everything."

A classic Marxist might see these signs and argue that part of the problem with "identity politics" is that they come to replace more materialist claims and demands. We disagree, as we see these different kinds of difference—including those related to race and immigration—

as deeply entwined with class in ways that may be impossible to disentangle. At the same time, we heed the warning that a lawn sign has not been, and never will be, enough.

Put another way, symbolic gestures of "wokeness" will not save us. Rattling off the "isms" and clinging onto California's exceptionalism, as some of the respondents did, will not make real inequalities more fixable. It will only serve to justify them, tie a bow around them, and relegate them to the background. Holding on too fiercely to the narrative that California is somehow beyond racism and xenophobia may make it even harder to address these very real issues in the state. What is clear is that valuing a vague diversity will never in and of itself guarantee the dignity or well-being of racially marginalized groups. To achieve that would require a long-term commitment to a collective pursuit. We would all also have to get more uncomfortable with inequality and human suffering and more comfortable with the redistribution of material goods and with rethinking of what belonging actually means in this state.

After all, who truly belongs in places that fashion themselves as progressive but that are also defined by enduring forms of racialized inequality? We can no longer wait to answer this question. The faster we barrel toward a future that continues to erase some, and that builds itself on the backs of others, the more we risk collective losses.

Conclusion

We have shared these stories of Californians because they underscore the need to think more critically about how differently situated people make sense of their lives while surrounded by deep inequalities. We are keenly aware that the rest of the nation is undergoing many of these same processes we discuss in this book. Every day, there are increasingly more people witnessing rising inequality in their regions and states. We argue that ideas about exceptionalism, place, and boundaries matter in these areas as well. For instance, we might expect that ideas about Washington, DC, as the "Chocolate City" or New York as the portal to the "Land of Immigrants" and the "City That Never Sleeps" likely shape the way that folks come to think about the many intersectional opportunities and inequalities they witness in these places.[10]

In this sense, while this book is based on the experiences of Californians, its message reaches farther. We hope to have identified processes by which inequality is tacitly normalized and accepted in today's society, with all its uncertainty. The exact logic of that acceptance varies by group and place, but what remains clear is that we have an enormous amount of work to do as we strive to create a society that provides true opportunity for all. Every day, our institutions, including our schools, churches, public offices, and state universities, have a new chance to do right by the communities that have been exploited, excluded, or abandoned for so long. Today, each one of us has the opportunity to see the inequalities around us with fresh eyes. It is our hope that in learning from and writing about the people of California, we have contributed to this effort, or that we have at least offered ideas on where to start.

EPILOGUE: OUR DREAM FOR CALIFORNIA

This book has been partly an intellectual exercise and partly a personal one. We believe it has begun to answer sociological questions about how people think about the world and their place in it, about the politics of place, and about how people navigate and understand inequality. It is also our letter to California. At times, it might be read as a love letter, other times a "Dear John" letter. This is not surprising as we embarked upon this book project with the many contradictions of the Golden State in mind. We also end with some ambivalence. We wrote this letter as daughters of California and also as mothers raising children of color in this state. Our children are economically privileged, growing up with all kinds of opportunities that we never experienced or could even dream of in our own childhoods. This fact might itself be read as testament to how the California Dream is alive and well for us, how our parents' sacrifices to get us here were ultimately worth it.

But raising children of color, even in a place like the Bay Area, is not for the faint of heart. We still have to have talks with our children about the racism and xenophobia they have and will inevitably experience in their everyday lives. We must do this even here, where everyone is supposed to belong and where people of color are very much the majority. We know that the social mobility we have experienced can save our children from some of the material dis-belonging that we talk about in this book. However, they will never be completely shielded from the entrenched inequalities in this state. They will experience them directly and even when they don't, they, like all of us, will have to navigate them in some form.

One thing we hope you take away from this book is that California is far from a monolith. It is not reducible to Los Angeles or San Francisco, even if the fame of those places profoundly shapes our sense of this place. We hope that you consider the parts of the state that some would rather hide from view, which are also the regions that do not easily conform to the idea of a woke utopia. In this book, we have only begun to touch the surface of those parts of California not associated with the dominant mythos of the state as diverse and valuing diversity, as progressive and "woke." For example, there is still much to learn about rural California and also about the most northern part of the state with its conservatism and its secession efforts aimed at creating an autonomous "State of Jefferson."[1] Today, what we can say is that even in a bastion of progressivism such as Los Angeles, people who consider themselves progressives and liberals often hold conflicting and contradictory ideas about progress, merit, and morality. They want affordable housing for Californians living in the most precarious conditions, but they often do not want it anywhere near them. They publicly support hard-working immigrants but sometimes wonder privately why they do not just "get in line."

We also want you to see the broader relevance of this work. We have already spoken about the ways that California often acts as a harbinger for the future of the country, a designation that is often highlighted by Californians—especially politicians—to claim this place as a leader, as an example, as a possible future for elsewhere in the nation. But if California tells us anything, it may be a cautionary tale. Indeed, if California is the future, then the future is one of extreme inequality, where wokeness, especially when it is performative and superficial, will not save us. It is a place in which having a structural view of inequality as it relates to race, immigration, and especially class, may frustrate many Californians but not enough to give up the dream of the place.

Social scientists have never been great at predicting the future. Sociologists in particular have sometimes shied away from actually giving policy advice for fear of being implicated in political battles, of being wrong, and, most importantly, of the finality of having a recommendation published on a page. Furthermore, offering up policy recommendations is difficult when we know that policies are situated in complex political and economic contexts, often requiring compromises that water down principled positions to settle for tacit agreements.

We both have analyzed this precise issue in our previous research. We are also aware that research is sometimes used to inform policy debates in ways that are not aligned with the researcher's intent. We are therefore apprehensive about giving any specific policy recommendations. At the same time, we did not want to miss this opportunity to dream up a better future. What we offer here is not a specific set of policies or a detailed position on existing policy debates but rather a vision of what we imagine as a better future, a way for California to move closer to the dream, toward a more egalitarian future.

We Dream of Racial Repair

We are experiencing a unique period in history, as political discussions about reparations for the descendants of enslaved Africans have advanced further than at any point since the initial commitments made during Reconstruction.[2] We are also witnessing the historic Land Back movement, which has strong roots in California, with infrastructure and practices that make the demands of indigenous communities for the reclamation of land more realistic than ever before.[3] These movements also reveal the profound constraints to fostering racial repair through reform and with a limited set of policy tools.

Discussions around reparations and land reclamation suggest the need for radical redistribution of material resources as well as a fundamental reconfiguration of how we think about power, property, and the collective good. Both sets of discussions are focused on the material and commodifiable, even as the main activists, organizers, and experts pushing for these changes have advocated for more expansive visions of change. It is encouraging to see California lead these national conversations about what to do in the wake of slavery and the deadly processes of land grabbing from indigenous communities that established the American West as we know it, and which are ongoing. Perhaps precisely because California is leading some of these discussions about repair and reclamation, it is here that we see their limits more clearly. We've already made it to what looked like a horizon and found that it may have only been a mirage.

Dreaming up a better future for Californians, regardless of their race, would mean tending to the racial violence, discrimination, and premature death that Black Californians have experienced and continue to experience in this state. It would also require serious work to unsettle the infrastructure of settler colonialism that made this state possible in the first place, including rematriation and rethinking commodifiable land rights alongside shifting our language about what this place is and who belongs here. Racial repair would also need to address the ways Latinos and Asians have been and are currently victimized by racism and how they have found themselves on the marginalized side of state and city policies that target them specifically.

In this dream, we find hope in the recent discussions around AB101, the historic bill that makes ethnic studies a high school graduation requirement in the Golden State. We see this as an important opportunity that, if handled with the serious reflection and commitment it deserves, could offer the children of California inroads to a better understanding of the ways that racial inequalities of various types have shaped our past and continue to structure our present and future. Ultimately, though, the work of addressing racial repair in California, if it were ambitious, would have to be, like all things related to race in California, on a large scale and done in a way that tends to the social complexity of this place. More fundamentally, it would have to be centered around deep empathy and connecting our stories of privilege and disadvantage to each other so that we might start to see ourselves and our futures as intertwined.

We Dream of Housing for All

On paper, cities like Los Angeles and San Francisco have done quite a lot to address the housing crisis, including finding creative solutions to building affordable housing, offering preferential/voucher programs to people previously displaced from a housing project, and building different types of facilities for the unhoused. On the surface, large cities seem to be moving toward addressing this dire situation, even as homeless encampments and extremely high rents have become all too normalized for people living there. But the pace of progress has been much too slow, outpaced by incredible need that seems to be transforming how we can relate to one another as neighbors.

For example, although elected officials in San Francisco created an ambitious long-range plan in 2022 to meet its housing needs over the following decade, the city has fallen far behind its annual building targets, especially with respect to low-income and affordable housing.

Housing advocates note that affordable housing permits continue to get mired in bureaucratic red tape, while luxury and above-moderate-income housing projects get fast-tracked. These delays are happening in a city where the average rental price is close to $3,500 a month and where families are sometimes displaced from one housing project only to be displaced again.[4] Reading the news, one might get the impression that the city is providing reparative solutions to the housing crisis but, in practice, it often offers convoluted, bureaucratic gestures that do not provide real access to tangible below-market housing, at least not for many.

This housing crisis is not contained to San Francisco. It exists in every major city in California. Only 17 percent of LA residents can afford a median-priced home in the city, and that rate drops to 11 percent in San Diego. And across all the major cities, people overwhelmingly report spending more than 30 percent of their income on rent. There are myriad stories of teachers, social workers, and full-time workers falling into housing instability at staggering rates. It is no wonder that the Golden State hosts 50 percent of the nation's unhoused population even as elected officials draft compassionate, ambitious, and visionary housing plans year after year.

What these disputes around housing reveal are the contradictions of belonging. What we need in California is a real response to the housing crisis, one that requires taking seriously the preferences of constituencies without succumbing to the tyranny of the home-owning class. NIMBYism should not be able to veto an otherwise just and pragmatic approach to inequality that offers a solution to a problem that everyone recognizes. What the partial and failed solutions to these problems reveal is that having a critique of corporations and the rich has never, on its own, given a single person food or shelter. For that we need more indignation, more compassion, more action. Ultimately, the question of who belongs here can most clearly be seen in the thousands of people who try to make a home for themselves on the streets of this beautiful state, in the most impossible of circumstances.

We Dream of Better Work Conditions and More Dignified Lives for Immigrants

California is currently home to over ninety Whole Foods Markets, often facetiously called "Whole Paycheck." That is by far the largest number of Whole Foods locations in any state in the nation. We mention

Whole Foods because California is a place where discourses about free-range, organic, and non-GMO foods abound and where a segment of the population is very used to paying a lot for those labels. California also has the distinction of producing about one-third of all domestic vegetables and three-quarters of all fruit and nuts.[5] In other words, we have no shortage of food here, something we see firsthand in the culture of going to farmers markets and farm stands nearly year-round. This practice makes us both close and far away from farmworkers, one of the most exploited labor sectors in this state and the country, one overwhelmingly composed of immigrants and the undocumented. The fact that the availability of our food, and therefore our lives, depend on immigrant labor implicates all of us.

We know that California has led the way in recent decades by passing progressive legislation allowing for the social ease and integration of immigrants—even sometimes the undocumented—in terms of driver's licenses, bilingual education, and health care. Indeed, in Oakland, a measure passed in 2022 allowing undocumented immigrant parents to vote in school board elections. Similar efforts are now being considered in other parts of the state. Without question, this is a state where, for the most part, and in most places, politicians have used the legislature and the tools of direct democracy to liberalize certain social processes that would give immigrants a more stable social footing.

Without minimizing these important moves, we also need to tend to the material aspects of immigrant lives. As we have discussed throughout this book, immigrants embody the California dream and at the same time reveal its limitations, its foreclosure, its extinguishing. One dream we have around immigration is that this state could become a true sanctuary for immigrants in every sense of the word—that in addition to living without the constant fear of deportation, we address some of the material precarity of immigrants—the kinds of things for which organizations like the United Farm Workers and the Coalition for Humane Immigrant Rights Los Angeles, among many others, have been valiantly fighting for decades. We dream that immigrants might not have to live in a constant, chronic, and backbreaking state of working poverty.

Solving California's increasingly vexing problems of inequality will be akin to ironing a shirt. Once the wrinkle is smoothed out in that one spot, and just after you've congratulated yourself for a job well done, you flip over the shirt only to find that the other side is now more wrinkled than it was before. With this framework, making life more livable for farmworkers, offering them the chance of actually living to old age, to become grandparents and great-grandparents, will most likely require consumers to pay more for the fruits and vegetables they buy at market that are delivered through the sweat, tears, and worn-down bodies of others. Paying more for fruits and vegetables would be a very hard pill to swallow for many in a state that already has the highest-priced groceries in the country,[6] where people already spend almost 30 percent their income on housing,[7] and where consumers pay 30 percent more than the rest of the nation for gas.[8] We are not looking to iron this shirt spot by spot. We instead need a bigger solution, one that matches our woke talk about diversity and immigrant dreams with real regard for immigrant families and their well-being. We need a solution that does not tie the exploitation of some to the mid-range gains of many or to the many excesses of the top one percent.

In her book on future imaginings, Ruha Benjamin wrote, "Who we imagine ourselves to be matters a great deal to who we will become."[9] Taking lessons from this, we believe that we must work to imagine a different California, an exercise that may also require new ways of thinking about what it means to truly belong here. We want to dream up a California where, in addition to seeing our interconnectedness, we also foreground real and honest conversations about how to change the structural conditions that work to widen divides between people. It is our hope that in so doing, in understanding and not minimizing the systemic inequalities that shape our lives and pull us apart, we can arrive at a common understanding of where we are and how we might build the new structures, systems, and beginnings that will bring us together.

And today, this kind of California Dream feels more important than ever. As masked federal agents kidnap our neighbors and friends at hardware stores, parks, schools, and even courthouses where they show up for their immigration hearings; as more and more families fall into homelessness; and as poverty rates skyrocket even among folks that work full-time, it feels more important than ever to keep striving for a different world. Inequality continues to grow here, even while so many people are overworking themselves for a dream that's out of reach, even as national government policies give way to fascism, and even as we stake signs on our lawns proclaiming resistance.

Despite it all, we believe that folks here do already have the seeds for change, if only because they are not completely blind to the structural explanations and effects of inequality. This, at least, is a starting point, one we hope will engender new possibilities, new demands, and new forms of interconnectedness. The people who shared their stories in this book deserve a more fully realized California Dream, as do the people they invoked while making sense of inequality. Our own children, Camilo, Marshawn, and Adela, also deserve this, as do the many diverse students entering classrooms and lecture halls throughout California, year after year, stepping into a world they have no choice but to inherit.

METHODOLOGICAL APPENDIX

We discussed our overall research design in the introduction of this book and highlighted in the preface some of the ways that our own positionalities have shaped this project from its inception. In this methodological appendix, we delve a bit deeper into our research design, including our approach to data collection and analysis of our survey and in-depth interview data.

Phase I: Survey Design

This initial phase of this research project was a survey of California residents that drew from two sources. The first was a random sample of registered voters in California run through the University of California, Berkeley Institute of Governmental Studies California Poll fielded in March of 2019. The Institute of Governmental Studies poll is a quarterly public opinion survey of Californians on important matters of politics, public policy, and public issues, including a battery of questions about local- and state-level dynamics. It includes standard demographic questions concerning gender, race, age, and location (zip code). It also includes information about the respondent's party affiliation, political ideology (on a scale from very conservative to very liberal). We included a host of questions on inequality, economic stability, and racial attitudes, including measures of racial contact, perceptions and experiences of discrimination, and racial ideology.

The second phase of our research involved panel data collected through a contract with Qualtrics Experience Management. The questions we

https://doi.org/10.7758/uybx4321.7739

asked in this survey were identical to the module included in the Institute of Governmental Studies poll, which was conducted in parallel in March 2019 and included both registered and nonregistered voter respondents.[1] We opted for this design because restricting the sample to registered voters would limit what we were able to say with the data, especially with regard to people in groups who are less likely to register or are not eligible to vote.

Our survey included new queries designed to capture opinions on contemporary and local dynamics, but we also included some standardized questions that echo previous regional surveys conducted in the state on race, inequality, and politics. The first of these is the 1986 Race and Politics Survey, conducted in the Bay Area just before the nativist propositions 187 and 227 were passed by California voters.[2] The survey asks a battery of questions about prejudice, race-based public policies, and race relations. The second is the 1994 Los Angeles Study on Urban Inequality, conducted soon after the Rodney King riots, which includes questions about racial positioning and neighborhood perceptions.[3] Finally, we included some questions from the 2016 Collaborative Multiracial Post-Election Survey, which includes an oversampling of Californians.[4]

The survey took about fourteen minutes to complete. The poll and Qualtrics panel data combined produced a sample of 6,163 California residents. Black respondents and residents of Central Valley counties were oversampled to achieve sufficient population numbers for our analysis.[5] We then applied poststratification weights to combine the two samples and align the resulting sample to the population characteristics of the entire state. Respondents were given the option to provide email addresses if they were interested in engaging in doing compensated in-depth follow-up interviews.

Ultimately, the survey data were important to our approach because they helped us understand general attitudinal patterns in California, ones that would ultimately inform the design of the in-depth interview guide. Survey findings also helped contextualize and compliment the qualitative findings we focus on in this book. While we ran more complex multivariate analyses throughout this project, we felt that those findings were better suited for article-length publications at a later date.

Phase II: In-Depth Interview Design

The heart of this book is the data derived from in-depth structured interviews. These were designed to help us better understand the meaning-making processes that undergird respondents' attitudes and ideas about inclusion and exclusion and to give us a better sense of how racial and economic inequality figures into people's daily lives. In addition, the interviews provided opportunities for respondents to answer open-ended queries and provide more background on their personal experiences. Research has shown that these multiple kinds of data are especially useful when questions are sensitive or can be interpreted in different ways.[6] This observation is especially important to consider in this moment of racial and political polarization.

The interviews were structured to probe for the subconscious narratives, beliefs, and values that individuals use to organize their political opinions, to draw group boundaries (for example, around race and class), and to take concrete action (such as through voting). Drawing on Arlie Hochschild's notion of a "deep story," the first several sections of the interview guide delve into personal histories and seek to understand a respondent's family background, educational history, working life, aspirations, and daily or weekly habits, including detailed descriptions of daily routines; working relationships and tasks; leisure time, including socializing and participation in clubs or organizations; commuting; and media consumption.[7] Interviewees were also asked to directly identify values they believe are important to teach to children.[8]

Following Nancy DiTomaso's work, respondents were asked a series of questions about their identities and views regarding class, the economy, race, social networks, and belonging.[9] Respondents were first asked to evaluate and or provide an explanation for cultural narratives (like the American Dream),[10] income inequality, the existence of race categories, discrimination, racial unity and disunity, the role of government, and claims of deservingness of government assistance. Views on race were further explored using racial thermometer and racial resentment questions drawn from the poll, formulated to probe the respondent's views on the group with which they identify and on groups with which they do not. For example, a Black respondent would be questioned on their perceptions of both Black communities and Latino, White, and Asian communities. Following Michelle Lamont's work on boundary formation, respondents were asked to describe the qualities that they look for in people they like or with whom they want to be associated as well as qualities of people with whom they prefer to avoid or do not want to be associated. To identify the degrees of social closure and socioeconomic diversity within their networks, respondents were asked to name their five closest friends, identify the race and class identities of these individuals, and talk about what made them feel close to these people. Throughout an interview, we asked multiple questions about place, some of which required respondents to think about their neighborhood, city, region, and state.

The concluding section of the interview focused on politics, posing direct questions about political affiliation, participation, and opinions on specific issues.[11] Respondents were asked to describe and evaluate local and national political issues of concern to them, and were probed to describe their understanding of various actors' political efficacy, views on the role of government, news sources, and analyses of how race and politics may interrelate. Respondents were also asked to give agree/disagree/why assessments for a wide range of national political issues, including immigration, special interests, national- and group-based division and unity, religion, and equal treatment. The interview closed with the opportunity for respondents to clarify or express anything they believed remained unstated or inadequately addressed.

For the in-depth interview and data analysis phases of the research, we hired a team of graduate student research assistants, including LA-based and Fresno-based interviewers who, along with the co-principal investigator of this research, carried out the in-depth interviews for this study.[12] We conducted racial matching for interviews so that, for example, Asian American respondents were interviewed by Asian American interviewers. We took this approach in part because of the sensitivity of some of the questions around experiences with race and racial discrimination as well as racial attitudes more generally.[13] However, we were not able to conduct matching beyond these broad racial categories, and all interviews were conducted in English. Research assistants attended a day-long orientation, conducted pilot interviews with co-principal investigators, and attended regular team meetings to brainstorm about the best locations for interviews, discuss recruitment strategies, and explore ways to improve interview techniques. Interviews were conducted from June to September 2019 and from January to February 2020.

We limited our interviews to people in the upper-working and lower-middle classes for pragmatic and analytic reasons, which we outline in the introduction of this book. The main criterion for inclusion in this group was household income. We considered those who made 80–120 percent of the average median income in their county to be part of this group. This approach helped us identify a sample of interviewees in the middle but still diverse in terms of the extent of their material conditions, education, household size, and wealth.[14] Many of the folks we interviewed lived in the liminal space between promise and precarity. Some had two jobs, others worked side gigs. Some worked full-time jobs in government or in education, others worked for nonprofit organizations or owned small businesses, and still others worked as freelancers. About two-thirds of the respondents had college degrees, but almost all did not feel "firmly" middle class or feared slipping downward.

We recruited interview respondents in two ways. The first was through the survey, as we had asked those interested to provide an email address for a potential follow-up interview. The other source of interviewees came from electronic mailing lists.[15] For some subgroups that proved to be harder to recruit, including Black respondents, we advertised with online flyers and electronic mailing lists and conducted some snowball sampling. These strategies were more than sufficient for recruiting a large number of respondents in Los Angeles. However, recruiting in Central Valley proved much more difficult, whether through the original survey sample or online. We suspect that this is in part because of potential distrust of a Bay Area university. Indeed, we hoped that having a principal researcher who had gone to high school in the region and research assistants who lived in the area and were affiliated with Fresno State and The University of California, Merced might eclipse any skepticism about outsiders coming into the region to extract information. Yet recruitment still proved to be difficult. We had a large number of no-shows and had to extend our time in the field by months.

This recruitment challenge was particularly high among Asians and Asian Americans in the Central Valley. And while Black respondents did not have a particularly low yield rate, their overall numbers in the

Central Valley made it challenging to recruit. We engaged in a great deal of direct recruitment for our Central Valley interviewees overall, including more follow up with original survey respondents, some snowball sampling, and physical flyers in areas with higher concentrations of Asian people in Fresno.[16]

In the end, we conducted 136 interviews—eighty-six in Los Angeles and fifty in the Central Valley.[17] Each interview lasted an average of two hours, with the shortest interview lasting forty-five minutes and the longest about four hours. In most cases, respondents were offered choices in terms of where they felt most comfortable meeting. The bulk of the interviews took place in coffee shops that were conveniently located for respondents. Interviewees were offered $50 gift cards in return for their time.

Data Analysis

Including two distinct California regions was important to us, as many studies of California reduce the state to its more populous, coastal cities. We instead wanted to understand how region might shape understandings of race, class and belonging. Moreover, we both were familiar with different versions of California, with Tianna S. Paschel having grown up mostly in the Central Valley between Sacramento, Fresno, and Bakersfield, and G. Cristina Mora in Los Angeles County. Having life experiences in these different regions in California is in part why we embarked on this project and why we asked questions about belonging in each iteration of our data collection.

Data was analyzed inductively by co-authors and a small team of research assistants using MaxQDA qualitative data analysis software. Interviews were transcribed professionally, including pauses and other utterances, as we agreed that they might yield important information. Co-authors conducted the first round of transcript reading to generate an initial set of codes. We then hired a team of graduate students and advanced undergraduates to begin the coding phase of the work. After conducted the initial phase of coding, we identified a number of new codes and finalized a more extensive coding scheme. The team held two initial intercoder reliability sessions to ensure that the applications of the codes were aligned. After some realignment, coders were cleared to begin analyzing the transcripts. We held biweekly meetings during the coding phase of the research to discuss the substance of what we were finding and to make sure that we maintained intercoder reliability.

Finally, we would like to mention one of the biggest challenges we faced during this project. While we knew that any research project, especially one of this scale, would encounter challenges along the way, we were not prepared for the COVID-19 pandemic. We initially planned to include interviews from the Bay Area in this project, but we had to stop those data collection efforts in March 2020, just as they were getting underway. We were also still in the midst of collection data in the Central Valley at that time, substantially complicating recruitment challenges. Rather than continue the Bay Area interviews or the rest of the Central Valley interviews via videoconference, we decided to close the data collection phase of the project in March 2020. We did not make this decision lightly but did so confidently as we wanted to avoid introducing two new variables into the project, which the switch to videoconferencing and the pandemic itself would have inevitably done. As we wrote up the results of this study, it became clear that the inclusion of the two sites (Central Valley and Los Angeles) provided enough data to discern the role of place in our analysis. Altogether, we hope that readers will see these efforts as a useful way to focus on sense-making and reveal the contemporary ways that inequality becomes normalized and reproduced.

NOTES

Introduction

1. Gould and Kandra 2021.
2. This rate is down from a high of about 40 percent in 2016. See Zucman 2019; Kuhn and Ríos-Rull 2025.
3. Anstey 2024; Dohrman and Fallick 2020.
4. We recognize that there are important debates within academia and political movements around naming the population of Latin American descent in the United States. We respect the invitation to think critically about how gender figures into such naming practices and think this is important. Because of this, we thoroughly debated the issue. We decided to use the term *Latino*, only because it would allow us to engage a wider set of audiences that might not be familiar with other terms. It is also important to note that the categories "Black" and "Latino" are not mutually exclusive. In 2020, about six million people—or 4 percent of the overall US Hispanic population identified as Afro-Latino (see Gonzalez-Barrera 2022). California had the second-highest number of Afro-Latinos with 237,000 self-identifying as such (see Galdámez et al. 2023).
5. Aladangady and Forde 2021.
6. See Perry et al. 2024.
7. Kotkin 2023.
8. Zillow 2025; Bentz 2025a; PayScale, n.d.
9. Wagner 2023b.
10. Sheehan 2022.
11. The Hmong people are an ethnic group originating in Southern China whose members fled to Laos, Thailand, and Vietnam in the mid-nineteenth century.
12. A note on context: Many Hmong families came to the United States in the wake of the Vietnam War. They had been recruited at high numbers by the Central Intelligence Agency to engage in anticommunist activities in Vietnam and in the "Secret War" in Laos. Families like Keej's were offered refugee

relocation assistance, which sometimes included special homeowner loans. See Yang 2001.

13. The Dong surname, which is of Chinese origin, is common among the Hmong population.
14. Public Religion Research Institute 2019.
15. The problem in accessing safe drinking water in the poorer farmworker communities in the Central Valley has escalated to the United Nations, which, in 2012, called on state and federal government agencies to address the issue. Yet ten years later, an audit of the State Water Resources Control Board found that the situation had gotten worse for many socioeconomically disadvantaged communities in the Central Valley. See State Water Resources Control Board 2022; Hashi and Morris 2023; Grossi 2014; Brown 2012.
16. State of California, Office of Governor Gavin Newsom 2024b.
17. The California Legislative Analyst Office estimates the cumulative growth rate for first-time homebuyer costs in Fresno Country since 2020 to be 102 percent. See Bentz 2025b.
18. See Reed 2004.
19. Parker 2018.
20. Google, Meta, Apple, Netflix, Airbnb, Salesforce, Uber, Instacart, Pinterest, and X (formerly Twitter), among others, were established in the San Francisco Bay Area and at the time of this writing all had headquarters in the area.
21. Varian 2025.
22. Paluch and Herrera 2023.
23. Kushel et al. 2023.
24. Thorman and Payares-Montoya 2025.
25. Fry 2024.
26. Bohn et al. 2023b.
27. Piketty and Saez 2014.
28. Anderson et al. 2024.
29. Orfield and Ee 2014; Miller 2022.
30. DiFeliciantonio 2022; Anderson et al. 2019.
31. State of California Civil Rights Department 2023
32. Davalos 2023; Ponder et al. 2024.
33. Babones 2008.
34. Lancee and Van De Werfhorst 2012; Fajnzylber et al. 2002.
35. See Masuoka and Junn 2022.
36. Antonsich 2010; Lamont 2023.
37. Ostrove and Long 2007; Trawalter et al. 2021.
38. Also see Lamont 2023, which refers to this as recognition.
39. Glenn 2004.
40. Polanyi 1944; Piketty 2014.
41. Tucker 1978; Polanyi 1944; Du Bois 1899; Bourdieu 1987.
42. Wright 2005; Robinson 2005; Burawoy 1982; López-Sanders 2024; Wilson 1980; Glenn 2004; Blauner 2001.

43. Stuart 2016; Jones 2018.
44. Oeur 2018; Stack 1983; Smith 2007; Rendón 2019; Rosales 2020.
45. See Sanchez Jankowski 2008, Lamont et al. 2010.
46. Rios 2011, 2017.
47. Silva 2013.
48. Hardy and Marcotte 2020; Leonce 2020.
49. Lareau 2011; Friedman 2013.
50. Hauser and Norton 2017. Note that the scholarship on perceptions of inequality in the United Kingdom has existed since the 1980s but has grown substantially in recent decades. The research on the United States is newer but also growing.
51. Gimpelson and Treisman 2017; Xian and Reynolds 2017; Isaacs et al. 2008.
52. Alesina et al. 2018.
53. Hadler 2005.
54. Lipset 1996.
55. Norton 2014.
56. Almås et al. 2019.
57. McCall 2013.
58. There is, of course, work that also posits a middle ground–meso-level framework. This framework involves a sort of interaction between peer groups, such as family and friends, with structural- and individual-level factors. See Homan et al. 2017.
59. Feagin 1972; Feagin 1975; Cech and Blair-Loy 2010; Kluegel and Smith 1986.
60. Heiserman et al. 2020; Trump 2020.
61. Kluegel and Smith 1986; Cech and Blair-Loy 2010.
62. Feagin 1972; Feagin 1975. Reynolds and Xian 2014.
63. Hadler 2005; McCall 2013.
64. Reynolds and Xian 2014; Homan, Valentino, and Weed 2017.
65. Alesina and Angeletos 2005; García-Sánchez et al. 2019.
66. McCall 2013.
67. Silva 2013; Ho 2024.
68. Hochschild 1996.
69. DiTomaso 2013.
70. Forman 2004; Bonilla-Silva 2010; Bobo 2001; Feagin 2013. Bonilla-Silva (2010) argues that in a post-civil-rights US context, in which holding explicitly racist attitudes carries some social stigma, the dominant form of racism that White people exhibit is colorblind racism. He defines this as claiming that racism does matter while still holding views that uphold racism. We use the terms "colorblind" and "colorblindness" in this book with a similarly critical lens.
71. Kraus et al. 2019.
72. Lopez and Pantoja 2004; Hunt 2007; Pew Research Center 2024a.
73. Fussell 2014. There are, of course, important studies that qualitatively probe how individuals think of immigrants, particularly Latino immigrants. And, to some extent, they describe how people understand immigrant welfare. However, this effort is secondary to the broader goal of describing immigration sentiment in the United States. See Parks-Yancy et al. 2009; Lacayo 2017.

74. Cech and Blair-Loy 2010.
75. Katz 2013.
76. See Collier 2013; Luttmer 2001; Pearce 2004; Gründler and Köllner 2020.
77. Kymlicka and Banting 2006.
78. Berger and Luckmann 2011.
79. Goffman 2017; Foucault 1995; Bourdieu 1987.
80. Berger and Luckmann 2011.
81. In *Prison Notebooks*, Gramsci (2011) argues that the main feature distinguishing modern economic and political rule from previous forms of rule is that while the previous forms were characterized mainly by force, modern forms of rule are always a delicate and often unstable balance between force or coercion and consent. To achieve consent, those in power must achieve and impose a commonsense or an unquestioned, assumed set of beliefs or worldview on civil society that serves to naturalize their authority and maintain power. While this more ancient form of power is sometimes called domination, Gramsci identifies the modern version as a more durable form of power called hegemony.
82. Wright's (2000) concept of "class compromise" acknowledges that contestation and agitation do happen in different forms, however, the blend of force and consent present in modern capitalist societies keep such contestation in check.
83. Omi and Winant 2014; Bonilla-Silva 2010. Hanchard (1998) has also conceptualized a particular kind of racial hegemony in the context of Brazil.
84. Hall 1997; Herman and Chomsky 1988.
85. The idea that there is no alternative to capitalism, or TINA, was a slogan popularized in the 1990s as part of the rise of neoliberal capitalism. It is associated with Margaret Thatcher and Ronald Reagan and widely regarded as an important cultural strategy to make alternatives to capitalism inconceivable. See de Sousa Santos 2006; Fisher 2022.
86. Even when society is successful in challenging these laws, as we saw with the civil rights movement, the vestiges of these systems continue to have what social theorist Pierre Bourdieu (1987) called symbolic power, or the unconscious power of cultural domination.
87. Stuart Hall (1997) reminds us that people do not simply adopt, whole-hog, dominant ideas about inequality and "the way things are." Instead, they wrestle with them, negotiate and contest them, and bend their meaning, sometimes in ways that amount to daily forms of resistance. At the same time, they can be seduced and comforted by them and ultimately resigned to accepting how things are. Hall argues that considering these cultural processes in the contexts in which they unfold is critical to understanding society today.
88. Almaguer 2023.
89. Tafoya et al. 2004. We know, though, from the context of Latin America and the Caribbean, racial fluidity can coexist with racial hierarchy, racism, and racial violence. See Smith 2016.
90. Frey 2018.

91. See Jones 2019 for an important look at how the South has come to grapple with similar issues related to increasing inequality and diversity.
92. We see California as a sort of extreme case study whose diversity and inequality bring into greater focus the relational processes involved in sense-making. Focusing on California allows us to see patterns that would be muted in places with less inequality and diversity. See Ermakoff 2014.
93. Kaye 2020.
94. Sharma 2018.
95. US Census Bureau 2024c.
96. Pew Research Center 2024b.
97. Nicolaides 2024; Saito 2023.
98. Lie and Abelmann 2009; Jones-Correa 2001; McClain et al. 2006; Telles et al. 2011.
99. According to Arthur Gailes and colleagues (2021), Los Angeles is sixth among the "most segregated metropolitan statistical areas." According to the Segregation Index, Los Angeles Unified School District is the fifth-most segregated large school district in the United States in terms of Black-White segregation and the sixth-most segregated in terms of Hispanic-White segregation.
100. Gibbons 2018.
101. Policy Link and the University of Southern California Program for Environmental and Regional Equity 2017.
102. See Holmes and Berube 2016.
103. Bonner 2025.
104. See United Way 2023.
105. Policy Link and the University of Southern California Program for Environmental and Regional Equity 2017.
106. Mejia et al. 2024b.
107. Starr 1996.
108. The nation's top three agricultural counties are all in California: Fresno, Tulare, and Kern.
109. California Water Science Center, n.d.; Escriva-Bou et al. 2023
110. US Census Bureau 2024a.
111. Leonard 2024.
112. Central Valley Community Foundation 2024.
113. California Association of Realtors 2024; Stacker 2022.
114. Central Valley Community Foundation 2024.
115. For more comprehensive, contemporary accounts of racial disparities in the Central Valley, see RACE COUNTS 2023.
116. McGhee 2020.
117. See Kimelman 2024.
118. There are valuable quantitative studies that engage in this comparative work, including many emerging from the Collaborative Multiracial Post-Election Survey. See also Vargas and Stainback 2015.
119. Bellah 1996.

120. Hauhart 2016.
121. Cullen 2004; Hanson and White 2011; Jillson 2016.
122. Lipset 1996.
123. Starr 1973; Starr 1997; Starr 2011.
124. Grandin 2019.
125. LaSalle 2021.
126. Perlmann 2005.
127. Fox 2012; Glenn 2004.
128. Davidai and Gilovich 2023; Markovits 2020.
129. Rodríguez-Muñiz 2024; Harris and Hahn 2011; Beckert and Suckert 2021.
130. Buunk and Mussweiler 2001, 467; Festinger 1954.
131. Blumer 1958.
132. Wills 1981; Gibbons and Gerrard 1989.
133. Goethals 1986: 271.
134. Lamont 2009; Lamont and Fournier 1992.
135. Valentine 1969; Lewis 1959, 1966, 1969.
136. Lamont et al. 2010.

Chapter One: From the American Dream to California Dreamin'

1. State of California, Office of Governor Gavin Newsom 2025.
2. The Mamas and The Papas 1965.
3. Friedersdorf 2021.
4. Zacchino 2016; Pastor 2018; Mathews and Paul 2010; Schrag 2004.
5. Owens 1999.
6. Brown 2022.
7. Jacobson 2008.
8. Bass and Cain 2008.
9. See Schachner 2022; Pew 2017.
10. See Nagel and Nivette 2023.
11. Levin 2021.
12. Blanco 2023.
13. Hagan et al. 2019.
14. Hauhart 2016; Rank et al. 2014.
15. Adams 2012.
16. Obama 2006.
17. Wolak and Peterson 2020.
18. McCormack 1987.
19. United Press International 2004.
20. Hanson and Zogby 2010.
21. Hanson and Zogby 2010.
22. Hanson and Zogby 2010.

23. Schwarz 2023.
24. Baldassare et al. 2023a.
25. Nichols 2008.
26. Young et al. 2023; The Investopedia Team 2024.
27. Mahler 2021.
28. Jones 2021.
29. Beltrán 2020.
30. Grandin 2019.
31. Montejano 2010; Almaguer 2023.
32. Molina 2014.
33. King 1960.
34. Hochschild 1996; Hauhart 2016; Rank et al. 2014.
35. Wiley et al. 2012; Hedegaard 2019.
36. DiTomaso 2013; Kluegel and Smith 1986.
37. Starr 2007.
38. US Census Bureau 2024b.
39. About 25,000 Mexican immigrants came to California between 1848 and 1852 alone. See Carrigan and Webb 2003.
40. According to Sucheng Chan 1986, by 1860, Chinese immigrants represented about 10 percent of the overall population and one-third of the total nonindigenous population in mining counties.
41. Pierce 2016.
42. Pierce 2016.
43. Wrobel 2002, 34, as cited by Pierce 2016.
44. Eric Avila (2006) notes that White migrants to Los Angeles found the small size of the Black population particularly appealing.
45. Avila 2006.
46. Kanazawa 2005.
47. Pfaelzer 2008.
48. Broussard 1993. It is important to note that some of this Black wealth was premised on the dispossession of Japanese Americans, whose internment had left parts of San Francisco, including the Fillmore, empty.
49. Flamming 2005, 36.
50. Sides 2003, 11.
51. Sides 2003, 39.
52. Sides 2003.
53. See Murch 2010; Broussard 1993; Sides 2003; Flamming 2005.
54. Sides 2003.
55. Gilmore 2007.
56. Tong 2004.
57. Glenn 1992.
58. Almaguer 2023.
59. Hayes-Bautista 2004.
60. Carrigan and Webb 2013.

61. Gonzales-Day 2006.
62. Cohen 2011.
63. This is our best estimate based on multiple data sources including the data compiled by José Cobas and colleagues (2018). In the early decades, estimates used the population of Mexican descent as a proxy for the Latino population more generally. In later years, the separation of a Hispanic ethnicity question meant that we had to make adjustments to offer a general picture of the trends. Finally, while the Native American population is not very visible on this graph, we do not want to contribute to their further erasure. The Native population in California stayed somewhat consistent at less than 1 percent over this 120-year period.
64. Almaguer 2023.
65. Telles and Ortiz 2008.
66. Catanzarite 2002.
67. Pitt 1998.
68. See Johnson 1996; Rojas 2010; Murch 2010; Rogers 2011; Pulido 2002; Paiz 2023.
69. Office of the Attorney General 2024.
70. On The Issues 2021.
71. Pham and Van 2024.
72. Cha et al. 2023; Finn 2023; Bohn and Schiff 2011; AP News 2024.
73. Andrews 2016.
74. Pierce 2016, 97.
75. Pierce 2016.
76. Grandin 2019, 3.
77. Starr and Orsi 2000.
78. Brilliant 2014.
79. McWilliams 1999; Turner 1893; Brilliant 2014. Mark Brilliant (2014) analyzes the life and legacy of Carey McWilliams, attorney and author, who thought that racial prejudice was a "malignant growth" on society and worked for decades litigating against formal segregation and writing about the possibilities of racial egalitarianism.
80. Brilliant 2014, 19.
81. Also see Avila 2006.
82. See Almaguer 2023.
83. Hosang 2010; Lytle Hernandez 2017.
84. Humes 2014.
85. Cohen 2008.
86. Hauhart 2016.
87. LaSalle 2021; Sternheimer 2014.
88. Nash 1972.
89. Starr 2007.
90. Starr 2011; Lindsey 1978.
91. Morris 2018.
92. Butler 1986.

93. Chavez 2008; Ana 2002; Daniel 1981; Armacost 1981; Lang and Hogue 1983.
94. Nash 1972.
95. Legislative Analyst's Office 1995.
96. Thorman and Payares-Montoya 2025.
97. Woods 2012, 192.

Chapter Two: Class Inequality in the Land of Plenty

1. Zhu et al. 2021.
2. Our findings indicating that most respondents across the political spectrum agreed that inequality was growing echoes a 2015 Institute of Governmental Studies survey. See Ahler et al. 2015.
3. Thorman and Payares-Montoya 2025; Sharma 2018.
4. Schafran 2018; Dougherty 2020.
5. Ahler et al. 2015.
6. Baldassare et al. 2021.
7. Nichols 2018.
8. Riquier 2018.
9. Ronayne 2021.
10. Roubenoff et al. 2023; Christopher 2020; Johnson and McGhee 2025.
11. Kanell 2018.
12. Prevatt 2021.
13. Kanell 2018; Friday, Jones, and Blake 2023.
14. Fadel 2022; LePard 2022.
15. This mirrors much survey research on structural thinkers—those who understand that inequality is tied to unfair advantages that stem from one's social location. See Kluegel and Smith 1986; Reynolds and Xian 2014.
16. Thomas 2021.
17. Johnson and McGhee 2025.
18. Baldassari 2024.
19. Henry et al. 2021.
20. Henry et al. 2021, 1.
21. Baldassare et al. 2023a.
22. Davidai and Gilovich 2018.
23. Frank 2017; Franko 2013.
24. Xu and Garand 2010.
25. Piketty 2014; Horowitz et al. 2020.
26. Rowlingson et al. 2010.
27. Sharot 2011.
28. Davidai and Gilovich 2018.
29. Rozsypal and Schlafmann 2023; Balleer et al. 2021; Conlon et al. 2018; Peetz and Buehler 2009.
30. Swidler 2001; Pugh 2015.

31. See also Ho 2024.
32. Christopher 2020; McGhee 2020.
33. Hall 2022; Bowen and Capozziello 2022.

Chapter Three: Racial Inequality in the Land of Multiracial Promise

1. Gilmore 2007.
2. Evans 1992.
3. Apple 1975
4. Sides 2003.
5. Hutchful 2018.
6. California Reparations Task Force 2023.
7. The Civil Rights Project 2014.
8. Hutchful 2018.
9. Proposition 187 (1993), which sought to deny undocumented immigrants access to health care, education, and social services, and Proposition 209 (1996), which effectively banned affirmative action in higher education, public jobs, and government contracting, stand out as notable examples. It is important to remember that Proposition 187 passed with 58 percent of the vote but was never fully implemented because of court rulings, including at the federal level. Both propositions would offer blueprints for anti-affirmative action to anti-immigrant legislators and lobbyists in other states in the following decades.
10. Ramirez and Bort 2024.
11. This is similar to the way that Mark Q. Sawyer (2005) describes "Latin American Exceptionalism" in the context of Cuba.
12. Kanter 1977.
13. See Junn 2007; Junn and Masuoka 2008.
14. It is worth noting that we collected this data before the upsurge in hate crimes against Asians in 2020 and 2021, which was partially fueled by the erroneous idea that the COVID-19 pandemic was "Asian" in origin and possibly created intentionally by China. This upsurge in Anti-Asian hate crime has subsided, with numbers now similar to pre-pandemic rates and much closer to the rate of "anti-White" crimes than to the hate crime rates against Latinos and especially Blacks. See Bonta 2022.
15. Kim 2003.
16. Feagin and Cobas 2015; Zamora 2022.
17. Ethington 2000; Pulido 2006; Wright et al. 2014.
18. Othering and Belonging Institute 2020.
19. Orfield and Ee 2014.
20. Fuller et al. 2019; Pinto-Coelho and Zuberi 2015.
21. Ethington 2000.
22. While there is no official count of people of Punjabi ancestry in the United States, most unofficial estimates point to California's Central Valley as a place

with one of the highest—or perhaps the highest—concentrations in the country (Wyatt 2024).

23. The most vivid and overt versions of Asian respondents minimizing their own experiences with racism came from male respondents, raising important questions about how constructions of masculinity might be shaping how they talk about their feelings. It is possible that these respondents shook off these experiences and were reticent to show signs of sadness and hurt because they were socialized not to, not specifically regarding racial incidents but in general. See Chua and Fujino (1999), Ocampo (2022).
24. See Smith (2016) and Shange (2019) for more on the prevalence of racial paradise narratives stacked on top of deep racial inequality and violence.
25. Perry 2023.
26. We asked survey respondents if they agreed with the following two statements: (1) Racism is alive and well in California; and (2) Racism is alive and well in the United States.
27. The gap was 14.1 percent for Black people and 13.6 percent for Latinos.
28. This reduction of California to its cities also happens in popular culture and to some extent in the extant research on contemporary California. Los Angeles or the Bay Area often serve as a stand-in for the state of California in such studies. Almaguer (2023), for example, guides our thinking in this research and at the same time, it uses data on the Bay Area to talk about California writ large.
29. It is important to note that sundown towns are designed to create and maintain racial segregation in the form of White enclaves. They almost always rely on racial violence or the threat of it but are established through a variety of means, including legal statutes, covenants, and redlining policies.
30. Pfaelzer 2008.
31. Loewen 2005.
32. It is important to note that this interview was conducted by a White graduate-student research assistant on our team. If the interview hadn't been racially matched, he might have been even less forthcoming.
33. We saw similar declarations when respondents talked about places like Orange County and other conservative and often less diverse places that they would rather excise from California than grapple with the messiness.
34. For incarceration rates, see Harris and Cremin 2024; for homelessness rates, see Benioff Homelessness and Housing Initiative 2024; for poverty rates, see McGhee 2023.
35. Hooker 2005; Ferguson 2012; Smith 2016; Shange 2019.
36. DelaRosa and Pereira 2023.
37. Swaine and Laughland 2015.
38. Embedded in Luv's comments is an uncomfortable awareness of Hmong people's status at the bottom of the Asian social totem pole in the United States. Nationally, we know that, whereas only 27 percent of Asians have less than a high school diploma, that rate is 48 percent among the Hmong population. In addition, incomes among the Hmong are lower, they have less wealth, and they

are much more likely to live in poverty than the Asian population as a whole. These dynamics are prevalent in California, which was once home to about 60 percent of the Hmong population in the United States (see Vang and Flores 1999). While outmigration has decreased that rate to about 30 percent, Fresno still has the second largest Hmong population in the country, after St. Paul, Minnesota. While there are not nationally representative data available, qualitative studies have shown that Hmong people report high levels of racial discrimination based on language and other factors (see Hein 2000). The Hmong respondents in this study often alluded to such discrimination but did not emphasize it.

39. Mora and Paschel 2020.
40. Kim 2003.

Chapter Four: Immigrant Inequality in the Land of Sanctuary

1. The formal program recruited Mexican agricultural migrants to work in fields in the United States with temporary status because the nation faced a labor shortage. Between 1942 and 1964, the program would bring in about 4.5 million migrant laborers to the United States. See Mize 2016; Library of Congress, n.d.
2. Kaiser Family Foundation 2025.
3. State of California, Office of Governor Gavin Newsom 2022.
4. Pham and Van 2020.
5. Mejia et al. 2024a.
6. The Children's Partnership 2021.
7. State of California, Office of Governor Gavin Newsom 2024c.
8. Fussell 2014; Gleeson 2016; Quijano 2020; Bond et al. 2020; Costa 2018.
9. California Department of Housing and Community Development 2023.
10. Bugarin and Lopez 1998.
11. Bohn and Schiff 2011.
12. Bohn et al. 2023a.
13. Camarota et al. 2023; Hall and Greenman 2013.
14. We did, however, find some clear variation by race of respondent. While only 11 percent of Asians strongly agreed that immigrants are treated unfairly in California, this rate nearly tripled when we asked the question about the United States. The group with the smallest gap between these two questions were Black respondents, who were overall more hesitant to embrace the idea that California was a fair place for immigrants. The gap among Latinos was also relatively small.
15. Phillips 2017.
16. Boak 2019.
17. See Jones 2019.
18. Catanzarite 2000.
19. Kim 2003; Mora and Paschel 2020.
20. California Immigrant Data Portal 2024.
21. Gleeson 2016.

22. Frank 2017; Markovits 2020.
23. Wagner 2023a.
24. Beacon Economics 2019.
25. Flores and Schachter 2018.
26. Wright et al. 2014; Levy and Wright 2020.
27. Baldassare et al. 2023b.
28. Watson and Thompson 2022.
29. Bonilla-Silva 2010.
30. Mora and Paschel 2020.
31. Obinna and Bacong 2024.
32. Chishti and Kamasaki 2014.
33. US Citizenship and Immigration Services 2022.
34. Bier 2023.
35. Menjívar 2006.
36. Hernández 2024.
37. Dietz et al. 2023.
38. Watson and Thompson 2022.
39. Watson and Thompson 2022.
40. Hernández 2024.
41. Bonilla-Silva 2010.
42. Alvarenga 2023.
43. Sklar 2019; City News Service 2019; Merl 2011.
44. Cadelago 2024.
45. Cadelago 2024.
46. Norman 2025.
47. Many cases have been reported in the Central Valley, including at Bullard High School in Fresno. (KSEE 2018). Also see ACLU Southern California 2016.
48. Benen 2024; Sullivan 2024; Jingnan and Garsd 2024.
49. Dávila 2008; Chavez 2008.

Chapter Five: Belonging in the Future

1. Du Bois (1903) 2009.
2. Weil (1958) 2001; Du Bois (1903) 2009. See Davidson 2020 for an analysis of Du Bois's theorizing of the future beyond teleology.
3. Davis 2006.
4. Mische 2014; Selin 2008; Rodríguez-Muñiz 2024.
5. Selin 2008.
6. Benjamin 2024.
7. Rodríguez-Muñiz 2024, 85.
8. Tutton 2017, 488.
9. De León and Rendon 2016.
10. Statista 2024.
11. Lazarow 2020.
12. See Playa Vista 2023.

13. Benjamin 2024.
14. Eigenheer 1976.
15. California Water Science Center, n.d.
16. State of California, Department of Finance 2024.
17. This is similar to the ways that the discussions about racism in California—as we show in other chapters—are often seen through eyes that compare it to places like the US South.
18. Metropolitan Transportation Commission 2008; Vartabedian 2022.
19. See Simon 2022; Galeano 1971; Anzaldúa 1987.
20. US Census Bureau 2023.
21. Day and Abraham 1993; Wong 2024.
22. Stoll 2024.
23. Cimini 2021; Ponder et al. 2024.
24. Harris and Cremin 2024.
25. Bohn et al. 2023a.
26. See Brandon 2021.
27. US Census Bureau 2023.
28. Sugrue and Carmona. 2023.
29. The State Bar of California, n.d.; Crontreras 2023; Association of Medical Colleges 2023; Musibay 2024.
30. Carmona and Barragan-Monge 2022.
31. US Government Accountability Office 2021; Martinez 2021.
32. See HOPE 2023; California Latino Legislative Caucus 2015.
33. See Chavez 2008; Rodríguez-Muñiz 2024.
34. Chavez 2008.
35. Hochschild 2018.
36. Telles et al. 2011.
37. It is also important to note that, whereas African Americans' negative perception of immigrants and sometimes of Latinos by proxy may stem from nativism, there is also a great deal of evidence of anti-Black racism in Latin America and the Caribbean, which fuels negative perceptions of African Americans and premigration distrust. These ideas of anti-Blackness are rooted in similar histories of settler colonialism and racialized slavery (see Zamora 2022).
38. Trudeau 2006; McKittrick 2006; Lefebvre 1992.
39. Smith et al. 2023; Case et al. 2023; Carmona et al. 2025; Carmona and Barragan-Monge 2022; UCLA Latino Policy and Politics Institute 2024.
40. McGhee 2023; Bonner and Ramos 2024.

Conclusion

1. See Hunt 2007; Mijs 2018.
2. Moreover, our findings dovetail with social psychology research that shows that individualist and structural understandings of inequality may not be opposite ends of a spectrum but rather distinct frameworks that can coexist, however seemingly contradictory they may be. See Hunt 2007 or Mijs 2018.

3. Xian and Reynolds 2017; Merolla et al. 2011.
4. Lukes 1973; O'Brien 2015; Eagleton 2014.
5. Lukes 1973; Eagleton 2014.
6. McKittrick 2006; Pulido 2006; Sánchez 2021; Cheng 2013.
7. As we think about the idea of place, it is important to note the absence of other regions of California in our research. Most conspicuously absent is the San Francisco Bay Area, at least in our methodological design. Of course, the Bay Area was present in this book as it was often mentioned by respondents in Los Angeles and the Central Valley. By the time the COVID-19 pandemic interrupted our data collection, we had already thought a great deal about the Bay Area since we had both lived there for over three decades. We thought it would be an important place to explore how Californians understand and navigate inequality in the state because it has increasingly come to embody the two ends of the spectrum of material inequalities—Silicon Valley and extreme homelessness. We believe our findings have important implications for how we might think about inequality and belonging in this part of the state and beyond.
8. Almaguer 2023; Sexton 2023; Jefferson 2022; Starr 1973.
9. Skoneki and Schweers 2023.
10. Summers (2019), for example, shows how Washington DC's history as the "Chocolate City" profoundly shapes the discourse and aesthetics of economic development there, just as it shapes how residents react to gentrification.

Epilogue: Our Dream for California

1. Hubler 2021; Vankin 2023.
2. California Reparations Task Force 2023.
3. State of California, Office of Governor Gavin Newsom 2023, 2024a; Cowan 2024.
4. Zillow Rentals 2024.
5. California Department of Food and Agriculture 2024.
6. Ruderman 2024.
7. Patoka 2023.
8. AAA 2024.
9. Benjamin 2024.

Methodological Appendix

1. The survey was fielded as part of the Berkeley Institute of Governmental Studies Poll, a quarterly public opinion survey of Californians on important matters of politics, public policy, and public issues, including a battery of questions about local- and state-level dynamics. The poll is an online survey conducted in English and Spanish, which recruits participants by emailing a stratified random sample of residents gleaned from registered voter lists and online directories. The panel sample was obtained through a contract with Qualtrics.
2. Sniderman and Piazza 1986.

3. There are also a few polls that have been conducted over the past decade that asked voters in California specific questions about racial attitudes and support for race- and class-based policies. We will also look at these more closely.
4. Frasure et al. 2016.
5. After processing our data, we applied poststratification weights to align the sample to the overall population characteristics of the state. While difficult to determine with certainty, it is likely that the results are subject to a sampling error of about 3 percentage points at a 95 percent confidence level. The survey included questions on issues including politics and ideology, the economic outlook, and immigration.
6. Small 2011.
7. Hochschild 2018.
8. Lamont 2009.
9. DiTomaso 2013.
10. Hochschild 2018.
11. DiTomaso 2013.
12. We also hired research assistants to conduct our Bay Area interviews, although as we explain later, that portion of the research was halted because of the COVID-19 pandemic.
13. We recognize that because race is a social construct and that there is great variation in phenotypes and ethnicities, interviewers had to navigate complex dynamics regarding insider-outsider status, racial membership, and other differences between themselves and the interviewees.
14. This approach had advantages and disadvantages. We had to return constantly to the demographics of the sample to make sure that the differences we were finding in terms of attitudes were not a function of the economic variation in the sample itself. Black and Latino respondents, for example, tended to be on the lower end of the income range included in the sample.
15. In the end, 22 percent of our interviews from the Los Angeles sample were recruited from the nested design (original survey), while 29 percent of the Central Valley interviews were from this source, reflecting the recruitment challenges we've outlined as well as the restrictions around income and need to achieve racial balance among interviewees.
16. Places we posted flyers included Asian Supermarket, TC Supermarket, RN Market, SF Supermarket, Korea Mart, Indian Mart, Golden Bowl Supermarket, and Hmong Community Alliance Church (all in Fresno).
17. Central Valley interviews were primarily conducted in Fresno, with a few in Merced and Bakersfield. The majority of the interviews were conducted between June and September 2019 and between January and February 2020. We originally planned to conduct more Central Valley interviews; however, we had to pause all interviews because of the COVID-19 pandemic. Rather than introduce another variable that might affect our results, we decided to close the interview data collection phase of our research.

REFERENCES

AAA. 2024. "Gas Prices." https://gasprices.aaa.com/?state=CA.

ACLU Southern California. 2016. "ACLU SoCal Statement on the Display of Confederate Flags by High School Students." Press release, September 7. https://www.aclusocal.org/en/press-releases/aclu-socal-statement-display-confederate-flags-high-school-students.

Adams, James Truslow. 2012. *The Epic of America*. Transaction Publishers.

Ahler, Douglas J., Beckett Kelly, Gabriel Lenz, Ethan Rarick, and Laura Stoker. 2015. "The IGS Survey: Californians' Beliefs About Income Inequality." Institute of Governmental Studies. https://escholarship.org/uc/item/0224560n.

Aladangady, Aditya, and Akila Forde. 2021. "Wealth Inequality and the Racial Wealth Gap." *FEDS Notes*. Board of the Governors of the Federal Reserve System. https://www.federalreserve.gov/econres/notes/feds-notes/wealth-inequality-and-the-racial-wealth-gap-20211022.html.

Alesina, Alberto, and George-Marios Angeletos. 2005. "Fairness and Redistribution." *American Economic Review* 95(4): 960–80. https://doi.org/10.1257/0002828054825655.

Alesina, Alberto, Stefanie Stantcheva, and Edoardo Teso. 2018. "Intergenerational Mobility and Preferences for Redistribution." *American Economic Review* 108(2): 521–54. https://doi.org/10.1257/aer.20162015.

Almaguer, Tomas. 2023. *Racial Fault Lines: The Historical Origins of White Supremacy in California*. University of California Press.

Almås, Ingvild, Alexander W. Cappelen, and Bertil Tungodden. 2019. "Cutthroat Capitalism Versus Cuddly Socialism: Are Americans More Meritocratic and Efficiency-Seeking Than Scandinavians?" *Journal of Political Economy* 128(5): 1753–88. https://doi.org/10.1086/705551.

Alvarenga, Emily. 2023. "'He Instigated A Lot of Hatred': Dolores Huerta, San Diegans Call to Remove Pete Wilson Statue Downtown." *The San Diego Union-Tribune*, June 19. https://www.sandiegouniontribune.com/2023/06/04/he-instigated-a-lot-of-hatred-dolores-huerta-san-diegans-call-to-remove-pete-wilson-statue-downtown/.

Ana, Otto Santa. 2002. *Brown Tide Rising: Metaphors of Latinos in Contemporary American Public Discourse*. University of Texas Press.

Anderson, Alissa, Kayla Kitson, Laura Pryor, Adriana Ramos-Yamamoto, and Monica Saucedo. 2024. "California's Poverty Rate Soars to Alarmingly High Levels in 2023." California Budget and Policy Center. https://calbudgetcenter.org/resources/californias-poverty-rate-soars-to-alarmingly-high-levels-in-2023/.

Anderson, Alissa, Sara Kimberlin, Amy Rose, Kayla Kitson, and Esi Hutchful. 2019. "California's Workers Are Increasingly Locked Out of the State's Prosperity California Budget and Policy Center." California Budget and Policy Center. https://calbudgetcenter.org/resources/californias-workers-are-increasingly-locked-out-of-the-states-prosperity/.

Andrews, George Reid. 2016. *Afro-Latin America: Black Lives, 1600–2000*. Harvard University Press.

Anstey, Chris. 2024. "The Middle Class Is Getting Squeezed by Debt Costs." *Bloomberg*, March 15. https://www.bloomberg.com/news/newsletters/2024-03-15/world-economy-latest-middle-class-squeeze.

Antonsich, Marco. 2010. "Searching for Belonging–An Analytical Framework." *Geography Compass* 4(6): 644–59.

Anzaldúa, Gloria. 1987. *Borderlands/La Frontera*. Aunt Lute Press.

Apple, R. W., Jr. 1975. "Black Students Quit Ghost Town." *New York Times*, June 4. https://www.nytimes.com/1975/06/04/archives/black-students-quit-coast-town-departure-follows-clash-with-white.html.

AP News. 2024. "California Lawmakers Pass Bill that Could Make Undocumented Immigrants Eligible for Home Loans." *AP News*, August 28. https://apnews.com/article/california-housing-loans-undocumented-immigrants-legislature-newsom-0882972ed1de9fd33e2800d1c699accd.

Armacost, Samuel H. 1981. "Immigration Wave Brings More Hispanics into Labor Force." *The American Banker*, August 22.

Association of Medical Colleges. 2023. "U.S. Physician Workforce Data Dashboard." http://www.aamc.org/data-reports/data/2022-physician-specialty-data-report-executive-summary#:~:text=In%202021%2C%2063.9%25%20of%20practicing,Other%20Pacific%20Islander%20(0.1%25).

Avila, Eric. 2006. *Popular Culture in the Age of White Flight: Fear and Fantasy in Suburban Los Angeles*. University of California Press.

Babones, Salvatore J. 2008. "Income Inequality and Population Health: Correlation and Causality." *Social Science & Medicine* 66(7): 1614–26. https://doi.org/10.1016/j.socscimed.2007.12.012.

Baldassare, Mark, Dean Bonner, Rachel Lawler, and Deja Thomas. 2021. "PPIC Statewide Survey: Californians and Their Economic Well-Being." Public Policy Institute of California, November. https://www.ppic.org/publication/ppic-statewide-survey-californians-and-their-economic-well-being-november-2021/.

Baldassare, Mark, Dean Bonner, Lauren Mora, and Deja Thomas. 2023a. "PPIC Statewide Survey: Californians and Their Economic Well-Being." Public Policy Institute of California, November. http://www.ppic.org/publication/ppic-statewide-survey-californians-and-their-economic-well-being-november-2023.

Baldassare, Mark, Dean Bonner, Rachel Lawler, and Deja Thomas. 2023b. "PPIC Statewide Survey: Californians and Their Government." Public Policy Institute of California, June. https://www.ppic.org/publication/ppic-statewide-survey-californians-and-their-government-june-2023/.

Baldassari, Erin. 2024. "California's Middle Class Declines as Low and High Incomes Surge, Study Shows." *KQED*, July 16. http://www.kqed.org/news/11975039/californias-middle-class-declines-as-low-and-high-incomes-surge-study-shows.

Balleer, Almut, Georg Duernecker, Susanne Forstner, and Johannes Goensch. 2021. "The Effects of Biased Labor Market Expectations on Consumption, Wealth Inequality, and Welfare." *SSRN Electronic Journal* (January). https://doi.org/10.2139/ssrn.3932035.

Barragan-Monge, Paul, and Gabriella Carmona. 2022. "From Disparity to Parity: Latino Representation in Appointed Positions Within California's Gubernatorial Cabinet, State Boards, and Commissions." Latino Policy & Politics Institute. https://latino.ucla.edu/research/ca-appointments-report/.

Bass, Sandra, and Bruce E. Cain. 2008. *Racial and Ethnic Politics in California: Continuity and Change*. IGS Press, Institute of Governmental Studies, University of California, Berkeley.

Beacon Economics. 2019. "The State of Diverse Businesses in California: Economic, Fiscal, and Social Impact Analysis." Cal Asian Chamber of Commerce. https://calasiancc.org/wp-content/uploads/2023/09/CalAsian-Chamber-Minority-Small-Businesses-Impact.pdf.

Beckert, Jens, and Lisa Suckert. 2021. "The Future as a Social Fact. The Analysis of Perceptions of the Future in Sociology." *Poetics* 84: 101499. https://doi.org/10.1016/j.poetic.2020.101499.

Bellah, Robert Neelly. 1996. *Habits of the Heart: Individualism and Commitment in American Life*. University of California Press.

Beltrán, Cristina. 2020. *Cruelty as Citizenship: How Migrant Suffering Sustains White Democracy*. University of Minnesota Press.

Benen, Steve. 2024. "Trump's Dehumanizing Anti-Immigrant Rhetoric Takes a Literal Turn." https://www.msnbc.com/rachel-maddow-show/maddowblog/trumps-dehumanizing-anti-immigrant-rhetoric-takes-literal-turn-rcna146159.

Benioff Homelessness and Housing Initiative. 2024. *Toward Equity: Understanding Black Californians' Experiences of Homelessness*. University of California San Francisco. https://homelessness.ucsf.edu/resources/reports/toward-equity-understanding-black-californians-experiences-homelessness.

Benjamin, Ruha. 2024. *Imagination: A Manifesto*. W. W. Norton.

Bentz, Alex. 2025a. "California Housing Affordability Tracker (Fourth Quarter 2024)." Legislative Analyst's Office, January 15. https://lao.ca.gov/LAOEconTax

/Article/Detail/793#:~:text=Housing%20Costs%20Have%20Grown%20More,$1%2C963.

Bentz, Alex. 2025b. "California Housing Affordability Tracker (2nd Quarter 2025)." Legislative Analyst's Office, July 24. https://lao.ca.gov/LAOEconTax/Article/Detail/793#:~:text=As%20shown%20above%2C%20monthly%20payments,costs%20on%20higher%20loan%20amounts.

Berger, Peter L., and Thomas Luckmann. 2011. *The Social Construction of Reality: A Treatise in the Sociology of Knowledge*. Open Road Media.

Bier, David. 2023. "Why Legal Migration is Nearly Impossible." Cato Institute. https://www.cato.org/policy-analysis/why-legal-immigration-nearly-impossible.

Blanco, Andrea. 2023. "California Police Officer Who Shot and Killed Kneeling Man Will Not Face Charges." *The Independent*, December 21. https://www.the-independent.com/news/world/americas/sean-monterrosa-police-shooting-jarrett-tonn-b2468111.html.

Blauner, Bob. 2001. *Still the Big News: Racial Oppression in America*. Temple University Press.

Blumer, Herbert. 1958. "Race Prejudice as a Sense of Group Position." *The Pacific Sociological Review* 1(1): 3–7. https://doi.org/10.2307/1388607.

Boak, Josh. 2019. "AP Fact Check: Trump Plays on Immigration Myths." *PBS News*, February 8. https://www.pbs.org/newshour/politics/ap-fact-check-trump-plays-on-immigration-myths.

Bobo, Lawrence D. 2001. "Racial Attitudes and Relations at the Close of the Twentieth Century." In *America Becoming: Racial Trends and Their Consequences: Volume 1*. National Academies Press. https://nap.nationalacademies.org/read/9599/chapter/10.

Bohn, Sarah, and Eric Schiff. 2011. "Immigrants and the Labor Market." Public Policy Institute of California, January 29. https://www.ppic.org/publication/immigrants-and-the-labor-market/.

Bohn, Sarah, Caroline Danielson, Sara Kimberlin, Patricia Malagon, and Christopher Wimer. 2023a. "Poverty in California." Public Policy Institute of California. https://www.ppic.org/publication/poverty-in-california/.

Bohn, Sarah, Caroline Danielson, Sara Kimberlin, Patricia Malagon, and Christopher Wimer. 2023b. "The Working Poor in California." Public Policy Institute of California. https://www.ppic.org/interactive/a-snapshot-of-californias-working-poor/.

Bohn, Sarah, Dean Bonner, Julien Lafortune, and Tess Thorman. 2020. "Income Inequality and Economic Opportunity in California." Public Policy Institute of California. https://www.ppic.org/wp-content/uploads/incoming-inequality-and-economic-opportunity-in-california-december-2020.pdf.

Bond, Timothy, Osea Giuntella, and Jakub Lonsky. 2020. "Immigration and Work Schedules: Theory and Evidence." *SSRN Electronic Journal* (January). https://doi.org/10.2139/ssrn.3602412.

Bonilla-Silva, Eduardo. 2010. *Racism Without Racists: Color-Blind Racism and the Persistence of Racial Inequality in the United States*. Rowman & Littlefield.

Bonner, Kacey. 2025. "Altadena's Black Community Disproportionately Affected by Eaton Fire, Report Shows." *PreventionWeb*, January 28. United Nations Office for Disaster Risk Reduction.

Bonner, Kacey, and Barbra Ramos. 2024. "Persistent Gaps for Black Californians Would Take Over 248 Years to Close." *UCLA Newsroom*, April 11. https://newsroom.ucla.edu/stories/state-of-black-california-2024.

Bonta, Rob. 2022. "Hate Crime in California." California Department of Justice. https://oag.ca.gov/system/files/attachments/press-docs/Hate%20Crime%20In%20CA%202022f.pdf.

Bourdieu, Pierre. 1987. *Distinction: A Social Critique of the Judgement of Taste*. Harvard University Press.

Bowen, Elizabeth A., and Nicole Capozziello. 2022. "Faceless, Nameless, Invisible: A Visual Content Analysis of Photographs in U.S. Media Coverage About Homelessness." *Housing Studies*, June, 1–20. https://doi.org/10.1080/02673037.2022.2084044.

Brandon, Sarah. 2021. "Inside the Fantastical World of Afro-Futurism, from P-Funk Mothership to the Black Panthers." Fast Company. https://www.fastcompany.com/90666376/inside-the-fantastical-world-of-afrofuturism-from-p-funks-mothership-to-black-panther.

Brilliant, Mark. 2014. "Re-Imagining Racial Liberalism." In *Making the American Century: Essays on the Political Culture of Twentieth Century America*, edited by Bruce J. Schulman. Oxford University Press.

Broussard, Albert S. 1993. *Black San Francisco: The Struggle for Racial Equality in the West, 1900–1954*. University Press of Kansas.

Brown, Rebecca. 2022. "The New 'Sanctuary State': United States Versus California and Lessons for Comprehensive Immigration Reform." *Loyola of Los Angeles Law Review* 55(1): 185–230.

Brown, Patricia Leigh. 2012. "The Problem Is Clear: The Water Is Filthy." *New York Times*, November 13. https://www.nytimes.com/2012/11/14/us/tainted-water-in-california-farmworker-communities.html.

Bugarin, Alicia, and Elias Lopez. 1998. *Farmworkers in California*. California State Library, California Research Bureau.

Burawoy, Michael. 1982. *Manufacturing Consent: Changes in the Labor Process Under Monopoly Capitalism*. University of Chicago Press.

Butler, David. 1986. "A Brew of Hope in California's Melting-Pot/Focus on West Coast US States Politics (958) /SCT." *The Times (London)*, March 12.

Buunk, Bram P., and Thomas Mussweiler. 2001. "New Directions in Social Comparison Research." *European Journal of Social Psychology* 31(5): 467–75. https://doi.org/10.1002/ejsp.77.

Cadelago, Christopher. 2024. "'Gov. Pete Wilson Was Right': California State Assembly candidate revives controversial immigration ad." *Politico*, January 29. https://www.politico.com/news/2024/01/29/california-controversial-immigration-ad-00138328.

California Association of Realtors. 2024. "2023 Housing Affordability by Ethnicity." Slide show (April).

California Department of Food and Agriculture. 2024. "California Agricultural Production Statistics." https://www.cdfa.ca.gov/Statistics/#:~:text=Over%20a%20third%20of%20the,the%202022%20crop%20year%20are%3A&text=Dairy%20Products%2C%20Milk%20—%20%2410.40%20billion,Grapes%20—%20%245.54%20billion.

California Department of Housing and Community Development. 2023. "Building Blocks a Comprehensive Housing-Element Guide to Assist Jurisdictions in Creating Comprehensive Housing Elements." https://www.hcd.ca.gov/planning-and-community-development/housing-elements/building-blocks/farmworkers.

California Immigrant Data Portal. 2024. "Employment: Immigrant Workers Comprise a Large Share of California's Workforce." https://immigrantdataca.org/indicators/employment.

California Latino Legislative Caucus. 2015. "2015 Priority Legislation." https://latinocaucus.legislature.ca.gov/news/april-08-2015-ca-latino-caucus-unveils-2015-priority-legislation.

California Reparations Task Force. 2023. "California Task Force to Study and Develop Reparation Proposals for African Americans." Office of the Attorney General. https://oag.ca.gov/system/files/media/full-ca-reparations.pdf.

California Water Science Center. n.d. "California's Central Valley." United States Geological Survey. Accessed October 10, 2024. http://ca.water.usgs.gov/projects/central-valley/about-central-valley.html.

Camarota, Steven, Bryan Griffith, and Karen Zeigler. 2023. "Mapping the Impact of Immigration on Public Schools." *Center for Immigration Studies*. https://cis.org/Report/Mapping-Impact-Immigration-Public-Schools.

Carmona, Gabriella, Aimee Benitez Aguirre, and Rodrigo Dominguez-Villegas. 2025. "Report Reveals Stark Latino Underrepresentation in California's Judiciary." UCLA Latino Policy & Politics Institute. https://latino.ucla.edu/press/balancing-the-bench/.

Carmona, Gabriella, and Paul Barragan-Monge. 2022. "From Disparity to Parity: Latino Representation in Appointed Positions Within California's Gubernatorial Cabinet, State Boards, and Commissions." Latino Policy & Politics Institute. https://latino.ucla.edu/research/ca-appointments-report/.

Carrigan, William D., and Clive Webb. 2003. "The Lynching of Persons of Mexican Origin or Descent in the United States, 1848 to 1928." *Journal of Social History* 37(2): 411–38. https://doi.org/10.1353/jsh.2003.0169.

Carrigan, William D., and Clive Webb. 2013. *Forgotten Dead: Mob Violence Against Mexicans in the United States, 1848–1928*. Oxford University Press.

Case, Ariana, Stacy L. Smith, and Katherine Pieper. 2023. "Hispanic/Latino Representation in Film: Erasure on Screen & Behind the Camera Across 1,600 Popular Movies." USC Annenberg Inclusion Initiative. https://assets.uscannenberg.org/docs/aii_11.3_hisp_latino_study_07-22.pdf.

Catanzarite, Lisa. 2000. "Brown-Collar Jobs: Occupational Segregation and Earnings of Recent-Immigrant Latinos." *Sociological Perspectives* 43(1): 45–75. https://doi.org/10.2307/1389782.

Catanzarite, Lisa. 2002. "Dynamics of Segregation and Earnings in Brown-Collar Occupations." *Work and Occupations* 29(3): 300–45. https://doi.org/10.1177/0730888402029003003.

Cech, Erin A., and Mary Blair-Loy. 2010. "Perceiving Glass Ceilings? Meritocratic Versus Structural Explanations of Gender Inequality Among Women in Science and Technology." *Social Problems* 57(3): 371–97. https://doi.org/10.1525/sp.2010.57.3.371.

Central Valley Community Foundation. 2024. "Our Valley." https://centralvalleycf.org/values-vision-mission/our-valley/.

Cha, Paullete, John Heintzman, and Patricia Malagon. 2023. "Health Conditions and Health Care among California's Undocumented Immigrants." Public Policy Institute of California. https://www.ppic.org/publication/health-conditions-and-health-care-among-californias-undocumented-immigrants/.

Chan, Sucheng. 1986. *This Bittersweet Soil: The Chinese in California Agriculture, 1860–1910.*

Chavez, Leo. 2008. *The Latino Threat: Constructing Immigrants, Citizens, and the Nation, Second Edition*. Stanford University Press.

Cheng, Wendy. 2013. *The Changs Next Door to the Díazes: Remapping Race in Suburban California*. University of Minnesota Press.

The Children's Partnership. 2021. "A Child Is a Child: Children in Immigrant Families." https://childrenspartnership.org/wp-content/uploads/2022/06/AChildIsaChild_Children-in-Immigrant-Families-2022-FINAL.pdf.

Chishti, Muzaffar, and Charles Kamasaki. 2014. "IRCA in Retrospect: Guideposts for Today's Immigration Reform." Migration Policy Institute. https://www.migrationpolicy.org/research/irca-retrospect-guideposts-today-s-immigration-reform.

Chua, Peter, and Dune C. Fujino. 1999. "Negotiating New Asian-American Masculinities: Attitudes and Gender Expectations." *The Journal of Men's Studies* 7(3): 391–413.

Christopher, Ben. 2020. "The Trumpiest and Most Anti-Trump Counties in California: Where Does Yours Rank?" *CalMatters*, December 28. http://calmatters.org/politics/2020/11/trumpiest-anti-trump-counties.

Cimini, Kate. 2021. "Black People Disproportionately Homeless in California." *Cal Matters*, February 27. https://calmatters.org/california-divide/2019/10/black-people-disproportionately-homeless-in-california/.

City News Service. 2019. "Former CA Gov. Endorses Maryott for 49th Congressional Seat." *Patch*, October 31. https://patch.com/california/sanjuancapistrano/former-ca-gov-endorses-maryott-49th-congressional-seat.

The Civil Rights Project. 2014. "California: The Most Segregated State for Latino Students." Press release, May 14. https://civilrightsproject.ucla.edu/press-releases/california-the-most-segregated-state-for-latino-students/.

Cobas, José, Joe R. Feagin, Daniel J. Delgado, Maria Chávez, eds. 2018. *Latino Peoples in the New America: Racialization and* Resistance. Routledge.

Cohen, Deborah. 2011. *Braceros: Migrant Citizens and Transnational Subjects in the Postwar United States and Mexico*. University of North Carolina Press.

Cohen, Lizabeth. 2008. *A Consumers' Republic: The Politics of Mass Consumption in Postwar America*. Vintage.

Collier, Paul. 2013. *Exodus: How Migration is Changing Our World*. Oxford University Press.

Conlon, John J., Laura Pilossoph, Matthew Wiswall, and Basit Zafar. 2018. "Labor Market Search with Imperfect Information and Learning." *National Bureau of Economic Research*. https://ideas.repec.org/p/nbr/nberwo/24988.html.

Costa, Daniel. 2018. "California Leads the Way: A Look at California Laws That Help Protect Labor Standards for Unauthorized Immigrant Workers." Economic Policy Institute. http://www.epi.org/publication/california-immigrant-labor-laws/.

Cowan, Jill. 2024. "In California, Tribal Members Are Reclaiming the 'Land of the Flowing Water.'" *New York Times*, June 16. https://www.nytimes.com/2024/06/16/us/california-native-american-tribes.html#.

Crontreras, Veronica. 2023. "Why Increasing the Number of Latino Physicians Is so Important for California." *CalMatters*, October 18. https://calmatters.org/commentary/2023/10/number-latino-physicians-important-california/.

Cullen, Jim. 2004. *The American Dream: A Short History of an Idea that Shaped a Nation*. Oxford University Press.

Daniel, Leon. 1981. "10,000 Indo Refugees to Become Citizens June 22." *United Press International*, June 20.

Davalos, Monica. 2023. "Homelessness Among Latinx Californians: An Alarming Increase." California Budget & Policy Center. https://calbudgetcenter.org/resources/homelessness-latinx-californians-an-alarming-increase/.

Davidai, Shai, and Thomas Gilovich. 2018. "How Should We Think About Americans' Beliefs About Economic Mobility?" *Judgment and Decision Making* 13(3): 297–304. https://doi.org/10.1017/s1930297500007737.

Davidai, Shai, and Thomas Gilovich. 2023. "How Should We Think About Americans' Beliefs About Economic Mobility?" *Judgment and Decision Making* 13(3): 297–304. https://doi.org/10.1017/s1930297500007737.

Davidson, Joe P. L. 2020. "Ugly Progress: W. E. B. Du Bois's Sociology of the Future." *The Sociological Review* 69(2): 382–95. https://doi.org/10.1177/0038026120954330.

Dávila, Arlene. 2008. *Latino Spin: Public Image and the Whitewashing of Race*. New York University Press.

Davis, Mike. 2006. *City of Quartz: Excavating the Future in Los Angeles*. Verso.

Day, Noel, and Zenophon Abraham. 1993. "The Unfinished Agenda: The Economic Status of African Americans in San Francisco 1964–1990." The Committee on African American Parity of the Human Rights Commission of San Francisco. https://www.sf.gov/sites/default/files/2022-11/The_Unfinished_Agenda . . . %20(1).pdf.

de Sousa Santos, Boaventura, ed. 2006. *Another Production Is Possible: Beyond the Capitalist Canon, Volume 2*. Verso.

DelaRosa, Monica, and Ivan Pereira. 2023. "'The Killing County': How Policing in One California County Became Notorious for its Alleged Brutality. *ABC News*,

February 3. https://abcnews.go.com/US/killing-county-countys-police-force-notorious-alleged-brutality/story?id=96314150.

De León, Kevin, and Anthony Rendon. 2016. "Joint Statement from California Legislative Leaders on Result of Presidential Election," November 9. California State Assembly. https://wclp.org/wp-content/uploads/2016/11/Joint-Statement-from-California-Legislative-Leaders-on-Result-of-Presidential-Election.pdf.

Dietz, Miranda, Laurel Lucia, Srikanth Kadiyala, et al. 2023. "California's Uninsured in 2024: Medi-Cal Expands to All Low-Income Adults, but Half a Million Undocumented Californians Lack Affordable Coverage Options." University of California Berkeley Center for Labor Research and Education. https://laborcenter.berkeley.edu/californias-uninsured-in-2024/.

DiFeliciantonio, Chase. 2022. "Gender and Racial Pay Gaps Persist Among California Companies." *Governing*, March 16. https://www.governing.com/work/gender-and-racial-pay-gaps-persist-among-california-companies.

DiTomaso, Nancy. 2013. *The American Non-Dilemma: Racial Inequality Without Racism*. Russell Sage Foundation.

Dohrman, Emily, and Bruce Fallick. 2020. "Is the Middle Class Worse off than It Used to Be?" Federal Reserve Bank of Cleveland. https://doi.org/10.26509/frbc-ec-202003.

Dougherty, Conor. 2020. *Golden Gates: The Housing Crisis and a Reckoning for the American Dream*. Penguin.

Du Bois, W. E. B. 1899. *The Philadelphia Negro: A Social Study*. University of Pennsylvania Press.

Du Bois, W. E. B. (1903) 2009. "Of the Meaning of Progress." In *The Souls of Black Folk*. Library of America.

Eagleton, Terry. 2014. *Ideology*. Routledge.

Eigenheer, Richard Allen. 1976. *Early Perceptions of Agricultural Resources in the Central Valley of California*. University of California, Davis.

Ermakoff, Ivan. 2014. "Exceptional Cases: Epistemic Contributions and Normative Expectations." *European Journal of Sociology* 55(2): 223–43. https://doi.org/10.1017/s0003975614000101.

Ethington, Philip. 2000. "Los Angeles and the Problem of Urban Historical Knowledge." *American Historical Review*, December.

Evans, Mark. 1992. "Kern County Town Struggling to Overcome Its Racist Image: Prejudice: Some Say Oildale No Longer Deserves that Reputation, but Others Say that Blacks Are Still Not Welcome in Community." *Los Angeles Times*, August 9. https://www.latimes.com/archives/la-xpm-1992-08-09-me-5918-story.html.

Fadel, Leila. 2022. "Ohio Ad Campaign Uses Edgy Billboards to Try to Lure Businesses from Other States." National Public Radio. https://www.npr.org/2022/01/31/1076895907/ohio-ad-campaign-uses-edgy-billboards-to-try-lure-businesses-from-other-states.

Fajnzylber, Pablo, Daniel Lederman, and Norman Loayza. 2002. "Inequality and Violent Crime." *The Journal of Law and Economics* 45(1): 1–39. https://doi.org/10.1086/338347.

Feagin, Joe R. 1972. "Poverty: We Still Believe That God Helps Those Who Help Themselves." *Psychology Today*, November.

Feagin, Joe R. 1975. *Subordinating the Poor: Welfare and American Beliefs*. Prentice-Hall.

Feagin, Joe R. 2013. *The White Racial Frame: Centuries of Racial Framing and Counter-Framing*. Routledge.

Feagin, Joe R., and José A. Cobas. 2015. *Latinos Facing Racism: Discrimination, Resistance, and Endurance*. Routledge.

Ferguson, Roderick A. 2012. "On the Specificities of Racial Formation: Gender and Sexuality in Historiographies of Race." In *Racial Formation in the Twenty-First Century*, edited by Daniel Martinez HoSang, Oneka LaBennett, and Laura Pulido. University of California Press. https://doi.org/10.1525/9780520953765-004.

Festinger, Leon. 1954. "A Theory of Social Comparison Processes." *Human Relations* 7(2): 117–40. https://doi.org/10.1177/001872675400700202.

Finn, Sam. 2023. "Newcomer Education in California." Policy Analysis for California Education. https://edpolicyinca.org/publications/newcomer-education-california.

Fisher, Mark. 2022. *Capitalist Realism: Is There No Alternative?* John Hunt Publishing.

Flamming, Douglas. 2005. *Bound for Freedom: Black Los Angeles in Jim Crow America*. University of California Press.

Flores, René D., and Ariela Schachter. 2018. "Who Are the 'Illegals'? The Social Construction of Illegality in the United States." *American Sociological Review* 83(5): 839–68. https://doi.org/10.1177/0003122418794635.

Forman, Tyrone A. 2004. "Color-Blind Racism and Racial Indifference: The Role of Racial Apathy in Facilitating Enduring Inequalities." In *The Changing Terrain of Race and Ethnicity*, edited by Maria Krysan and Amanda Lewis. Russell Sage Foundation.

Foucault, Michel. 1995. *Discipline and Punish: The Birth of the Prison*. Vintage.

Fox, Cybelle. 2012. *Three Worlds of Relief: Race, Immigration, and the American Welfare State from the Progressive Era to the New Deal*. Princeton University Press.

Frank, Robert H. 2017. *Success and Luck: Good Fortune and the Myth of Meritocracy*. Princeton University Press.

Franko, William W. 2013. "Political Inequality and State Policy Adoption: Predatory Lending, Children's Health Care, and Minimum Wage." *Poverty & Public Policy* 5(1): 88–114. https://doi.org/10.1002/pop4.17.

Frasure, Lorrie, Janelle Wong, Edward Vargas, and Matt Bareto. 2016. "Collaborative Multi-racial Post-election Survey (CMPS), United States, 2016." Inter-University Consortium for Political and Social Research. https://doi.org/10.3886/ICPSR38040.v2.

Frey, William H. 2018. "The US Will Become 'Minority White' in 2045, Census Projects." *The Brookings Institution*, March 14. https://www.brookings.edu/articles/the-us-will-become-minority-white-in-2045-census-projects/.

Friday, Baylee, Savannah Jones, and Chris Blake. 2023. "Texas Wants to Know: What's Driving so Many People and Businesses From California to Texas?" *NBC 5*

Dallas-Fort Worth, January 5. https://www.nbcdfw.com/news/business/whats-driving-so-many-people-and-businesses-from-california-to-texas/3163338/.

Friedersdorf, Conor. 2021. "The California Dream Is Dying." *The Atlantic*, July 21. https://www.theatlantic.com/ideas/archive/2021/07/california-dream-dying/619509/.

Friedman, Hilary Levey. 2013. *Playing to Win: Raising Children in a Competitive Culture*. University of California Press.

Fry, Wendy. 2024. "Pandemic Social Safety Net Programs Expire: 2024 California Income Inequality Year in Review." *CalMatters*, December 31. https://calmatters.org/california-divide/2024/12/income-inequality-2024-review/.

Fuller, Bruce, Yoonjeon Kim, Claudia Galindo, et al. 2019. "Worsening School Segregation for Latino Children?" *Educational Researcher* 48(7): 407–20. https://doi.org/10.3102/0013189x19860814.

Fussell, Elizabeth. 2014. "Warmth of the Welcome: Attitudes Toward Immigrants and Immigration Policy in the United States." *Annual Review of Sociology* 40(1): 479–98. https://doi.org/10.1146/annurev-soc-071913-043325.

Gailes, Arthur, Stephen Menendian, and Samir Gambhir. 2021. "The Roots of Structural Racism Project." *Othering and Belonging Institute*, June 21. https://belonging.berkeley.edu/roots-structural-racism.

Galdámez, Misael, Morís Gomez, Rocio Perez, et al. 2023. "Centering Black Latinidad: A Profile of the U.S. Afro-Latinx Population and Complex Inequalities." UCLA Latino Policy & Politics Institute Policy Report. https://latino.ucla.edu/research/centering-black-latinidad.

Galeano, Eduardo. 1971. *Open Veins of Latin America; Five Centuries of the Pillage of a Continent*. Siglo Veintiuno.

García-Sánchez, Efraín, Danny Osborne, Guillermo B. Willis, and Rosa Rodríguez-Bailón. 2019. "Attitudes Towards Redistribution and the Interplay Between Perceptions and Beliefs About Inequality." *British Journal of Social Psychology* 59(1): 111–36. https://ƒdoi.org/10.1111/bjso.12326.

Gibbons, Andrea. 2018. *City of Segregation: 100 Years of Struggle for Housing in Los Angeles*. Verso Books.

Gibbons, Frederick X., and Meg Gerrard. 1989. "Effects of Upward and Downward Social Comparison on Mood States." *Journal of Social and Clinical Psychology* 8(1): 14–31. https://doi.org/10.1521/jscp.1989.8.1.14.

Gilmore, Ruth Wilson. 2007. *Golden Gulag: Prisons, Surplus, Crisis, and Opposition in Globalizing California*. University of California Press.

Gimpelson, Vladimir, and Daniel Treisman. 2017. "Misperceiving Inequality." *Economics and Politics* 30(1): 27–54. https://doi.org/10.1111/ecpo.12103.

Gleeson, Shannon. 2016. *Precarious Claims: The Promise and Failure of Workplace Protections in the United States*. University of California Press.

Glenn, Evelyn Nakano. 1992. "From Servitude to Service Work: Historical Continuities in the Racial Division of Paid Reproductive Labor." *Signs* 18(1): 1–43. https://doi.org/10.1086/494777.

Glenn, Evelyn Nakano. 2004. *Unequal Freedom: How Race and Gender Shaped American Citizenship and Labor*. Harvard University Press.

Goethals, George R. 1986. "Social Comparison Theory." *Personality and Social Psychology Bulletin* 12(3): 261–78. https://doi.org/10.1177/0146167286123001.

Goffman, Erving. 2017. *Interaction Ritual: Essays in Face-to-Face Behavior*. Taylor & Francis.

Gonzalez-Barrera, Ana. 2022. "About Six Million U.S. Adults Identify as Afro-Latino." *Pew Research Center*, May 2. https://www.pewresearch.org/short-reads/2022/05/02/about-6-million-u-s-adults-identify-as-afro-latino/.

Gonzales-Day, Ken. 2006. *Lynching in the West, 1850–1935*. Duke University Press.

Gould, Elise, and Jori Kandra. 2021. "Inequality in Annual Earnings Worsens in 2021." Economic Policy Institute. https://www.epi.org/publication/inequality-2021-ssa-data/#:~:text=The%20share%20of%20earnings%20enjoyed,of%20total%20earnings%20in%202021.

Gramsci, Antonio. (1929–1933) 2011. *Prison Notebooks Volume 2*. Columbia University Press.

Grandin, Greg. 2019. *The End of the Myth: From the Frontier to the Border Wall in the Mind of America*. Metropolitan Books.

Grossi, Mark. 2014. "Water Crisis in Tulare County's Seville Trigger State Help, Short-term Fixes." *The Fresno Bee*, July 10. https://www.fresnobee.com/news/local/water-and-drought/article19522113.html/.

Gründler, Klaus, and Sebastian Köllner. 2020. "Culture, Diversity, and the Welfare State." *Journal of Comparative Economics* 48(4): 913–32. https://doi.org/10.1016/j.jce.2020.05.003.

Hadler, Markus. 2005. "Why Do People Accept Different Income Ratios?" *Acta Sociologica* 48(2): 131–54. https://doi.org/10.1177/0001699305053768.

Hagan, Chris, Nick Miller, Ben Adler, et al. 2019. "No Criminal Charges for Sacramento Police Officer Who Fatally Shot Stephon Clark." *National Public Radio*, March 2. https://www.npr.org/2019/03/02/699719214/officers-in-stephon-clark-shooting-wont-be-charged-says-sacramento-d-a.

Hall, Matthew, and Emily Greenman. 2013. "Housing and Neighborhood Quality Among Undocumented Mexican and Central American Immigrants." *Social Science Research* 42(6): 1712–25. https://doi.org/10.1016/j.ssresearch.2013.07.011.

Hall, Sarah. 2022. "Media Coverage of Homelessness Skews Public Perception." *Invisible People* (October). http://invisiblepeople.tv/media-coverage-of-homelessness-skews-public-perception.

Hall, Stuart. 1997. "The Work of Representation." In *Representation: Cultural Representation and Signifying Practices*, edited by Stuart Hall. Sage.

Hanchard, Michael G. 1998. *Orpheus and Power: The Movimento Negro of Rio de Janeiro and São Paulo, Brazil 1945–1988*. Princeton University Press.

Hanson, Sandra L., and John Zogby. 2010. "Trends: Attitudes About the American Dream." *Public Opinion Quarterly* 74(3): 570–84. https://doi.org/10.1093/poq/nfq010.

Hanson, Sandra, and John Kenneth White. 2011. *The American Dream in the 21st Century*. Temple University Press.

Hardy, Bradley L., and Dave E. Marcotte. 2020. "Education and the Dynamics of Middle-Class Status." The Brookings Institution. https://www.brookings.edu/wp-content/uploads/2020/06/Final-Report_Education-Middle-Class-Status-1.pdf?utm_source=chatgpt.com.

Harris, Adam J. L., and Ulrike Hahn. 2011. "Unrealistic Optimism About Future Life Events: A Cautionary Note." *Psychological Review* 118(1): 135–54. https://doi.org/10.1037/a0020997.

Harris, Heather, and Sean Cremin. 2024. "California's Prison Population." Public Policy Institute of California. https://www.ppic.org/publication/californias-prison-population/#:~:text=Black%20men%20and%20women%20are%2028%25%20and,account%20for%20about%2037%25%20of%20both%20populations.

Hashi, Aya, and Jesse Morris. 2023. "As Toxins Taint Central Valley Water, Community and Political Leaders Face Uphill Battle." *Fresnoland*. October 17. https://fresnoland.org/2023/10/17/unsafe-water/.

Hauhart, Robert C. 2016. *Seeking the American Dream: A Sociological Inquiry*. Palgrave Macmillan.

Hauser, Oliver P., and Michael I. Norton. 2017. "(Mis)Perceptions of Inequality." *Current Opinion in Psychology* 18: 21–25. https://doi.org/10.1016/j.copsyc.2017.07.024.

Hayes-Bautista, David. 2004. *La Nueva California: Latinos in the Golden State*. University of California Press.

Hedegaard, Troels Fage. 2019. "Migration and Meritocracy: Support for the Idea that Hard Work Will Get You Ahead in Society Among Nine Migrant Groups in Denmark, the Netherlands and Germany." *Nordic Journal of Migration Research* 9(1): 1. https://doi.org/10.2478/njmr-2019-0002.

Hein, Jeremy. 2000. "Interpersonal Discrimination Against Hmong Americans: Parallels and Variation in Microlevel Racial Inequality." *Sociological Quarterly* 41(3): 413–29. https://doi.org/10.1111/j.1533-8525.2000.tb00085.x.

Heiserman, Nicholas, Brent Simpson, and Robb Willer. 2020. "Judgments of Economic Fairness Are Based More on Perceived Economic Mobility Than Perceived Inequality." *Socius Sociological Research for a Dynamic World* 6. https://doi.org/10.1177/2378023120959547.

Henry, Mary Kay, James Manyika, Roy Bahat, et al. 2021. "A New Social Compact for Work and Workers." *California Future of Work Commission*. Institute for the Future. https://www.labor.ca.gov/wp-content/uploads/sites/338/2021/02/ca-future-of-work-report.pdf.

Herman, Edward S., and Noam Chomsky. 1988. *Manufacturing Consent: Power and Inequality*. Pantheon Books.

Hernández, César Cuauhtémoc García. 2024. *Welcome the Wretched: In Defense of the Criminal Alien*.

Ho, Jacqueline. 2024. "Agentic Selves, Agentic Stories: Cultural Foundations of Beliefs About Meritocracy." *American Journal of Cultural Sociology* 12(3): 379–409. https://doi.org/10.1057/s41290-023-00201-9.

Hochschild, Arlie Russell. 2018. *Strangers in Their Own Land: Anger and Mourning on the American Right*. The New Press.

Hochschild, Jennifer L. 1996. *Facing Up to the American Dream: Race, Class, and the Soul of the Nation*. Princeton University Press.

Holmes, Natalie. and Alan Berube. 2016. "City and Metropolitan Inequality on the Rise, Driven by Declining Incomes." *Brookings Institution*, January 14.

Homan, Patricia, Lauren Valentino, and Emi Weed. 2017. "Being and Becoming Poor: How Cultural Schemas Shape Beliefs About Poverty." *Social Forces* 95(3): 1023–48. https://doi.org/10.1093/sf/sox007.

Hooker, Juliet. 2005. "Indigenous Inclusion/Black Exclusion: Race, Ethnicity and Multicultural Citizenship in Latin America." *Journal of Latin American Studies* 37(2): 285–310. https://doi.org/10.1017/s0022216x05009016.

HOPE. 2023. "Latina Representation in California Government." Hispanas Organized for Political Empowerment. https://www.latinas.org/wp-content/uploads/HOPE-Latina-Representation-Report-2023-FINAL.pdf.

Horowitz, Juliana Menasce, Ruth Igielnik, and Rakesh Kochhar. 2020. "1. Trends in Income and Wealth Inequality." Pew Research Center. https://www.pewresearch.org/social-trends/2020/01/09/trends-in-income-and-wealth-inequality/.

HoSang, Daniel Martinez. 2010. *Racial Propositions: Ballot Initiatives and the Making of Postwar California*. Vol. 30. University of California Press.

Hubler, Shawn. 2021. "The State of California's 'State of Jefferson.'" *New York Times*, May 26. https://www.nytimes.com/2021/05/26/us/california-jefferson-secession.html.

Humes, Edward. 2014. *Over Here: How the G.I. Bill Transformed the American Dream*. Diversion Books.

Hunt, Matthew O. 2007. "African American, Hispanic, and White Beliefs About Black/White Inequality, 1977–2004." *American Sociological Review* 72(3): 390–415. https://doi.org/10.1177/000312240707200304.

Hutchful, Esi. 2018. "The Racial Wealth Gap: What California Can Do About a Long-Standing Obstacle to Shared Prosperity." California Budget and Policy Center. https://calbudgetcenter.org/resources/the-racial-wealth-gap/#:~:text=For%20Latinx%20families%2C%20median%20wealth,a%20typical%20Latinx%20family%20has.

The Investopedia Team. 2024. "What Is the American Dream? Examples and How to Measure It." *Investopedia*, July 2. https://www.investopedia.com/terms/a/american-dream.asp.

Isaacs, Julia B., Isabel V. Sawhill, and Ron Haskins. 2008. "Getting Ahead or Losing Ground: Economic Mobility in America." Education Resources Information Center. https://eric.ed.gov/?id=ED500256.

Jacobson, Robin D. 2008. *The New Nativism: Proposition 187 and the Debate over Immigration*. University of Minnesota Press.

Jefferson, Alison Rose. 2022. *Living the California Dream: African American Leisure Sites During the Jim Crow Era*. University of Nebraska Press.

Jillson, Cal. 2016. *The American Dream: In History, Politics, and Fiction*. University Press of Kansas.

Jingnan, Huo, and Jasmine Garsd. 2024. "JD Vance Spreads Debunked Claims About Haitian Immigrants Eating Pets." *NPR*, September 10. https://www.npr.org/2024/09/10/nx-s1-5107320/jd-vance-springfield-ohio-haitians-pets.

Johnson, Hans, and Eric McGhee. 2025. "Who's Leaving California—And Who's Moving In?" *Public Policy Institute of California* (blog), February 5. http://www.ppic.org/blog/whos-leaving-california-and-whos-moving-in.

Johnson, Troy R. 1996. *The Occupation of Alcatraz Island: Indian Self-Determination and the Rise of Indian Activism*. University of Illinois Press.

Jones, Jennifer. 2019. *The Browning of the New South*. Chicago, Chicago University Press.

Jones, Nikki. 2018. *The Chosen Ones: Black Men and the Politics of Redemption*. University of California Press.

Jones, Reece. 2021. "How the Statue of Liberty Became a Symbol for a National Myth." *University of Hawai'i News*, October 29. https://www.hawaii.edu/news/2021/10/29/statue-of-liberty-symbol-for-a-national-myth/.

Jones-Correa, Michael. 2001. *Governing American Cities: Inter-Ethnic Coalitions, Competition, and Conflict*. Russell Sage Foundation.

Junn, Jane. 2007. "From Coolie to Model Minority." *Du Bois Review Social Science Research on Race* 4(2): 355–73. https://doi.org/10.1017/s1742058x07070208.

Junn, Jane, and Natalie Masuoka. 2008. "Asian American Identity: Shared Racial Status and Political Context." *Perspectives on Politics* 6(4): 729–40. https://doi.org/10.1017/s1537592708081887.

Kaiser Family Foundation. 2025. "Key Facts on Health Coverage of Immigrants." https://www.kff.org/racial-equity-and-health-policy/key-facts-on-health-coverage-of-immigrants/.

Kanazawa, Mark. 2005. "Immigration, Exclusion, and Taxation: Anti-Chinese Legislation in Gold Rush California." *Journal of Economic History* 65(3). https://doi.org/10.1017/s0022050705000288.

Kanell, Michael E. 2018. "For Fleeing Californians, Atlanta Is a Top Destination." *Atlanta Journal-Constitution*, June 1. https://www.ajc.com/business/for-fleeing-californias-atlanta-top-destination/uGx08Y3VNiQqhshTGcx6AP/.

Kanter, Rosabeth Moss. 1977. *Work and Family in the United States: A Critical Review and Agenda for Research and Policy*. Russell Sage Foundation.

Katz, Michael B. 2013. *The Undeserving Poor: America's Enduring Confrontation with Poverty: Fully Updated and Revised*. Oxford University Press.

Kaye, Loren. 2020. "California Is the Place to Be—Unless You're Middle Income and Need an Affordable Place to Live." *CalMatters*, February 13. https://calmatters.org/economy/2020/02/california-is-the-place-to-be-unless-youre-middle-income-and-need-an-affordable-place-to-live/.

Kim, Claire Jean. 2003. *Bitter Fruit: The Politics of Black-Korean Conflict in New York City*. Yale University Press.

Kimelman, Jeremia. 2024. "Did Your County Back Trump More this Time than 2020?" *Cal Matters*, December 5. https://calmatters.org/politics/elections/2024/12/california-election-results-trump-vote-2024/.

King, Martin Luther, Jr. 1960. "'The Negro and the American Dream,' Excerpt from Address at the Annual Freedom Mass Meeting of the North Carolina State Conference of Branches of the NAACP." The Martin Luther King, Jr. Research and Education Institute. https://kinginstitute.stanford.edu/king-papers/documents/negro-and-american-dream-excerpt-address-annual-freedom-mass-meeting-north#:~:text=But%20ever%20since%20the%20founding,practiced%20the%20antithesis%20of%20democracy.

Kluegel, James R., and Eliot R. Smith. 1986. *Beliefs About Inequality: Americans' Views of What Is and What Ought to Be*. Transaction Publishers.

Kotkin, Joel. 2023. *The Coming of Neo-Feudalism: A Warning to the Global Middle Class*. Encounter Books.

Kraus, Michael W., Ivuoma N. Onyeador, Natalie M. Daumeyer, Julian M. Rucker, and Jennifer A. Richeson. 2019. "The Misperception of Racial Economic Inequality." *Perspectives on Psychological Science* 14(6): 899–921. https://doi.org/10.1177/1745691619863049.

KSEE. 2018. "Seven Students Involved in Hanging Confederate Flag at Fresno High School." *KRON4 News*, May 25. https://www.kron4.com/news/california/7-students-involved-in-hanging-confederate-flag-at-fresno-high-school/.

Kuhn, Moritz, and José-Víctor Ríos-Rull. 2025. "Income and Wealth Inequality in the United States: An Update Including the 2022 Wave." National Bureau of Economic Research Working Paper 33823. https://doi.org/10.3386/w33823.

Kushel, Margot, Tiana Moore, Jennafer Birkmeyer, et al. 2023. "Toward a New Understanding: The California Statewide Study of People Experiencing Homelessness." UCSF Benioff Homelessness and Housing Initiative. https://homelessness.ucsf.edu/sites/default/files/2023-06/CASPEH_Report_62023.pdf.

Kymlicka, Will, and Keith Banting. 2006. "Immigration, Multiculturalism, and the Welfare State." *Ethics & International Affairs* 20(3): 281–304. https://doi.org/10.1111/j.1747-7093.2006.00027.x.

Lacayo, Celia Olivia. 2017. "Perpetual Inferiority: Whites' Racial Ideology Toward Latinos." *Sociology of Race and Ethnicity* 3(4): 566–79. https://doi.org/10.1177/2332649217698165.

Lamont, Michèle. 2009. *The Dignity of Working Men: Morality and the Boundaries of Race, Class, and Immigration*. Harvard University Press.

Lamont, Michèle. 2023. *Seeing Others: How Recognition Works—And How It Can Heal a Divided World*. Simon and Schuster.

Lamont, Michèle, and Marcel Fournier. 1992. *Cultivating Differences: Symbolic Boundaries and the Making of Inequality*. University of Chicago Press.

Lamont, Michèle, Mario Luis Small, and David J. Harding. 2010. "Introduction: Reconsidering Culture and Poverty." *The Annals of the American Academy of Political and Social Science* 629(1). https://dash.harvard.edu/bitstream/handle/1/10494213/Small-Harding-Lamont_Introduction-Reconsidering-Culture-and-Poverty.pdf?sequence=1.

Lancee, Bram, and Herman G. Van De Werfhorst. 2012. "Income Inequality and Participation: A Comparison of 24 European Countries." *Social Science Research* 41(5): 1166–78. https://doi.org/10.1016/j.ssresearch.2012.04.005.

Lang, John S., and Juanita R. Hogue. 1983. "Still the Land of Opportunity? Busboy to Millionaire." *U.S. News & World Report*, July 4.

Lareau, Annette. 2011. *Unequal Childhoods: Class, Race, and Family Life*. University of California Press.

LaSalle, Mick. 2021. *California in the Movies*. Heyday Books.

Lazarow, Alex. 2020. "Beyond Silicon Valley: How Start-Ups Succeed in Unlikely Places." *Harvard Business Review* (March–April). https://hbr.org/2020/03/beyond-silicon-valley.

Lefebvre, Henri. 1992. *The Production of Space*. Wiley-Blackwell.

Legislative Analyst's Office. 1995. "The California Economy." https://lao.ca.gov/1995/010195_calguide/cgep1.html.

Leonard, Christian. 2024. "How Fresno Region Became One of California's Fastest-Growing Areas." *San Francisco Chronicle*, March 17. https://www.sfchronicle.com/california/article/fresno-population-2023-18969597.php.

Leonce, Tesa E. 2020. "The Inevitable Rise in Dual-Income Households and the Intertemporal Effects on Labor Markets." *Compensation & Benefits Review* 52(2): 64–76. https://doi.org/10.1177/0886368719900032.

LePard, Clay. 2022. "Billboards in Major U.S. Cities Take Quirky Approach to Encourage People to Move to Ohio." *News 5 Cleveland WEWS*, April 15. https://www.news5cleveland.com/news/state/billboards-in-major-u-s-cities-take-quirky-approach-to-encourage-people-to-move-to-ohio.

Levin, Sam 2021. "Oscar Grant's Family on the Chauvin Conviction: 'This Is Huge. We've Been Let Down So Many Times.'" *Guardian*, April 20. https://www.theguardian.com/us-news/2021/apr/20/derek-chauvin-verdict-oscar-grant-family.

Levy, Morris, and Matthew Wright. 2020. *Immigration and the American Ethos*. Cambridge University Press. https://doi.org/10.1017/9781108772174.

Lewis, Oscar. 1959. *Five Families: Mexican Case Studies in the Culture of Poverty*. Basic Books.

Lewis, Oscar. 1966. *La Vida: A Puerto Rican Family in the Culture of Poverty—San Juan and New York*.

Lewis, Oscar. 1969. "The Culture of Poverty/Oscar Lewis." In *On Understanding Poverty: Perspectives from the Social Sciences*, edited by Daniel P. Moynihan. Basic Books.

Library of Congress. n.d. "A Latinx Resource Guide: Civil Rights Cases and Events in the United States: 1942: Bracero Program." Accessed October 10, 2024. https://guides.loc.gov/latinx-civil-rights/bracero-program.

Lie, John, and Nancy Abelmann. 2009. *Blue Dreams: Korean Americans and the Los Angeles Riots*. Harvard University Press.

Lindsey, Robert. 1978. "Young Are Swelling New Migration to California." *New York Times*, February 19. https://www.nytimes.com/1978/02/19/archives/young-are-swelling-a-new-migration-to-california-after-decades.html.

Lipset, Seymour Martin. 1996. *American Exceptionalism: A Double-Edged Sword*. W. W. Norton.

Loewen, James. 2005. *Sundown Towns: A Hidden Dimension of American Racism.* The New Press.

Lopez, Linda, and Adrian D. Pantoja. 2004. "Beyond Black and White: General Support for Race-Conscious Policies Among African Americans, Latinos, Asian Americans and Whites." *Political Research Quarterly* 57(4): 633–42. https://doi.org/10.1177/106591290405700411.

López-Sanders, Laura. 2024. *The Manufacturing of Job Displacement: How Racial Capitalism Drives Immigrant and Gender Inequality in the Labor Market.* New York University Press.

Lukes, Steven. 1973. *Individualism.*

Luttmer, Erzo F. P. 2001. "Group Loyalty and the Taste for Redistribution." *Journal of Political Economy* 109(3): 500–28. https://doi.org/10.1086/321019.

Lytle Hernandez, Kelly. 2017. *City of Inmates: Conquest, Rebellion, and the Rise of Human Caging in Los Angeles, 1771–1965.* University of North Carolina Press.

Mahler, Sarah J. 2021. *American Dreaming: Immigrant Life on the Margins.* Princeton University Press.

The Mamas and The Papas. 1965. "California Dreamin'." *If You Can Believe Your Eyes and Ears.* Dunhill Records.

Mathews, Joe, and Mark Paul. 2010. *California Crackup: How Reform Broke the Golden State and How We Can Fix It.* University of California Press.

Markovits, Daniel. 2020. *The Meritocracy Trap: How America's Foundational Myth Feeds Inequality, Dismantles the Middle Class, and Devours the Elite.* Penguin.

Martinez, Fidel. 2021. "Latinx Files: Netflix Has a Latinx Problem." *Los Angeles Times*, March 4. http://www.latimes.com/world-nation/newsletter/2021-03-04/latinx-files-streaming-services-diversity-latinx-files.

Masuoka, Natalie, and Jane Junn. 2022. *The Politics of Belonging: Race, Public Opinion, and Immigration.* University of Chicago Press.

McCall, Leslie. 2013. *The Undeserving Rich: American Beliefs about Inequality, Opportunity, and Redistribution.* Cambridge University Press.

McClain, Paula D., Niambi M. Carter, Victoria M. DeFrancesco Soto, et al. 2006. "Racial Distancing in a Southern City: Latino Immigrants' Views of Black Americans." *The Journal of Politics* 68(3): 571–84. https://doi.org/10.1111/j.1468-2508.2006.00446.x.

McCormack, Patricia. 1987. "Survey: American Dream Threated by Drugs." *United Press International Archive: Domestic News*, February 4. https://advance-lexis-com.libproxy.berkeley.edu/document?crid=b53da3f2-c9cf-4b29-8624-b25a2bea9c07&pddocfullpath=%2Fshared%2Fdocument%2Fnews%2Furn%3AcontentItem%3A3SJB-JF30-001X-W562-00000-00&pdsourcegroupingtype=&pdcontentcomponentid=8076&pdmfid=1519360&pdisurlapi=true.

McGhee, Eric. 2020. "California's Political Geography 2020." Public Policy Institute of California. http://www.ppic.org/publication/californias-political-geography.

McGhee, Eric. 2023. "California's African American Community." *Public Policy Institute of California* (blog), February 22. https://www.ppic.org/blog/californias-african-american-community/.

McKittrick, Katherine. 2006. *Demonic Grounds: Black Women and the Cartographies of Struggle*. University of Minnesota Press.

McWilliams, Carey. 1999. *California: The Great Exception*. University of California Press.

Mejia, Marisol Cuellar, Cesar Alesi Perez, and Hans Johnson. 2024a. "Immigrants in California." Public Policy Institute of California, January. http://www.ppic.org/publication/immigrants-in-california.

Mejia, Marisol Cuellar, Hans Johnson, and Julien LaFortune. 2024b. "California's Housing Divide." *Public Policy Institute of California* (blog), October 21. https://www.ppic.org/blog/californias-housing-divide/.

Menjívar, Cecilia. 2006. "Liminal Legality: Salvadoran and Guatemalan Lives in the U.S." *American Journal of Sociology* 11(4): 999–1036. https://doi.org/10.1086/499509.

Merl, Jean. 2011. "Pete Wilson Endorses in Area Congressional." *Los Angeles Times*, December 16. https://www.latimes.com/archives/blogs/politi-cal/story/2011-12-15/pete-wilson-endorses-in-area-congressional-race.

Merolla, David M., Matthew O. Hunt, and Richard T. Serpe. 2011. "Concentrated Disadvantage and Beliefs About the Causes of Poverty: A Multi-Level Analysis." *Sociological Perspectives* 54(2): 205–27. https://doi.org/10.1525/sop.2011.54.2.205.

Metropolitan Transportation Commission. 2008. "High-Speed Rail Bond Measure Passes." November 28. http://mtc.ca.gov/news/high-speed-rail-bond-measure-passes.

Mijs, Jonathan J. B. 2018. "The Paradox of Inequality: Income Inequality and Belief in Meritocracy Go Hand in Hand." *Socio-Economic Review* 19(1): 7–35. https://doi.org/10.1093/ser/mwy051.

Miller, Jenesse. 2022. "Segregation Index Shows U.S. Schools Remain Highly Separated by Race, Ethnicity and Economic Status." *USC Today*, May. https://today.usc.edu/new-segregation-index-shows-u-s-schools-remain-highly-segregated-by-race-ethnicity-and-economic-status/.

Mische, Ann. 2014. "Measuring Futures in Action: Projective Grammars in the Rio +20 Debates." *Theory and Society* 43(3–4): 437–64. https://doi.org/10.1007/s11186-014-9226-3.

Mize, Ronald L. 2016. *The Invisible Workers of the U.S.–Mexico Bracero Program: Obreros Olvidados*. Lexington Books.

Molina, Natalia. 2014. *How Race is Made in America: Immigration, Citizenship and the Historical Power of Racial Scripts*. University of California Press.

Montejano, David. 2010. *Anglos and Mexicans in the Making of Texas, 1836–1986*. University of Texas Press.

Mora, G. Cristina, and Tianna S. Paschel. 2020. "Antiblackness as a Logic for Anti-Immigrant Resentment: Evidence From California." *Sociological Forum* 35(S1): 918–40. https://doi.org/10.1111/socf.12601.

Morris, Wright. 2018. *Love Among the Cannibals*. University of Nebraska Press.

Murch, Donna Jean. 2010. *Living for the City: Migration, Education, and the Rise of the Black Panther Party in Oakland, California*. University of North Carolina Press.

Musibay, Oscar. 2024. "Engineering Degree Attainment for Hispanics Is Key to Closing Critical US Job Gap." *Society of Hispanic Professional Engineers (SHPE)*, July 23. http://shpe.org/news-posts/el-pais-article-feature.

Nagel, Christof and Amy Nivette. 2023. "The Rodney King Incident and Verdict Revisited: Examining Opinion-Mobilizing Effects Using Data from Southern California in 1991 and 1992." *Journal of Criminal Justice* 85(101989). https://doi.org/10.1016/j.jcrimjus.2022.101989

Nash, Gerald D. 1972. "Stages of California's Economic Growth, 1870–1970: An Interpretation." *California Historical Quarterly* 51(4): 315–30. https://doi.org/10.2307/25157401.

Nichols, Chris. 2018. "Ted Cruz's Misleading Claim: California 'Is Hemorrhaging Population.'" *Politifact*. September 28. https://www.politifact.com/factchecks/2018/sep/28/ted-cruz/ted-cruzs-misleading-claim-california-hemorrhaging/.

Nichols, John. 2008. "George Carlin: American Radical." *The Nation*, June 23. https://www.thenation.com/article/archive/george-carlin-american-radical/.

Nicolaides, Becky M. 2024. *The New Suburbia: How Diversity Remade Suburban Life in Los Angeles After 1945*. Oxford University Press.

Norman, Michelle. 2025. "MAGA Sheriff Running for CA Governor Vows to End 'Sanctuary' Laws." *Politico*, February 17. https://www.politico.com/news/2025/02/17/california-end-sanctuary-law-trump-00204600.

Norton, Michael I. 2014. "Unequality: Who Gets What and Why It Matters." *Policy Insights from the Behavioral and Brain Sciences* 1(1): 151–55. https://doi.org/10.1177/2372732214550167.

Obama, Barack. 2006. *The Audacity of Hope: Thoughts on Reclaiming the American Dream*. Three Rivers Press.

O'Brien, John. 2015. "Individualism as a Discursive Strategy of Action." *Sociological Theory* 33(2): 173–99. https://doi.org/10.1177/0735275115588353.

Obinna, Dina and Adrian Bacong. 2024. "Barriers to Entry: the Impacts of Visa Queues and National Origin on Family Migration to the United States." *Identities* 1–20. https://doi.org/10.1080/1070289X.2025.2510772

Ocampo, Anthony Christian. 2022. "Brown and Gay in LA: The Lives of Immigrant Sons." *Brown and Gay in LA*. New York University Press.

Oeur, Freeden Blume. 2018. *Black Boys Apart: Racial Uplift and Respectability in All-Male Public Schools*. University of Minnesota Press.

Office of the Attorney General. 2024. "Attorney General Bonta Reminds California Immigrants of Their Rights and Protections Under the Law," December 17. Department of Justice, State of California. https://oag.ca.gov/news/press-releases/attorney-general-bonta-reminds-california-immigrants-their-rights-and.

Omi, Michael, and Howard Winant. 2014. *Racial Formation in the United States*. Routledge.

On The Issues. 2021. "Arnold Schwarzenegger on Immigration." https://www.ontheissues.org/celeb/Arnold_Schwarzenegger_Immigration.htm.

Orfield, Gary, and Jongyeon Ee. 2014. "Segregating California's Future: Inequality and Its Alternative 60 Years After Brown V. Board of Education." Civil Rights Project. https://civilrightsproject.ucla.edu/research/k-12-education/integration-and-diversity/segregating-california2019s-future-inequality-and-its-alternative-60-years-after-brown-v.-board-of-education/orfield-ee-segregating-california-future-brown-at.pdf.

Ostrove, Joan M., and Susan M. Long. 2007. "Social Class and Belonging: Implications for College Adjustment." *The Review of Higher Education* 30(4): 363–89.

Othering and Belonging Institute. 2020. "Change in Segregation, 1990–2019." Othering & Belonging Institute. https://belonging.berkeley.edu/change-segregation-1990-2019.

Owens, Louis. 1999. "Where Things Can Happen: California and Writing." *Western American Literature* 34(2): 150–55.

Paiz, Christian O. 2023. *The Strikers of Coachella: A Rank-And-File History of the UFW Movement*. The University of North Carolina Press.

Paluch, Jennifer, and Joseph Herrera. 2023. "Homeless Populations Are Rising Around California." *Public Policy Institute of California* (blog). https://www.ppic.org/blog/homeless-populations-are-rising-around-california.

Parker, John. 2018. "Why One of America's Richest States Is Also Its Poorest." *The Economist*, October 27. https://www.economist.com/united-states/2018/10/27/why-one-of-americas-richest-states-is-also-its-poorest.

Parks-Yancy, Rochelle, Johanna Shih, Nancy DiTomaso, and Corinne Post. 2009. "Talking About Immigration and Immigrants: A Qualitative Exploration of White Americans' Attitudes." *International Review of Modern Sociology* 35(2): 285–306. http://www.jstor.org/stable/41421359.

Pastor, Manuel. 2018. *State of Resistance: What California's Dizzying Descent and Remarkable Resurgence Mean for America's Future*. The New Press.

Patoka, Josh. 2023. "Average Rent by State." *Forbes Advisor*, November 15. https://www.forbes.com/advisor/mortgages/average-rent-by-state/.

PayScale. n.d. "Cost of Living in Los Angeles, CA." Accessed March 1, 2025. https://www.payscale.com/cost-of-living-calculator/California-Los-Angeles.

Pearce, Nicholas. 2004. "Diversity Versus Solidarity: A New Progressive Dilemma?" *Renewal* 12(3): 79–87. https://researchportal.bath.ac.uk/en/publications/diversity-versus-solidarity-a-new-progressive-dilemma.

Peetz, Johanna, and Roger Buehler. 2009. "Is There a Budget Fallacy? The Role of Savings Goals in the Prediction of Personal Spending." *Personality and Social Psychology Bulletin* 35(12): 1579–91.

Perlmann, Joel. 2005. *Italians Then, Mexicans Now: Immigrant Origins and the Second-Generation Progress, 1890–2000*. Russell Sage Foundation.

Perry, Andre M., Hannah Stephens, and Manann Donoghoe. 2024. "Black Wealth Is Increasing, but So Is the Racial Wealth Gap." *The Brookings Institution*,

January 9. https://www.brookings.edu/articles/black-wealth-is-increasing-but-so-is-the-racial-wealth-gap/.

Perry, Imani. 2023. *South to America: A Journey Below the Mason Dixon to Understand the Soul of a Nation*. Ecco.

Pew Research Center. 2017. "Intermarriage Across the United States by Metro Area." Report, May 18. https://www.pewresearch.org/social-trends/feature/intermarriage-across-the-u-s-by-metro-area/.

Pew Research Center. 2024a. "On Views of Race and Inequality, Blacks and Whites Are Worlds Apart." Report, June 27. https://www.pewresearch.org/social-trends/2016/06/27/on-views-of-race-and-inequality-blacks-and-whites-are-worlds-apart.

Pew Research Center. 2024b. "Filipino Americans: A Survey Data Snapshot." Report, October 4. https://www.pewresearch.org/race-and-ethnicity/2024/08/06/filipino-americans-a-survey-data-snapshot/.

Pfaelzer, Jean. 2008. *Driven Out: The Forgotten War Against Chinese Americans*. University of California Press.

Pham, Huyen, and Pham Hoang Van. 2020. "Measuring the Climate for Immigrants: A State-by-State Analysis." In *Strange Neighbors: The Role of States in Immigration Policy*, edited by Carissa Byrne Hessick and Gabriel J. Chin. New York University Press.

Pham, Huyen, and Pham Hoang Van. 2024. "The Immigrant Climate Index." Data set. https://vpham415.github.io/ICI/.

Phillips, Amber. 2017. "'They're Rapists.' President Trump's campaign Launch Speech Two Years Later, Annotated." *Washington Post*, June 16. https://www.washingtonpost.com/news/the-fix/wp/2017/06/16/theyre-rapists-presidents-trump-campaign-launch-speech-two-years-later-annotated/.

Pierce, Jason Eric. 2016. *Making the White Man's West: Whiteness and the Creation of the American West*. University Press of Colorado.

Piketty, Thomas. 2014. *Capital in the Twenty-First Century*. Harvard University Press. https://doi.org/10.4159/9780674369542.

Piketty, Thomas, and Emmanuel Saez. 2014. "Inequality in the Long Run." *Science* 344(6186): 838–43. https://eml.berkeley.edu/~saez/piketty-saezScience14.pdf.

Pinto-Coelho, Joanna Marie, and Tukufu Zuberi. 2015. "Segregated Diversity." *Sociology of Race and Ethnicity* 1(4): 475–89. https://doi.org/10.1177/2332649215581057.

Pitt, Leonard. 1998. *Decline of the Californios: A Social History of the Spanish-Speaking Californians, 1846–1890*. University of California Press.

Playa Vista. 2023. "Our Story." January 12. https://playavista.com/the-campus/.

Polanyi, Karl. 1944. *The Great Transformation: The Political and Economic Origins of Our Time*. Beacon Press.

Policy Link and the University of Southern California Program for Environmental and Regional Equity. 2017. "An Equity Profile of the Los Angeles Region." https://dornsife.usc.edu/eri/publications/equity-profile-los-angeles-region/.

Ponder, Kara Young, Tiana Moore, Sila Adhiningrat, Regina Sakoda and Margot Kushel. 2024. "Toward Equity: Understanding Black Californians' Experiences of

Homelessness Findings from the California Statewide Study of People Experiencing Homelessness." Benioff Homelessness and Housing Initiative, University of California, San Francisco. https://homelessness.ucsf.edu/resources/reports/toward-equity-understanding-black-californians-experiences-homelessness.

Prevatt, Mike. 2021. "Is California Ruining Nevada?" *Nevada Public Radio*, May 21. https://knpr.org/show/knprs-state-of-nevada/2021-05-21/is-california-ruining-nevada.

Public Religion Research Institute. 2019. "The Working Lives and Struggles of Asian Americans and Pacific Islanders in California." *PRRI*, November 18. https://www.prri.org/research/the-working-lives-and-struggles-of-asian-americans-and-pacific-islanders-in-california/.

Pugh, Allison J. 2015. *The Tumbleweed Society: Working and Caring in an Age of Insecurity*. Oxford University Press.

Pulido, Laura. 2002. "Race, Class, and Political Activism: Black, Chicana/O, and Japanese-American Leftists in Southern California, 1968–1978." *Antipode* 34(4): 762–88. https://doi.org/10.1111/1467-8330.00268.

Pulido, Laura. 2006. *Black, Brown, Yellow, and Left: Radical Activism in Los Angeles*. University of California Press.

Quijano, Josselyn Andrea Garcia. 2020. "Workplace Discrimination and Undocumented First-Generation Latinx Immigrants." Crown Family School of Social Work, Policy, and Practice. https://crownschool.uchicago.edu/student-life/advocates-forum/workplace-discrimination-and-undocumented-first-generation-latinx.

RACE COUNTS. 2023. "Economic Opportunity." https://www.racecounts.org/issue/economic/.

Ramirez, Nikki McCann, and Ryan Bort. 2024. "Every State's Song at the DNC Roll Call to Nominate Harris." *Rolling Stone*, August 20. https://www.rollingstone.com/politics/politics-news/dnc-roll-call-songs-every-state-chose-nominate-harris-1235084163/.

Rank, Mark Robert, Thomas A. Hirschl, and Kirk A. Foster. 2014. *Chasing the American Dream: Understanding What Shapes Our Fortunes*. Oxford University Press.

Reed, Deborah. 2004. "Recent Trends in Income and Poverty." Public Policy Institute of California. https://www.ppic.org/publication/recent-trends-in-income-and-poverty/.

Rendón, María G. 2019. *Stagnant Dreamers: How the Inner City Shapes the Integration of the Second Generation*. Russell Sage Foundation.

Reynolds, Jeremy, and He Xian. 2014. "Perceptions of Meritocracy in the Land of Opportunity." *Research in Social Stratification and Mobility* 36(121): 121–37. https://www.sciencedirect.com/science/article/abs/pii/S0276562414000122#bib0115.

Rios, Victor M. 2011. *Punished: Policing the Lives of Black and Latino Boys*. NYU Press.

Rios, Victor M. 2017. *Human Targets: Schools, Police, and the Criminalization of Latino Youth*. University of Chicago Press.

Riquier, Andrea. 2018. "With No Letup in Home Prices, the California Exodus Surges." *Real Estate News & Insights*, May 3. https://www.realtor.com/news/real-estate-news/no-letup-home-prices-california-exodus-surges/.

Robinson, Cedric J. 2005. *Black Marxism: The Making of the Black Radical Tradition*. University of North Carolina Press.

Rodríguez-Muñiz, Michael. 2024. *Figures of the Future: Latino Civil Rights and the Politics of Demographic Change*. Princeton University Press.

Rogers, Ibram H. 2011. "The Black Campus Movement and the Institutionalization of Black Studies, 1965–1970." *Journal of African American Studies* 16(1): 21–40. https://doi.org/10.1007/s12111-011-9173-2.

Rojas, Fabio. 2010. *From Black Power to Black Studies: How a Radical Social Movement Became an Academic Discipline*. JHU Press.

Ronayne, Kathleen. 2021. "California Losing Congressional Seat for First Time." Associated Press, April 26. https://apnews.com/article/census-2020-government-and-politics-california-dd4a4f3ce3070231b0aecdc1cac3e97b.

Rosales, Rocío. 2020. *Fruteros: Street Vending, Illegality, and Ethnic Community in Los Angeles*. University of California Press.

Roubenoff, Ethan, Jasmijn Slootjes, and Irene Bloemraad. 2023. "Spatial and Sociodemographic Vulnerability: Quantifying Accessibility to Health Care and Legal Services for Immigrants in California, Arizona, and Nevada." *Socius: Sociological Research for a Dynamic World* 9: 1–22. https://doi.org/10.1177/23780231231157683.

Rowlingson, Karen, Michael Orton, and Eleanor Taylor. 2010. "Do We Still Care About Inequality?" In *British Social Attitudes: The 27th report: Exploring Labour's Legacy*, edited by Alison Park, John Curtice, Elizabeth Clery, and Catherine Bryson. Sage.

Rozsypal, Filip, and Kathrin Schlafmann. 2023. "Overpersistence Bias in Individual Income Expectations and Its Aggregate Implications." *American Economic Journal Macroeconomics* 15(4): 331–71. https://doi.org/10.1257/mac.20190056.

Ruderman, Owen. 2024. "California Has the Highest Grocery Prices in the US, According to HelpAdvisor Report." *The Press Democrat*, February 16. https://www.pressdemocrat.com/article/news/california-has-the-highest-grocery-prices-in-the-u-s-according-to-helpadv/.

Saito, Leland T. 2023. *Race and Politics: Asian Americans, Latinos, and Whites in a Los Angeles Suburb*. University of Illinois Press.

Sánchez, George J. 2021. *Boyle Heights: How a Los Angeles Neighborhood Became the Future of American Democracy*. University of California Press.

Sanchez Jankowski, Martin. 2008. *Cracks in the Pavement; Social Change and Resilience in Poor Neighborhoods*. University of California Press.

Sawyer, Mark Q. 2005. *Racial Politics in Post-Revolutionary Cuba*. Cambridge University Press.

Schafran, Alex. 2018. *The Road to Resegregation: Northern California and the Failure of Politics*. University of California Press.

Schachner, Jared. 2022. "Racial Stratification and School Segregation in the Suburbs; Evidence from LA County." *Social Forces* 101(1): 309–40 https://doi.org/10.1093/sf/soab128.

Schrag, Peter. 2004. *Paradise Lost: California's Experience, America's Future—Updated with a New Preface*. University of California Press.

Schwarz, Gonzalo. 2023. "American Dream 2023 Snapshot: The Health and State of the American Dream." The Archbridge Institute. https://www.archbridgeinstitute.org/wp-content/uploads/2023/06/2023-American-Dream-Snapshot_Final-1.pdf.

Selin, Cynthia. 2008. "The Sociology of the Future: Tracing Stories of Technology and Time." *Sociology Compass* 2(6): 1878–95. https://doi.org/10.1111/j.1751-9020.2008.00147.x.

Sexton, Jason S. 2023. *Redemptive Dreams: Engaging Kevin Starr's California*. Taylor & Francis.

Shange, Savannah. 2019. *Progressive Dystopia: Abolition, Antiblackness, and Schooling in San Francisco*. Duke University Press.

Sharma, Amita. 2018. "California's Middle Class Is in Decline, Despite the State's Immense Wealth." *CalMatters*, March 8. https://calmatters.org/economy/2018/03/california-middle-class-decline-despite-states-immense-wealth/.

Sharot, Tali. 2011. *The Optimism Bias: A Tour of the Irrationally Positive Brain*. Vintage Books.

Sheehan, Tim. 2022. "Housing Costs and Rent Up in Fresno, Valley Since 2020. Here's By How Much and Where." *Fresno Bee*. https://www.fresnobee.com/news/local/article292571469.html.

Sides, Josh. 2003. *L.A. City Limits: African American Los Angeles from the Great Depression to the Present*. University of California Press.

Silva, Jennifer M. 2013. *Coming Up Short: Working-Class Adulthood in an Age of Uncertainty*.

Simon, Joshua. 2022. "Overcoming the Other America: Jose Marti's Critique of the Unionist Paradigm" *The Review of Politics* 81(4): 55–79. https://doi.org/10.1017/S0034670521000735.

Sklar, Debbie L. 2019. "Former Gov. Pete Wilson Endorses Republican Brian Maryott for Congress." *Times of San Diego*, November 1. http://timesofsandiego.com/politics/2019/10/31/former-gov-pete-wilson-endorses-republican-brian-maryott-for-congress/.

Skoneki, Mark, and Jeffrey Schweers. 2023. "'If You Want to Do Things Like Gender Ideology, Go to Berkeley,' says Anti-DEI DeSantis." *The Orange County Register*, May 15. https://www.ocregister.com/2023/05/15/desantis-bans-diversity-equity-and-inclusion-in-colleges/.

Small, Mario Luis 2011. "How to Conduct a Mixed Methods Study: Recent Trends in a Rapidly Growing Literature." *Annual Review of Sociology* 37(1): 57–86.

Smith, Christen A. 2016. *Afro-Paradise: Blackness, Violence, and Performance in Brazil*. University of Illinois Press.

Smith, Sandra Susan. 2007. *Lone Pursuit: Distrust and Defensive Individualism Among the Black Poor*. Russell Sage Foundation.

Smith, Stacy L., Katherine Pieper, and Sam Wheeler. 2023. "Inequality in 1,600 Popular Films: Examining Portrayals of Gender, Race/Ethnicity, LGBTQ+ & Disability From 2007 to 2022." USC Annenberg Inclusion Initiative. https://assets.uscannenberg.org/docs/aii-inequality-in-1600-popular-films-20230811.pdf.

Sniderman, Paul M., and Thomas Piazza. 1986. "San Francisco Bay Area Race and Politics Survey, 1986." Inter-University Consortium for Political and Social Research. https://doi.org/10.3886/ICPSR38168.v2.

Stack, Carol B. 1983. *All Our Kin: Strategies for Survival in a Black Community*. Basic Books.

Stacker. 2022. "The Black Homeownership Gap in Fresno." March 22. https://stacker.com/california/fresno/black-homeownership-gap-fresno.

Starr, Kevin. 1973. *Americans and the California Dream, 1850–1915*. Oxford University Press.

Starr, Kevin. 1996. *Endangered Dreams: The Great Depression in California*. Oxford University Press.

Starr, Kevin. 1997. *The Dream Endures: California Enters the 1940s*. Oxford University Press.

Starr, Kevin. 2007. *California: A History*. Modern Library.

Starr, Kevin. 2011. *Golden Dreams: California in an Age of Abundance, 1950–1963*. Oxford University Press.

Starr, Kevin, and Richard J. Orsi. 2000. *Rooted in Barbarous Soil: People, Culture, and Community in Gold Rush California*. University of California Press.

The State Bar of California. n.d. "Diversity 2022 California Licensed Attorneys." Accessed October 10, 2024. http://publications.calbar.ca.gov/2022-diversity-report-card/diversity-2022-california-licensed-attorneys.

State of California, Civil Rights Department. 2023. "Second Annual Release of Pay Data Findings Suggest Significant Overrepresentation of Women and Communities of Color Among the State's Lowest Paid Workers." https://calcivilrights.ca.gov/2023/08/31/civil-rights-department-releases-statewide-demographic-breakdown-of-employee-pay-data-for-2021/#:~:text=The%20data%20shows%20that:%20*%20Women%20made,*%20Pay%20disparities%20remain%20a%20persistent%20challenge.

State of California, Department of Finance. 2024. "Population and Housing Estimates for Cities, Counties, and the State—January 1, 2023 and 2024." State of California. http://dof.ca.gov/forecasting/demographics/estimates-e1.

State of California, Office of Governor Gavin Newsom. 2022. "MediCal Expansion Provided 286,000 Undocumented Californians with Comprehensive Health Care." Press release, July 24. https://www.gov.ca.gov/2022/10/19/medi-cal-expansion-provided-286000-undocumented-californians-with-comprehensive-health-care/.

State of California, Office of Governor Gavin Newsom. 2023. "Over Forty Acres of Ancestral Land Returned to Native American Tribe." https://www.gov.ca.gov/2023/12/01/over-40-acres-of-ancestral-land-returned-to-native-american-tribe/.

State of California, Office of Governor Gavin Newsom. 2024a. "A Step Towards Healing and Restoration: California to Support the Return of Ancestral Tribal

Lands and Lands Management Projects." https://www.gov.ca.gov/2024/04/26/a-step-towards-healing-and-restoration-california-to-support-the-return-of-ancestral-tribal-lands-and-lands-management-projects/.

State of California, Office of Governor Gavin Newsom. 2024b. "California Remains the World's Fifth Largest Economy." http://www.gov.ca.gov/2024/04/16/california-remains-the-worlds-5th-largest-economy.

State of California, Office of Governor Gavin Newsom. 2024c. "Governor Newsom Proclaims Immigrant Heritage Month." Proclamation, June 18. https://www.gov.ca.gov/2024/06/18/governor-newsom-proclaims-immigrant-heritage-month-2024/.

State of California, Office of Governor Gavin Newsom. 2025. "California is Now the Fourth Largest Economy in the World." Press release, April 23. https://www.gov.ca.gov/2025/04/23/california-is-now-the-4th-largest-economy-in-the-world/.

State Water Resources Control Board. 2022. "State Water Resources Control Board: It Lacks the Urgency Necessary to Ensure That Failing Water Systems Receive Needed Assistance in a Timely Manner." Auditor of the State of California. https://information.auditor.ca.gov/reports/2021-118/index.html.

Statista. 2024. "Top States in the U.S. with the Highest Tech Economic Impact as Share of Total State Economy in 2023." October 9. https://www.statista.com/statistics/1301507/tech-economic-impact-in-the-us-by-state/#:~:text=Tech%20economic%20impact%20in%20the%20U.S.%20as%20a%20share,state%20economy%202022%2C%20by%20state&text=The%20state%20with%20the%20highest,Massachusetts%20with%20nearly%2013%20percent.

Sternheimer, Karen. 2014. *Celebrity Culture and the American Dream: Stardom and Social Mobility*. Routledge.

Stoll, Michael A. 2024. "The State of Black California: Assessing Twenty Years of Black Progress in the Golden State." UCLA Ralph Bunche Center. https://bunchecenter.ucla.edu/wp-content/uploads/2025/12/Interactive-2024-SOBC-Report_red.pdf.

Stuart, Forrest. 2016. *Down, Out and Under Arrest: Policing and Everyday Life in Skid Row*. University of Chicago Press.

Sugrue, Noreen M., and Tonantzin Carmona. 2023. "Closing the Latino Wealth Gap: Exploring Regional Differences and Lived Experiences." *The Brookings Institution*, October 24. https://www.brookings.edu/articles/closing-the-latino-wealth-gap-exploring-regional-differences-and-lived-experiences/.

Sullivan, Kate. 2024. "Trump Suggests Undocumented Immigrants Who Commit Murder Have 'Bad Genes.'" *CNN*, October 7. https://www.cnn.com/2024/10/07/politics/trump-undocumented-immigrants-bad-genes/index.html.

Summers, Brandi Thompson. 2019. *Black in Place: The Spatial Aesthetics of Race in a Post-Chocolate City*. University of North Carolina Press.

Swaine, Jon, and Oliver Laughland. 2015. "The County: The Story of America's Deadliest Police." *The Guardian*, December 1. https://www.theguardian.com/us-news/2015/dec/01/the-county-kern-county-deadliest-police-killings.

Swidler, Ann. 2001. *Talk of Love: How Culture Matters*. University of Chicago Press.

Tafoya, Sonya M. Laura Hill, and Hans Johnson. 2004. "California's Multiracial Population." *California Counts* report (August). Public Policy Institute of California. https://www.ppic.org/publication/californias-multiracial-population/

Telles, Edward E., and Vilma Ortiz. 2008. *Generations of Exclusion: Mexican-Americans, Assimilation, and Race*. Russell Sage Foundation.

Telles, Edward, Mark Sawyer, and Gaspar Rivera-Salgado. 2011. *Just Neighbors? Research on African American and Latino Relations in the United States*. Russell Sage Foundation.

Thomas, Deja. 2021. "Work Is Satisfying for Many but Views on Discrimination Persist." *Public Policy Institute of California* (blog), December 8. https://www.ppic.org/blog/work-is-satisfying-for-many-but-views-on-discrimination-persist/.

Thorman, Tess, and Daniel Payares-Montoya. 2025. "Income Inequality in California." Public Policy Institute of California. https://www.ppic.org/publication/income-inequality-in-california/.

Tong, Benson. 2004. "Race, Culture, and Citizenship Among Japanese American Children and Adolescents During the Internment Era." *Journal of American Ethnic History*, 3–40.

Trawalter, Sophie, Kelly Hoffman, and Lindsay Palmer. 2021. "Out of Place: Socioeconomic Status, Use of Public Space, and Belonging in Higher Education." *Journal of Personality and Social Psychology* 120(1): 131–44. https://doi.org/10.1037/pspi0000248.

Trudeau, Daniel. 2006. "Politics of Belonging in the Construction of Landscapes: Place-Making, Boundary-Drawing and Exclusion." *Cultural Geographies* 13(3): 421–43. https://doi.org/10.1191/1474474006eu366oa.

Trump, Kris-Stella. 2020. "When and Why Is Economic Inequality Seen as Fair." *Current Opinion in Behavioral Sciences* 34: 46–51. https://doi.org/10.1016/j.cobeha.2019.12.001.

Tucker, Robert C., ed. 1978. "The Eighteenth Brumaire of Louis Bonaparte." In *The Marx-Engels Reader*. W. W. Norton.

Turner, Frederick Jackson. 1893. *The Significance of the Frontier in American History*.

Tutton, Richard. 2017. "Wicked Futures: Meaning, Matter and the Sociology of the Future." *The Sociological Review* 65(3): 478–92. https://doi.org/10.1111/1467-954x.12443.

UCLA Latino Policy and Politics Institute. 2024. "As More Latinos Run for U.S. Congress Ahead of the 2024 Elections, Study Finds They Remain Significantly Underrepresented in Elected Offices." Press release, October 28. https://latino.ucla.edu/press/latino-representation-in-congress/.

United Press International. 2004. "Many Believe 'American Dream' Out of Reach." *United Press International Archive: General News*, September 27.

United Way. 2023. "The 2023 State of Black L.A. Makes the Case for More Resource-Rich Communities." October 10.

US Census Bureau. 2023. "Vintage 2022 Estimates of National, State, and County Population by Age, Sex, Race, and Hispanic Origin; and Estimates of Puerto

Rico Commonwealth and Municipios Population by Age and Sex." US Department of Commerce. http://www.census.gov/newsroom/press-kits/2023/population-estimates-characteristics.html.

US Census Bureau. 2024a. "Fresno City, California." US Department of Commerce. https://data.census.gov/profile/Fresno_city;_California?g=160XX00US0627000.

US Census Bureau. 2024b. "Net International Migration Drives Highest U.S. Population Growth in Decades." US Department of Commerce. https://www.census.gov/newsroom/press-releases/2024/population-estimates-international-migration.html.

US Census Bureau. 2024c. "New Estimates Highlight the Difference in Growth Between Hispanic and Non-Hispanic Populations." https://www.census.gov/newsroom/press-releases/2024/population-estimates-characteristics.html#:~:text=Harris%20County%2C%20Texas%2C%20had%20the,the%20lowest%20share%20in%202023.

US Citizenship and Immigration Services. 2022. "Unlawful Presence and Admissability." https://www.uscis.gov/laws-and-policy/other-resources/unlawful-presence-and-inadmissibility.

US Government Accountability Office. 2021. "Workforce Diversity: Analysis of Federal Data Shows Hispanics Are Underrepresented in the Media Industry," September 21. http://www.gao.gov/products/gao-21-105322.

Valentine, Charles A. 1969. "Culture and Poverty: Critique and Counter-Proposals." *Current Anthropology* 10(2/3): 181–201. https://doi.org/10.1086/201071.

Vang, Tony, and Juan Flores. 1999. "The Hmong Americans: Identity, Conflict, and Opportunity." *Multicultural Perspectives* 1(4): 9–14. https://doi.org/10.1080/15210969909539923.

Vankin, Jonathan. 2023. "State of the State of Jefferson: How This Secessionist Movement Started and Where It Stands Today." *California Local*, March 24. https://californialocal.com/localnews/statewide/ca/article/show/31200-state-of-jefferson-california-north-counties-sisikiyou-oregon/.

Vargas, Nicholas, and Kevin Stainback. 2015. "Documenting Contested Racial Identities Among Self-Identified Latina/Os, Asians, Blacks, and Whites." *American Behavioral Scientist* 60(4): 442–64. https://doi.org/10.1177/0002764215613396.

Varian, Ethan. 2025. "Bay Area Homeless Population Rose to a Record 38,891 People in 2024." *The Mercury News*, January 6. https://www.mercurynews.com/2025/01/05/bay-area-homeless-population-2024/.

Vartabedian, Ralph. 2022. "Governor, Legislators Won't Budge in High-Speed Rail Dispute." *CalMatters*, May 6. http://calmatters.org/politics/2022/05/california-high-speed-rail-standoff.

Wagner, David. 2023a. "Immigrant Entrepreneurs Continue to Shape California's Economy." *CalMatters*, May 24. https://calmatters.org/california-divide/2019/06/immigrant-entrepreneurs-california-economy/.

Wagner, David. 2023b. "Only 17% of LA Residents Can Afford to Buy a Home There." *LAist*, April 17. https://laist.com/news/housing-homelessness/california

-association-realtors-homebuying-house-affordability-report-2022-housing-los-angeles.

Watson, Tara, and Kalee Thompson. 2022. *The Border Within: The Economics of Immigration in an Age of Fear*. University of Chicago Press.

Weil, Simone. (1958) 2001. *Oppression and Liberty*. Routledge.

Wiley, Shaun, Kay Deaux, and Carolin Hagelskamp. 2012. "Born in the USA: How Immigrant Generation Shapes Meritocracy and Its Relation to Ethnic Identity and Collective Action." *Cultural Diversity & Ethnic Minority Psychology* 18(2): 171–80. https://doi.org/10.1037/a0027661.

Wills, Thomas A. 1981. "Downward Comparison Principles in Social Psychology." *Psychological Bulletin* 90(2): 245–71. https://doi.org/10.1037/0033-2909.90.2.245.

Wilson, William J. 1980. *The Declining Significance of Race: Blacks and Changing American Institutions*. University of Chicago Press.

Wolak, Jennifer, and David A. M. Peterson. 2020. "Trump Keeps Invoking the 'American Dream.' Americans Are Pessimistic That They Can Achieve It." *Washington Post*, September 21. https://www.washingtonpost.com/politics/2020/09/21/trump-keeps-invoking-american-dream-americans-are-pessimistic-that-they-can-achieve-it/.

Wong, Greg. 2024. "Where San Francisco's Black Population Stands—And Where It Goes from Here." *San Francisco Examiner*, February 27. https://www.sfexaminer.com/news/the-city/how-black-san-francisco-has-dwindled-since-harlem-west-days/article_42b6f538-d5a4-11ee-85ea-df19cc90bd0d.html#:~:text=By%202020%2C%20the%20Black%20population,the%20Bayview%2DHunters%20Point%20neighborhood.

Woods, Clyde. 2012. *Black California Dreamin': The Crises of California's African-American Communities*. https://escholarship.org/uc/item/63g6128j.

Wright, Erik Olin, ed. 2005. *Approaches to Class Analysis*. Cambridge University Press.

Wright, Erik Olin. 2000. "Working-Class Power, Capitalist-Class Interests, and Class Compromise." *American Journal of Sociology* 105(4): 957–1002.

Wright, Matthew, Morris E. Levy, and Jack Citrin. 2014. "Conflict and Consensus on American Public Opinion on Illegal Immigration." *SSRN*, May 10. https://doi.org/10.2139/ssrn.2476001.

Wrobel, David M. 2002. *Promised Lands: Promotion, Memory, and the Creation of the American West*. University Press of Kansas.

Wyatt, Dennis. 2024. "Punjabi Americans, Sikhs and Their Deep California Roots." *The Bulletin*, May 4. https://www.mantecabulletin.com/news/local-news/punjabi-americans-sikhs-their-deep-california-roots/.

Xian, He, and Jeremy Reynolds. 2017. "Bootstraps, Buddies, and Bribes: Perceived Meritocracy in the United States and China." *Sociological Quarterly* 58(4): 622–47. https://doi.org/10.1080/00380253.2017.1331719.

Xu, Ping, and James C. Garand. 2010. "Economic Context and Americans' Perceptions of Income Inequality." *Social Science Quarterly* 91(5): 1220–41. https://doi.org/10.1111/j.1540-6237.2010.00729.x.

Yang, Kou. 2001. "Research Note: The Hmong in America: Twenty-Five Years After the US Secret War in Laos." *Journal of Asian American Studies* 4(2): 165–74.

Young, Caitlin, Amalie Zinn, and Jung Hyun Choi. 2023. "Rethinking Homeownership as 'The American Dream.'" *Urban Wire*, June 26. https://www.urban.org/urban-wire/rethinking-homeownership-american-dream?utm_source=chatgpt.com.

Zacchino, Narda. 2016. *California Comeback: How a Failed State Became a Model for the Nation*. Thomas Dunne Books.

Zamora, Sylvia. 2022. *Racial Baggage: Mexican Immigrants and Race Across the Border*. Stanford University Press.

Zillow. 2025. "Los Angeles County, CA Housing Market." https://www.zillow.com/home-values/3101/los-angeles-county-ca/.

Zillow Rentals. 2024. "Average Rental Price in San Francisco, CA and Market Trends." https://www.zillow.com/rental-manager/market-trends/san-francisco-ca/.

Zucman, Gabriel. 2019. "Global Wealth Inequality." *Annual Review of Economics* 11(1): 109–38.

Zhu, Linna, Evgeny Burinskiy, Jorge De la Roca, Richard. K. Green, and Marlon G. Boarnet. 2021. "Los Angeles' Housing Crisis and Local Planning Responses: An Evaluation of Inclusionary Zoning and the Transit-Oriented Communities Plan as Policy Solutions in Los Angeles." *Cityscape* 23(1): 133–60. https://www.jstor.org/stable/26999943.

INDEX

Tables and figures are listed in **boldface**.